BDSM Primer

First Edition

Published by The Nazca Plains Corporation
Las Vegas, Nevada
2007

ISBN: 978-1-887895-56-9

Published by

The Nazca Plains Corporation ®
4640 Paradise Rd, Suite 141
Las Vegas, NV 89109-8000

PUBLISHER'S NOTE
BDSM Primer is a work of fiction created wholly by *Ralph Whites'* imagination. All characters are fictional and any resemblance to any persons living or deceased is purely by accident. No portion of this book reflects any real person or events.

Cover Photo, Martin Carlsson
Art Direction, Blake Stephens

Dedication

This work is dedicated to
slave dee kitten
the woman who makes my life
easier each and every day, and
wirh whom I intend to spend
the rest of my days

Acknowledgements

Over the time I worked on this book, a number of people have contributed ideas that were incorporated into the finished work. For obvious reasons, I either can't or won't use real names here, but they know who they are.

I first started this work after separating from my second wife "E". The story in the second chapter titled "The Ceremony" was inspired by my dreams of what could have been.

"First Date" in chapter four was inspired by "L" who I was talking to at the time. She is a sweet person. We just didn't "click".

In chapter five, the story "The Diet" was suggested by a gentleman in a Yahoo discussion group. I never actually knew his name, but he was looking in real life for his wife/ mistress to help him lose weight.

The story in chapter eight, "Bad Boys" was suggested by "K" a friend of several years. "K", I hope you find the special One for you!

"Christmas" was inspired by my own dee kitten and a friend "J". It is a fantasy story that I once hoped could become real.

The final story in the book was inspired by "L" (not the same "L" as earlier).

I want to thank "Joy from the Yahoo discussion group named 'GDsN'" for her topic suggestions, and for proof-reading the first few chapters.

Finally, I want to thank my loving slave girl who is proof-reading the final layout right now. girl, without you by my side it wouldn't be worth the effort to write this book.

-- Ralph White

BDSM Primer

Ralph White

Contents

Author's Forward

This book started life as just a collection of fictional erotic stories that had a BDSM theme. But, over the years I have come to understand that there are a great many things that those new to the lifestyle have questions about. There are also some things that are frequently topics in the "I wish somebody had told me" category. I decided to use this volume to provide some of these answers; or, at least, how I view some of the answers. At a minimum, it should give you information that will make you better equipped to find your own answers.

The first word of caution I will offer is that there are no rules. No matter what anyone tells you, you must decide what is "right" for you. There is a certain percentage of people in the lifestyle who are of the opinion that what works for them is, by definition, "correct" for everyone. That just isn't the case. So, I encourage you to approach your journey with an open mind. But, make your own decisions on what is "right" for you from your own investigations.

The second word of caution is that nothing is constant. Like all human beings, you are on a journey from what you were yesterday to what you will become tomorrow. There is a certain amount of change that you will undergo in the process of becoming what you are destined to be. What may surprise you is that your single biggest enemy in your progress will be your own thoughts and emotions. The human organism resists change. That is a fact. Anyone who tells you otherwise has a vested interest in encouraging you to change in the way that THEY want you to change. This will not always be in your best interest. Ultimately, you are the only one responsible for seeing that your own best interests are protected. (Although, eventually, you may trust another person enough to allow him/her to protect you, it is still, ultimately, your responsibility.)

All books must have a certain amount of "entertainment value." Particularly those that you are electing to read by your own choice. In this book you will find various short stories. These stories are not related to each other (although, I have had a few requests to do a follow-up to one of them). They are not, in any way related to real persons or events, and are provided to be entertaining, adult reading. However, it is my hope that through these stories, you will get a flavor of how relationships in this lifestyle might work. As they say, your actual mileage may vary.

The stories in this volume are a collection of FICTIONAL short stories that center around a BDSM lifestyle. The stories are all totally fictional, and the people in them bear no relationship to any person or persons in real life. The events described are provided for your entertainment. I don't necessarily recommend that you actually do anything described here, and some things do involve health risks. Before doing any real play activity, you should talk to other more experienced people to make sure that what you are doing is safe!

One final word of warning… Be aware of any health factors that may impact your activities. If you have any increased risk factors, consult a physician. Be sure that any play partners are also aware of these risks as well.

Chapter 1: So, you think you're kinky?

Well, you're reading this book, so someone thinks you are kinky (or maybe they just want you to become that way). But, just what does "kinky" mean? That is a much different question. For some people, "kink" is just adding a little spice to their sex life. For others, it is a pattern of behavior that permeates all areas of their life. For some people, it is a simple matter of adding rope and handcuffs to the drawer in the table beside the bed. Others don't even have rope in the house.

Bondage, Discipline, Domination, Submission, Sado-Masochism

Let's start with the term "BDSM". Traditionally, it is expanded to: "BD", "DS" and "SM", which is admittedly more confusing. "BD" stands for "Bondage and Discipline", "DS" stands for "Dominance and Submission", and "SM" stands for "Sado-Masochism". Each of these terms represent components that MAY or MAY NOT be part of your life and relationship. You and your partner have to decide what is right for you, and to what degree. But, we need to start somewhere, so we'll start with these terms. It may seem a little confusing at first, and there is also a certain blending of ideas between the terms too.

"Bondage" is the one part of "kinky" that most people know about, or at least think that they know about. It can involve any kinds of restraints or toys. Common items include: rope, chain, duck tape, leather cuffs, handcuffs/shackles, or even a belt, neck tie, or shoe strings can be used. I would include blindfolds, hoods, and gags in this category since they are used to limit sensory perceptions. Toys that you might encounter could include: dildos, clamps, and a multitude of things that can be inserted into a body cavity opening. (Even a soda bottle counts!) The goal of "bondage" is to limit the subject's freedom of movement and/or perceptions of the world around them.

"Discipline" is, just like it sounds, giving pain to an individual to modify an undesirable behavior into a more desirable one. This pain can be physical, but it can also be emotional or psychological. The key is that it not be something the person being disciplined enjoys. There can be assorted reasons for using discipline. First, discipline is used for punishment. In a Dominant/submissive relationship (often abbreviated "D/s"), there are typically rules that the submissive must obey. For a rule to be an effective way to control a person's activities there must be consequences if it is broken. (We will talk more about "Dominant/submissive" in the next paragraph, and throughout the rest of the book.) Punishment can take various forms: standing naked in a corner, for example, or maybe seven strokes with a cane. This is a very traditional interpretation of discipline. But, in the BDSM sense, discipline can be simply inflicting pain on another person because it gives them pleasure. I know of one person who says: "It's my birthday" every month at a local party. She does this for the sole reason of getting "birthday spankings" from anyone willing to give them to her. In no way is a spanking a punishment to her. This is perhaps one of the hardest things to get people to understand… the fact that there are those people who like receiving (and others who enjoy giving) pain. In fact, my housemate pronounces that, by definition, this is a "sick" person. There are many, many ways to discipline someone. For punishment, I have a heavy wooden spoon that I use. For fun, I have floggers and a rattan cane. I will probably buy a paddle in the near future. For a good old-fashioned spanking, nothing is better than your hand.

We will consider "dominance and submission" together since they are two sides of the same coin. In fact, there are many couples in the "vanilla" (non-BDSM) world who practice this part of BDSM. At its simplest level, dominance and submission means one person leads and the other follows. Even in a traditional marriage, typically one person does the cooking virtually all of the time. The other person, usually, sits down at the table and eats what is put in front of them. Are there exceptions? Of course there are. There are various degrees to how far the dominant and submissive roles extend in the relationship. What really matters is: "Does it work for you?" We will spend a whole chapter later in this book talking about the dominant / submissive aspects of relationships. A word of caution is appropriate though. Sometimes a dominant person will believe that because another person has a submissive personality that they should submit to EVERY dominant. Nothing is further from the truth. A submissive person has a natural desire to submit to another person. But, it is still a choice that they have to make as to who they will submit to. It is definitely improper for a dominant to demand all submissives to submit to them.

One thing that you must be careful to note and understand is that "dominance" or "submissivness" is not constant. How dominant a Dominant person is will depend of the situation they are in. There are some individuals who are both dominant and submissive (not at the same time) depending on who they are with or the situation they are in. We call these people "switches". For most switches, they either behave in a mostly dominant or mostly submissive manner.

Sado-Masochism, like dominance and submission, are flip sides to the same dynamic. There are individuals who get pleasure from receiving painful stimuli, and others who get pleasure from giving it. Regardless of how you personally feel about it, these people do exist.

Safe, Sane, and Consensual

In the BDSM community there is a term used called SSC, and a second called RACK, that stress a healthy perspective on our lifestyle. SSC stands for "Safe, Sane, and Consensual" and RACK means "Risk-Aware Consensual Kink". Not to get into a religious debate over one term or the other, they are essentially the same concept. (Advocates of the latter disagree with the assertion that what we do should be called "safe", for example.)

The concepts of being "safe" or of being "risk-aware" are essentially the same thing. It means being as safe as possible in the activity that you are doing. It is a fact that you cannot remove all risk or danger from life. This isn't really a foreign concept, and not as alien as it might seem at first. Most of us drive or ride a car every day of our lives. Nobody would make the assertion that cars are safe. The news broadcasts every day have reports of automobile accidents that claim lives or result in serious bodily injury. Clearly, cars today are safer than they were ten years ago. But, if history has taught us anything, it is that we must assume that cars today are not as safe as they will be ten years from now. However, it is a fact that advertisers have made a lot of money claiming that their cars are safe. So, let's look at what is really being said. In advertising, they are saying that the particular car they want you to buy is as safe as they can make it, and they want you to assume that that their car is better than others.

Make no mistake, there is risk of injury in some activities that are done in the BDSM lifestyle, and I am not trying to discount that risk in any way. The best way to deal with the risks it to know what they are, and assess whether you are willing to take them or not. Secondarily, there are some risks that can be controlled. I'll give you an example. In doing rope bondage the set up can be rather elaborate and time consuming. This will result in the one being tied up to have parts of their body immobilized for extended periods of time. Unfortunately, if the ropes are a little too tight they can cut off circulation. There is also the possibility of muscle cramps. Either of these situations can result in the need to free the one being bound rapidly. A way of reducing the risk of injury when you are doing rope bondage it to (1.) never leave the one being tied up alone and unmonitored and (2.) have sharp medical-type scissors handy to cut the ropes. Cutting the rope will result in the need to buy a new rope. But, that is a far better option then injuring the one being tied up. The bottom line is that you are taking risks, and you should do whatever you can to reduce that risk, and you should acknowledge that what you are doing has risks associated with it.

The other major part of SSC / RACK is the word consensual. The idea of consent is absolutely central to the healthy expression of "What It Is That We Do" (also written "WIITWD"). From the dominant's side, most consider "consent" as a passive thing. It is something received from the submissive. But, in a very real sense, the dominant consents to doing whatever He/She is doing to the submissive. Of course, informed consent is important from the submissive as well. The moment that consent is withdrawn, whatever is being done changes from play to abuse.

This whole issue of consent and of abuse is a crucial one. Many people outside of the lifestyle do not understand the whole thing. Many people who are not in the lifestyle cannot conceive that someone would want, or even enjoy, being spanked. Their only understanding is that spanking is abusive. You cannot convince a person who cannot conceive any opinion other than their own is valid that you do, in fact, want and enjoy what you are doing. They feel duty-bound to protect you from yourself. In fact, according to United States federal law at the time of this writing, you cannot lawfully consent to being spanked. Therefore, by law, anyone who spanks you is abusing you. This makes it doubly important that you exercise caution in what you do and who you do it with. It is also important that you are very upfront about the fact that consent is being given. It is vitally important! If you get into a legal situation, it may be the only defense you have.

If you haven't already, you will probably hear some Dominant addressed as "Master" or "Mistress" or you will hear a submissive called "slave". At first, this is confusing to some. In traditional slavery the slave is considered the property of the Master / Mistress. In this they had no voice. They were captured and then sold. In the BDSM culture you will hear the term "consensual slavery" used to contrast it from the traditional form. A consensual slave is a slave because they give their consent to be treated that way. A slave has no say in what happens to them, they don't get a vote. However, there is a subtle, but very critical, difference. A consensual slave always has the ability to withdraw their consent. Once consent is taken away, the relationship is dissolved. The other thing that needs to be added is that the Master / Mistress consents to "own" the slave as well. This consent can be withdrawn as well. In that case, the slave is said to have been "released." We will talk more about this topic later in this book.

While we are on the topic of risks, it is important to understand that the legal system moves slowly, and not always in our favor. There are still quite a number of states where oral sex is against the law! Most of these states do not generally enforce such laws, but they are on the books. It is interesting to note that in terms of per capita numbers, there is a higher percentage of the military and law enforcement that are in the lifestyle than there are from other professions. You will also find a high number of medical and educational professionals involved. For such persons, being "outted" (having their lifestyle publicly disclosed) is a risk to their employment or worse.

Our Story

That leads us to our first story. Remember, these stories are complete fiction. Any resemblance to real persons is purely coincidence. In our first story, the setting is an intimate dinner party for three couples, held at one of the couple's home. As I mentioned in this chapter, there is no one set of rules that all kinksters follow. In this story, you will see rules as part of the story. That doesn't mean that these are rules for everyone.

The other thing that you will find in this story is that the couples involved are pretty casual about nudity. Nudity is common in the BDSM lifestyle, but is by no means universal. If you are in a situation where you are not sure if nudity is appropriate, wait until someone else strips down, or ask the host if it is okay. Alternatively, just leave your clothes on. Nobody (except maybe the person you are there with) is going to force you to take your clothes off if you don't want to. Initially, you will probably be self-conscious that you don't have the perfect body, and that everyone will be looking at your flaws. If they are looking at your flaws, it will probably be so that they can see that your flaws are not as bad as theirs are, and probably a little admiration that you had the courage that they didn't have.

Story: "The Dinner Party"

It was about a half hour drive from their house to Ralph and Michelle's house for the dinner that they had been invited to. Before they left, Terry had given Wendy her orders; she wasn't sure she could keep them all tonight, but she was going to give it her best effort. As a warning, he had whipped her tender bottom briefly with the flogger before leaving home. Even now her bottom was still tingling in remembrance of the sweet pain of the lashes on her bare flesh. He promised her that if she was good and obeyed all of his rules tonight, and he would reward her when they got home. But, if not, that he would punish her there in front of everyone. Even now, she reviewed his list…

- ☐ He had not allowed her to wear any undergarments at all. He had even picked out the dress that she was wearing. It was the sleeveless black one (he liked her in black) with the low-cut square neckline. It was a neckline in the style that she preferred because it accentuated the collar that she wore around her neck.
- ☐ He put their wrist and ankle cuffs on her before they left the house. Of course, she wore his collar like she did at all times.
- ☐ She was seat belted into her seat in the car and her wrists were attached to the ring on her collar.
- ☐ He had told her that she was required to sit with her bare bottom touching the seat at all times that evening. Even now, in their car, her dress was pulled up so that her naked flesh was against the seat. Even before he had fastened her hands to her collar it had been hard to pull the dress down enough to cover her private parts.
- ☐ He had told her that she was not allowed to make eye contact with anyone that evening.
- ☐ She was required to address him as "Master" and the other two masters as "Sir" at all times… How could she remember that, he never required her to do that before. Even at home, calling him "Master" had always been her choice. She liked to call him that because it showed that she respected him. She knew that she would be punished tonight, and the thought both scared her a little and excited her a lot.
- ☐ She was only allowed to refer to herself in the third person.
- ☐ He had fastened the silver chain leash to her collar before they left the house, and had told her that tonight she was not allowed to let the slack out of the chain. If he felt the leash get tugged, he would punish her.
- ☐ His last rule for the night was that when it was time for dinner that she would take her dress off, without being told, and then her hands would be fastened behind her back, and that he would feed her.

This was going to be a night that would live on in her mind for months to come. Terry had told her that Ralph and Michelle had just put some finishing touches on their new dungeon and that it was ready for use. By the twinkle in his eye, she knew that he wanted very much to get her into the dungeon to have his way with her. She had talked to Michelle earlier that day, and Michelle had said something about "the chair" but refused to discuss it any more than that.

"Wendy?" said Terry as they turned into Ralph and Michelle's driveway.

"Yes, Master?" (Whew, she remembered.)

"You remember our rules for tonight?"

"Yes, Master, this one remembers."

He got out of the car and went around to her door and opened it. He unfastened her seat belt, and before he unfastened her wrists, he pulled her dress up, exposing not only her private parts, but her breasts as well. He smiled at her, very pleased, when he noticed the star burst nipple shields that she had put on.

"Good, just checking. Well done my Pet."

"Thank you Master. This one only wishes to please you Master."

He allowed her dress to fall back down to cover her once more, and unfastened her wrists. He took her hand and helped her out of the car. She stood there in front of him, not entirely sure what to expect from him this evening. He straightened her dress and smoothed out the wrinkles. He asked her for her hair brush and brushed her hair for her. (She always liked the way He cared for her.) Before handing the brush to her so that she could put it away, he quickly lifted her dress and swatted her bare bottom with it twice.

"Eek!" she squealed in surprise.

"Just a reminder, Honey." He whispered.

He took the leather handle to her leash in her hand and reached behind the seat and pulled out their bag of toys.

She just stared at him in surprise. She hadn't seen him put the bag in the car. Looking closer, she saw a small package wrapped in gift paper in the bag.

Terry just smiled at her and said: "Later." As he turned and walked to the house, she almost left the slack out of her leash. She hurried to catch up with him. (Oh no, this is not looking good, she thought.) She noticed that Ed and Marie's minivan was already there, so all were present and accounted for.

They reached the front door and Ralph opened the door to invite them in. He had seen them pull in. She suspected that he had been watching as Terry got her out of the car too.

As they entered the house, Wendy saw Michelle standing with her nose in the corner. She had her pants around her ankles and her shirt pulled up to her shoulders. Seeing Wendy gaze at Michelle, Ralph said: "She was bad just before you got here. She will be joining us in a few moments. But, it is the house rule that everyone who enters while she is in the corner must rub her butt as they come in for good luck."

Terry and Wendy each gave Michelle's but a brief rub for luck. Michelle felt a small shudder go through her when they touched her. Having Ralph put her on display both embarrassed her and excited her tremendously.

Ralph led Terry and Wendy to the living room where Ed and Marie waited for them. Like Wendy, Marie was wearing her leash, collar, and cuffs. She had on elegant navy blue slacks and a matching blazer. She wore nothing under the blazer, but, at the moment, her body was covered. She was sitting at Ed's feet on a silk pillow that matched the color of her pants.

"Excuse me a moment." Ralph said and went over to where Michelle was standing.

Gently, he pulled her pants up and straightened her blouse. He then turned her to face him and said: "Next time watch the baking instead of the internet." He tenderly brushed the tears from her face and kissed her. "Come say hello to our guests."

With a flush on her cheeks, she greeted each master first.

"Hello Mr. Ed, Sir."

"Good evening Michelle."

"May I have permission to greet Marie, Sir?"

"Yes you may."

"Hello Sis, how are you tonight?"

"I'm fine thank you. Looking forward to the dinner you fixed. It smells really great."

"Hello Mr. Terry, Sir."

"Hello Michelle."

"May I have permission to greet Wendy, Sir?"

"Yes you may."

"Hey Sis, how are you tonight. You look great!"

"Thank you, Sis. This one is doing very well tonight. Aren't you going to change for the party?"

"Ummmm... I don't know, my Master has not given me permission yet."

Michelle turned to her Master, bowing respectfully. "Master, may I change clothes for the party please?"

"Yes, Dear One, you may. I put a blouse and skirt on the bed for you, and some new... ummm... jewelry that I want you to wear."

She turned to the other masters and said: "Would you excuse me a moment, please, Sirs?"

As both indicated that she could leave the room, she hurried to change. As she walked down the hall, she heard her master call her... "Michelle?"

"Yes, Master?"

"Nothing but what is on the bed."

"Yes, Master, Okay, Master."

As she closed the bedroom door, she heard her Master begin serving drinks to their guests.

In a hurry to get back to their guests, Michelle stripped her clothes off. Only then did she see the new "jewelry" that he had bought her… a pair of nipple clamps with a short length of chain between them. Tears of joy filled her eyes as she looked at her Master's gift of love. He knew how she liked them, and hers had gotten lost on vacation last month. She wondered for a moment about the chain between the two tiny clips… Her old clips were not chained together.

Quickly she pulled on each nipple and rolled it between her fingers to get it hard and fastened the clamp tightly to it. As she walked over to look at the clothes he had pocked out for her, she could feel the chain tighten and tug the clamp on her nipples with every step she took. Tonight he was going to kill her with pleasure!

She picked up the blouse that he had laid out for her… it was her sheer white, see through blouse, and her white miniskirt, the one with the cutouts in the back so that her butt was on display for everyone. She quickly dressed and as she walked to the door, she noticed the shoes… white stiletto heels! What a way to complete her ensemble!

She took one last look in the mirror and quickly ran a brush through her hair… she thought that she looked great, even though the blouse didn't hide a whole lot.

As she walked down the hall, she heard her Master begin singing (only slightly off key)… "Here she comes, Miss America…"

When she got back to the living room, they were all standing in a semicircle with drinks in their hands, watching her enter. At a signal from her Master, she turned around to let them all see her butt showing through her skirt. When she was facing them again, her Master handed her a nice mug of coffee, fixed just the way she liked it, and gave her his special smile that always made her melt.

They returned to sit down again and talk about the day's news. Each Master sitting in a chair in the living room, with his slave sitting at their feet. Wendy, remembering her master's rule had pulled up the back of her skirt as she sat down on the red silk pillow. Marie was reclining back against her master's legs, and her blazer was hanging open to show off her breasts. Michelle sat at Ralph's feet on a white silk pillow. Her clamped nipples showing clearly through her blouse now. The fabric of her shirt rubbing against them, combined with the tugging of the clamps caused by the chain was beginning to drive her to distraction. She could feel the moisture beginning to build in her vagina.

When the timer in the kitchen went off, Michelle and her master went to the kitchen to bring dinner to the table and Terry, Wendy, Ed, and Marie remained seated and continued talking.

Once they were alone, Ralph wrapped his arms around her, pressing her tender breasts tightly to his chest. He lifted her skirt and grabbed her bottom with both hands. His mouth covered hers as a soft moan tried to escape from all of the stimulation she was receiving. "Later, honey." He whispered to her.

Dinner began with a spicy sausage soup. Ralph and Michelle brought the steaming bowls to the table and summoned their guests to the dining room.

The four from the living room came into the dining room and each master took his place at the table, each one leaving an empty chair beside them for their slave.

After their masters were seated, each slave took the vacant seat to the right of their master. Ralph asked God's blessing on their meal, and they began to eat.

After her third spoonful of soup, Wendy belatedly remembered Terry's rules. Immediately she said: "Master, this one is sorry that she forgot to undress and allow you to feed her. May this one please be allowed to do so now?"

"Yes you may" he answered her "But… you will need to be punished for forgetting."

With tears in her eyes, she responded: "Yes, master. This one understands." She then stood and removed her dress, and held her arms behind her back to allow him to fasten her wrists together. Then she turned and faced him and said: "Master, may this one ask what this one's punishment is?"

"Yes, you may. You will go to each person at the table and ask them to forgive you for the disrespect that you have shown."

"Yes, Master. Thank you, Master."

She turned to the person to her right, which happened to be Ralph. "Mr. Ralph, Sir. This one asks to be forgiven for the disrespect of disobeying her master. May this one be forgiven, Sir?"

"Yes, you are forgiven."

She walked around the table to where Michelle was seated. "Sister Michelle, this one asks to be forgiven for the disrespect of disobeying her master. May this one be forgiven?"

"Yes, you are forgiven."

Continuing around the table to where Ed was seated. "Mr. Ed, Sir. This one asks to be forgiven for the disrespect of disobeying her master. May this one be forgiven, Sir?"

"Yes, you are forgiven."

She walked around the table to where Marie was seated. "Sister Marie, this one asks to be forgiven for the disrespect of disobeying her master. May this one be forgiven?"

"Yes, you are forgiven."

Finally, she returned to her place at her master's side. Kneeling before him, she quietly said: "Master, this one begs to be forgiven for disrespecting you. May this one be forgiven?"

With love in his heart for the words she had just offered to him, knowing the sincerity of them from their time together, he stood up, helped her to her feet, wrapped his arms around her, kissed her tenderly and said: "Yes, love, all is forgiven. Be seated and have some soup." Having closed the incident, he helped her get comfortable in the chair and fed her soup to her, returning to his own soup only when he had fed her all of hers.

As the dinner progressed through the salad course and the main course, Terry continued to feed Wendy before eating his own food. (The main course was penne pasta with a fresh garlic and basil sauce, served with grilled chicken.)

As the coffee was poured for the dessert course, Terry turned to Wendy and asked her to stand.

"My dearest love, you have behaved wonderfully through the dinner. As a reward, I will loosen your hands and you may feed yourself dessert."

"Thank you, master. This one only wishes to please you master."

"You have pleased me very much. Please be seated."

"Master, may this one be allowed to put her dress back on?"

Terry looked at both Ed and Ralph. This was the question that they had agreed upon. Returning his gaze to Wendy, he said: "No, you may not, please be seated again."

Ralph turned to Michelle and said: "Dear One, it is only proper that since Wendy is undressed, that you should be as well. Please remove your clothes."

Michelle stood up and began unbuttoning her blouse. "Master, does that include removing my new jewelry too?"

"No, dear one, those stay on for now."

As she removed her blouse and dropped her skirt to the floor, everyone in the room could see how red and swollen her nipples now were. She returned to her seat and took the stiletto heels off too.

Ed now looked at Marie and said: "Beloved, it is time for you to join Michelle and Wendy."

Marie stood and removed both her blazer and pants.

After all three women were naked, Ralph stood and announced: "We have a special dessert. Please go into the living room while I get it ready.

Ralph went into the kitchen to prepare their treat, and Michelle ushered everyone else into the living room.

Once in the living room, Michelle told each master to sit on the silk pillow that his slave had occupied earlier with his legs crossed. Then she told each slave to lie on her back in front of her master. Michelle assumed her position on the floor in front of the white pillow that her master would occupy.

When Ralph returned from the kitchen, he held a tray with three plates on it. He handed one to each of the other masters and them assumed his position on the white pillow beside Michelle. Looking at each in turn, he said: "Dessert tonight is 'Hot apple pie, a la mode, served on a nude slave." With that, he took his plate holding the warm pie and cold ice cream and dumped it on Michelle's tummy, motioning for the other couples to do the same.

The sudden warmth of the pie and the cold of the ice cream made Michelle draw in a sharp breath of surprise. Gently, tenderly, each master began feeding dessert to his slave, and ate his portion of the dessert himself.

When they were finished eating dessert, Ralph gave each master a warm wash cloth. But, for his Michelle, he bent down and licked her tummy clean with his tongue. Only after she was as clean as his tongue could make her did he finally wash her with his own wash cloth.

Michelle and Ralph quickly gathered up the dishes from the meal and put them in the dishwasher. Barely controlling his anticipation, Ralph asked the other masters if they would like to see the dungeon that he and Michelle had just finished. Both nodded their heads enthusiastically, and Ralph started to lead them all down to the basement.

As they walked, Michelle whispered: "Master, haven't you forgotten something?"

"Oh yes, thank you Dear One" and turned to the other two masters. "Our rule is: No clothes in the dungeon. So, you will have to leave your clothes here."

The troop of six naked people headed down the stairs to the basement.

Ralph opened a rather innocent looking door to reveal their dungeon. As they entered the room, he began to point out the special features that he and Michelle had designed in.

The first initially looked like two boards nailed together to form the letter X. At the bottom there were footpads that the slave would place her feet. Then going all the way up the arms of the X were leather straps with buckles. In the middle were straps big enough to go around the slave's torso, and on the upper arms of the X were more leather straps. Ralph described that "the slave would be securely strapped to the frame, and then" he said pointing to the garage door rails set on the wall and ceiling "you can move the whole frame up so that she is suspended from the ceiling, or at any angle in between."

On the opposite wall, he pointed out his "spinning wheel." Like the X frame, this two had arm, leg, and torso bindings. However, instead of moving up to hang the slave from the ceiling, this one allowed her body to be rotated at any angle from the floor that the master desired. In fact, there was also a small motor that could be used to turn the wheel rotisserie-style.

The other things he showed them were hooks for hanging the slave from the ceiling, or fastening her to the floor. Various floggers and whips. Blindfolds and several gags. He also pointed out that he had covered the walls and ceiling, and even the back of the door with six-inch baffled foam for sound-proofing. He told them that he had closed the door and told Michelle to scream as loudly as she could. Standing outside the door, he couldn't hear anything.

"Well, that's about it."

Wendy looked around and asked Terry: "Master, may this one ask a question?"

"Yes you may."

"Mr. Ralph, Sir, what it that in the corner covered over with a blanket?"

"Ah! That's the latest addition to our little play room." (He pulled away the blanket.) "I call it 'the chair'."

What they saw was a vertical post with five arms coming out of it. On the bottom, about thirty inches off the floor, were three arms. There was one short arm in back that was parallel to the floor, and had two pegs sticking up out of it, and the two forward ones that were slightly tilted up. About two feet higher, were two more arms also tilted up.

Ralph explained: "The slave sits here" (pointing to the short arm with the two pegs sticking up) "one peg goes into her vagina and the other into her anus. Then her legs are strapped to the other two arms on the bottom. After that, you strap her arms to the upper arms of the chair, and she is ready for whatever you care to do to her. I have added a hook on the back side that allows me to take the chain on Michelle's nipple clamps and use it to pull her breasts upward away from her body."

Eyeing the chair, Marie looked at her master with begging eyes. Ed looked at Ralph and said: "May we use your dungeon for a little while?"

"Of course you may. We will be up stairs having coffee."

Terry, Wendy, Ralph, and Michelle returned to the living room, still naked, and had their coffee. Terry turned to Wendy and said: "Love, we have a problem."

"We do master? Can this one ask what that problem is?"

"Yes you may. The problem is that you have been making eye contact with everyone since dessert, and that was one of the rules."

"Yes master, you are right. This one forgot the rule about eye contact. May this one be punished for her mistake, please?"

"Yes, your punishment is that you will get a spanking."

"Thank you master." (She gets on her hands and knees.)

S-M-A-C-K

After twenty-five strong smacks on her butt with his hand, he tells her, once again that all is forgiven, pulls her into his lap and cradles her in his arms.

"Master, may this one ask you about the present in our toy bag?"

"Yes you may, there are two, actually. The larger one is for you and the smaller one is for Ralph and Michelle."

Unable to restrain herself any more, Wendy tore into her package. "Master, what are these for?"

"Those are called 'spreader bars' they are used to force you to keep your legs apart when I have you tied up."

"Thank you, master. Your slave loves them."

"You're welcome, love. But, don't you think that Ralph and Michelle should open their present?"

"Yes master, this one is sorry master. This one should have allowed Ralph and Michelle to open their gift first." (She hands the smaller gift to Michelle.)

Michelle looks to her master to find out if she should open it. At his nod, she rips the paper from the small package and looks at it. "Master, what in the world is an anal pl…. Oh no, master, not THAT!!"

"Yes, Dear One, that. Go into the bedroom and get some lubricant."

(Michelle leaves and returns with the K-Y Jelly.)

Ralph removes the anal plug from its package and liberally lubricates the end. He tells Michelle to bend over, and gently begins to work the lubricated plug into her anus. Gradually, she is relaxed enough to take the plug inside her body and keep it there.

With her new toy in place, she says thank you to Terry and Wendy and returns to her pillow at her master's feet. She smiles, enjoying the feeling of the plug filling her ass. And everyone returns to sipping their coffee.

About the time that they were ready to begin their third cup of coffee, Ed and Marie pop up out of the basement door.

"Mr. Ralph, Sir, that chair is great! Ed tied me to it and then used your flogger on me until I was ready to lose it. I screamed and screamed. It was WONDERFUL!!! Thank you for sharing Mr. Ralph, Sir."

"You are very welcome Marie."

As Ed returned to his chair and Marie to her pillow, Ralph noticed that her bottom was about as red as his coffee mug. But her face had a glow about it. The glow of someone in sub space, who cares only about her master taking her to the next level.

"Hey sis, look what I got." Wendy said showing off her new spreader bars. "Michelle got a new toy too… show her, sis!"

Michelle looked up at her master, and again he just nodded. She stood up and bent over, and holding her cheeks apart showed Ed and Marie the plug in her butt.

The rest of the evening was spent in the relaxing camaraderie of friends who know that their life is the best that it can ever be because they are married to the O/one.

Chapter 2: Kinkiness and Religion

Perhaps the greatest influence for good in our society at large is religion. Paradoxically, it is also the greatest vehicle to create harm. People become fanatical zealots promulgating their own personal view to the exclusion of all else. The problem with all religions is that they depend on man interpreting what God meant when He said X. Or, even worse, projecting what God would have said if He had said anything on topic Y.

This book is not about theology or comparative religion. It isn't intended to be one. I do have strong religious beliefs that are very deep. You may, or may not, believe as I believe. In fact, you may not believe in God at all. It is not my purpose to convince you one way or the other. Perhaps I shall write that book one day. But this isn't that book.

There is no religion where the written guidelines that came from God, be it the Torah, the Bible, the Quran, or whatever other holy book there is, cover the totality of the human experience. Unfortunately, the devout of each religion must ask: "Given what I know, what do I believe God thinks about X?" From what that person knows about what God has said, they then infer what He would have said if He had spoken on that subject. Most often, the answer to that question concludes that what the devotee wants to believe is correct. This conclusion typically takes the form of: "God doesn't say anything about X, therefore He must not object to it." Or, alternatively: "God didn't say that X was okay, so therefore it isn't." But, it is never that simple.

An example of creative religious thinking

Let's take, for example, the issue of nudity that I introduced in chapter 1. Since the Christian perspective is the one that I am more familiar with, I will discuss it from that aspect. The traditional arguments against nudity are:
- God clothed Adam and Eve in the book of Genesis, therefore clothing is what He intended.
- Paul writes that women should dress modestly.
- The Bible teaches against lust. It is not possible to see a naked person of the opposite sex without lusting after them. Therefore, clothing is required.

Each of these makes assumptions about what was meant. We'll examine each point individually. On each of these issues you will have to decide what you believe. I am presenting it purely as an example of creative thinking that prevails in all religions. As a believer in whatever you believe, the burden is on you to decide WHY you believe what you do.

Argument number 1

It is always dangerous to assume that you know what God intended. If you read the account recorded in Genesis, you will find that Adam and Eve were created naked. In fact, clothing wasn't God's idea at all. Once Adam and Eve ate the fruit that God had forbidden them, they clothed themselves with aprons made of fig leaves. In the King James Bible, God asks: "Who told you that you were naked?" Which the church has taught for years implied that Adam and Eve now knew that nakedness was wrong, where as they hadn't known of their sin before. However, God created them sinless... sinless AND naked. So, just being naked couldn't be sinful. Furthermore, this interpretation of God's question implies that before they sinned, Adam and Eve were too stupid to know that they were not wearing clothes. This is clearly not the case since the Bible records that they were naked and not ashamed. We need to come up with some way to resolve this.

If we look at the actual Hebrew words for God's question, perhaps another translation would resolve the issue. It would be more accurate to say that God asked: "Who told you that being naked was a problem?" This translation doesn't assume that Adam and Eve were too dumb to know that they were not wearing clothes, and it doesn't indicate that nudity was a problem for God. What is indicates it that Adam and Eve's perception of their nudity had changed, and God was asking: "What happened?"

Argument number 2

This argument assumes that God views nudity as immodest and therefore that it is a problem. This is a case of our culture's definitions being applied to a culture that died over eighteen hundred years ago. This would be like saying that everyone who lived then was functionally illiterate because they didn't know how to operate a computer. Today's standards do not apply to that culture. So, just what do we know about that culture?

- ☐ In all sporting competitions the participants competed in the nude.
- ☐ Every major Roman city (the Apostle Paul was a citizen of Rome) had public baths. These baths were the social clubs of their time. Historians now tell us that they were definitely co-ed, and that any well-to-do Roman would visit them daily.
- ☐ Historians now believe that, because of their worship of the sun god, and because of their climate, that nudity was common in ancient Egypt.
- ☐ It is a fact that Roman criminals were crucified totally naked.
- ☐ Documents from the early church indicate that co-ed baptisms were held in the nude.

If simple nudity were immodest, as some assert, the Bible would have been required to speak out against all of these things. It doesn't.

Argument number 3

For this argument, all of the cases discussed in "Argument 2" also apply. But, more than that, there were cases where God actually commanded His prophet to go about nude. In fact, nudity was often viewed as a sign of holiness. If nudity always produces lustful thoughts, God could not have commanded it because it would have been a violation of His nature.

Translation Issues

Many people will quote text from the King James Bible to prove their point. But, the KJV was a translation from the Latin Vulgate, which was a translation from the Greek, which was, in turn, a translation from the original manuscripts. Many times in translation there is no exact equivalent from one language to the other. It depends on the translator to make a decision as to what was meant. In the case of the KJV, there can be a cascade effect of these translation inaccuracies. For example, one of the Ten Commandments reads "Thou shalt not kill." However, the correct translation should have been: "Thou shalt not commit murder." This is a drastic difference. Even in modern translations from the original manuscripts, the translators relied on tradition to deal with any ambiguities.

Conclusion

I am not telling you what to believe. I am certainly not telling you that what you believe is wrong. But neither am I telling you that it is right. What I am telling you is that you must research it and decide for yourself if you believe that a particular practice is wrong or right. And that you should do so with intelligent, open eyes; not believing blindly what some cleric tells you.

Our Story

The story for this chapter is titled "The Ceremony". It is about a collaring ceremony between a Master and a slave. It is one of my stories that moves me to tears almost every time I read it (and I wrote it!). Collaring and collaring ceremonies will be discussed in greater detail in the next chapter, but a little background is probably appropriate here.

A collar (yes, like a dog collar) is a symbolic representation of the relationship that exists between a dominant and a submissive. It can be compared to a wedding ring because its meaning is so deep to the two who share it. There are other reasons people wear a collar, just like someone might put on a ring to keep people from hitting on them at a party.

A collar can literally be anything that would go around a submissive's neck. If it is intended that the submissive wear it 24/7, a necklace might be a better choice than a wide leather and chain affair with rings for fastening her to a wall. (Then again, your actual mileage may vary.) It should also be noted that not all use a collar. Some may use a bracelet or an anklet, or perhaps a symbolic piercing.

More about collars in the next chapter; on to our story…

Story: "The Ceremony"

She had never been as nervous as she was today. Even their wedding just one short year ago paled in comparison. What she was about to do could never be undone. Her lawyer had cautioned her. Urged her. Pleaded with her. In fact, she had almost walked off the case entirely once she understood what Shelly was asking for. But her Master insisted that they have a formal written accord of what was about to transpire. A document that fully outlined what she was giving him, and his promises to her in return. Even now she held it in her hands… "Contract Of Legal Ownership"… it seemed so simple. In her heart, she had signed the contract months ago, as she knew he had as well. This short three page document will make her his legal property.

It had been a very strange week. He had started that week telling her that he was dedicating this step in their lives to God, and that as an outward demonstration that they were going to spend the week in prayer and Bible study. He had disconnected the television and the radio. He had stopped the newspaper delivery for that week. He had turned off the ringer on the telephone, allowing the machine to answer. They had agreed to return only "important" calls, like work or family emergencies. He even decided that they would spend three days of total fasting so that they could focus on God.

As a surprise this morning, he had gotten up and fixed her a special breakfast: coffee, orange juice, eggs, potatoes, toast, and bacon-wrapped filet mignon. He brought it up to her in bed just as she was waking up. He brought out a pair of shiny handcuffs, and cuffed her hands behind her back. "You don't need your hands this morning. I will care for you." She was surprised that he did not seem to have any food for himself. When she looked at him, he simply whispered that he had already eaten. Then to her delight, he sat down and began to feed her, telling her the whole time of his love for her.

As he put the last bite of steak into her mouth, he told her that he had a surprise for her. He showed her a flat square box wrapped in tissue paper. He opened it and she saw a beautiful sterling silver collar. She blinked back tears. They had a studded leather collar that they used in their play sessions. She had assumed that the ceremony would use that one too, and that she would just be wearing it permanently from that point on. She looked at him through her tears… "But I thought… It's beautiful… How can we use it…" A thousand emotions filled her mind.

He just took her in his arms, brushed the tears from her cheeks, and whispered: "The other one is fine for play. We will still use it. But, for today and forever, you needed to have the best."

He removed the breakfast tray and helped her to her feet. She was naked the way that she had slept since graduating college. He gently led her to their bathroom. He had been there before her and had set out lighted candles that filled the room with a vanilla-strawberry scent. He gave her a few moments privacy so that she could use the toilet and told her to call him when she was done.

She finished and called him. He came back in and turned the shower on. He helped her to her to her feet and helped her into the shower, her hands still bound behind her back. He then washed her body starting at her feet. She had never had another person shave her legs before. She was surprised at how gently yet deftly he moved the razor over her skin. After washing her body, he brought out a second pair of hand cuffs, unfastened one of her wrists, and fastened each wrist to the curtain rod. Taking the razor again, he tenderly shaved her under arms. Finally, after washing her body, he shampooed her long dark hair. Not once, but twice!

He turned the shower off, and, with her hands still fastened to the curtain rod, began drying her off. Once she was dry, he unfastened the cuffs from the curtain rod, and led her back to their bedroom. He motioned her to kneel down on the floor in front of him. He walked around behind her and fastened the dangling cuffs to her ankles.

He left her there for a moment and returned carrying the candles, a hair brush, and a blow dryer. He leaned over and kissed her luscious lips and then walked around behind her and knelt down to dry and brush her hair. She was in ecstasy because of his special attentions to her this morning. He knew her better than she knew herself.

After her hair was dry, he removed her hand cuffs. He led her to the bed and told her to lay down on her stomach on the bed. He went over to her dresser and got her body lotion. He then rubbed and massaged every inch of her body to relax her even more than she was already. He had her roll over and finished with her lotion and massage.

He went over to her dresser and retrieved a white lace bra and matching panties. He returned to the bed and began dressing her. She stood there and waited for him, thinking: "This is different. He never dressed me before. Undressed, yes, but never dressed." He walked to the closet and picked out a dress covered with large flowers that looked like it came from the sixties. His favorite... She should have known! He gently pulled the dress over her head and pulled her arms through the openings where the arm holes were. He gently zipped up the back.

To complete the ensemble, he put a white knee sock on each foot, and topped them off with her patent leather shoes.

He looked at her. Pleased with what he saw. He motioned her over to her dressing table and told her to sit down. He hand cuffed her wrists to the chair and whispered: "I will do this too today." It was all she could do to keep from arguing with him. He was NOT doing her makeup for her! No, no, no, no, NO!!! Her control faltered and she began to tremble. "Please, Master, not that." She whispered as tears fell down her cheeks.

He knelt down before her and stared into her watery eyes. He gave her the special smile that was hers alone and said: "My darling, you have promised me your trust, tonight you are giving me everything that you are. Have I ever betrayed your trust in me? You know how important today is for us, would I take any risk at betraying that trust in this day?"

She stared back into his eyes for a moment, and then looked away. She was giving this man her very life, in fact, in her heart it was his already, how could she be afraid to let him do her makeup for her?… She looked back at him again, seeing nothing but love in his eyes, and whispered: "Master, my life and all that I am is yours. You have never betrayed my trust. Please forgive my moment of weakness" As the truth of her words washed through her mind, her tears stopped and her trembling body calmed.

He waited, patiently watching her to see her trust in him return like the waters of a flood. He waited just a moment longer, and then turned her chair so that she could not watch in the mirror as he completed her look for the day. She was now the canvas on which he would paint his masterpiece. This is why he had been secretly taking classes in applying makeup. It had been so hard to keep the secret from her so that he could complete this surprise for her.

He began with an orange eye shadow to match the predominant color of her dress. He slowly faded the color to be almost non existent at the top of her eye lids. Then he added a heavy white line just above her eye lashes, keeping with a sixties motif. Next he added a light foundation and just a hint of color on her cheeks. To her lips he applied a vivid red lip gloss, and as a final touch, he added small black triangles to the outside corners of her eyes to give just a hint of an Egyptian face.

Before letting her see the completed image, he needed to braid her hair. He didn't want all of her hair braided. The look that he was after was to give the image of a thick band of hair holding her hair back so that all could see the collar that represented his ownership of her. More importantly, he wanted every man in the room to see her, and to know beyond all doubt that she was his for the rest of their natural lives, and that they could never have her.

When he had finally finished feeding her and preparing her for the day. It had been four hours since he had entered the room with breakfast. Four hours that he had enjoyed immensely because he had the pleasure of caring for her. He could see in her face that she wanted very much to see what he had done to her face. But, that would have to wait for a little while longer.

He went over to the play drawer and retrieved a number of leather straps. He returned to her and bound her arms and legs to the chair so that she was not able to move. He told her: "Honey, I have to get ready myself, and you have to wait here until I am ready so that you get to see the final image all at once. I am going to shower and shave and get dressed. When I return to the room I will tell you to close your eyes, and then I will unbind you from the chair, will stand you up and turn you around and stand beside you. Only then will you open your eyes. Do you understand?"

"Yes Master, I understand."

He went to the closet and retrieved a garment bag that she had never seen before and went to the bathroom to get ready. He quickly shaved, showered, and got dressed. Returning to their room he called in that she was to close her eyes. He went to the closet and retrieved the while platform shoes that he had special ordered for today and put them on. He finally returned to where she was sitting and removed all of her restraints. He helped her to her feet and turned her to face their full length mirror. Then he stood next to her and told her that she could open her eyes.

She took in her hair and makeup. She was in awe. She couldn't have done her hair and makeup as nicely as he had done. She looked over her dress and foot wear. Then she looked at his image in the mirror. He was wearing a stark white leisure suit with an orange turtle neck. It was all topped off with white platform shoes. The final image totally over powered her and she could do nothing but fall to her knees at his feet in gratitude for how he cared for her.

He gently picked her up and sat down with her bundled in his arms. He could see that she was ready to cry and told her that she wasn't allowed to ruin her makeup… yet.

They were just sitting there enjoying their moment when the doorbell rang. He had been watching the time, and knew who it was. In fact, they were five minutes late. He whispered that she should answer the door while he cleaned up things in there.

After she left the room, he quickly gathered up her new collar and the two suitcases that he had secretly packed with clothes and toys. She had no idea that they wouldn't be returning home tonight. He was right behind her when she opened the door. Standing on their porch was the driver for the limousine that he had hired for the day.

He escorted her to the limo and made sure that she was seated comfortably before having the driver put their bags in the car. He climbed in beside her. He fastened her seatbelt securely, and then fastened his own.

They rode to the hotel in a pleasant silence. She was lost in her love for him. In her need to do whatever it took to please him. Right now she wanted nothing more than to put on his collar. To show the world that he owned her. She leaned against him and reached for his strong hand… she suddenly needed him to touch her… to feel the warmth and strength of his hands… As her hand reached his, the limo pulled into the hotel parking lot, and they had to get out. Their driver quietly opened the door for her Master who quickly got out and closed the door. As the driver opened the trunk so that the bellboy could get their bags, her door opened too. To her surprise, her Master was holding the door for her, and helping her out of the car.

Her Master had her sit down and wait for him as he went over to the front desk to check on the meeting room that they had rented for the day. He tipped the bellboy and had him take their bags to the bridal suite that he had secretly checked into the day before. He gave him an extra tip to being a bottle of chilled Champagne up to their room too.

Master then led her over to the meeting room that they had rented for the occasion. They had paid to have the room decorated as a sixties-style disco. The design was better than she had imagined it would be. The DJ that they hired would be there within the hour, and the caterer was just setting up. It was about two hours before the first guests would arrive. Some of them were in for a surprise. They were not in the lifestyle, and wouldn't know what to expect. Even her parents didn't fully understand, even though she had tried many times to explain it to them.

Her Master took her hand and escorted her up to their room. She had no idea that he had rented it for them. "Oh, Master! It looks just like it did on our wedding night!"

(Well, almost the same he thought.) He led her over to the corner where he had set up some dividers to isolate the corner from the rest of the room. He had her kneel down on a pillow that he had left there. He went back and got her new collar and a candle and placed each in front of her. He told her that for the next half hour that she was to pray and meditate about what she was about to do and that he would be doing the same elsewhere. He lit the candle and moved the room divider to close her off from the rest of the world.

She began to pray: "Father God, You were with me as I began walking down this path many years ago. You know more about me than even I know about myself. You brought this man into my life as my husband a year ago. You have molded us together to become one, and I thank You so much for him. In my heart, he is my Master, and I am just his lowly slave. Yet, I yearn for nothing more than to please him. Father, I pledged my service to You before You gave me to him, and he has never forced me to break my service to You. In fact, he has led me in new ways to serve You as I serve him. Today it is my intent to enter into a pledge and contract that will legally bind me to him as his property for the rest of my life. Father, I now come before you one last time to ask Your blessing on what I am about to do. I wait on You, Father, and I ask for Your guidance in the name of Your Son who died for me. Amen."

She knelt quietly before the light of the candle. She picked up her Master's collar and looked at it. Suddenly an overpowering sense of profound peace and calm filled every corner of her mind. She knew that her heavenly Father had just blessed what she was about to do. She was so full of joy that she had to sing. She sang every song of praise that she knew, tears of pure joy streaming down her face. She was happier than she had ever been in her life. Her Father was pleased that she was giving herself to her Master. She was so profoundly happy that she thought she would surely pass out because of it.

At the end of the half hour, her Master had finished his own prayers and came and removed the room dividers that had separated them. Seeing her tears, and the joy on her face, he said: "Come, honey, we have just enough time to fix your makeup again."

She jumped to her feet literally jumping into his arms. "Dad gave us His blessing!!! I am so happy."

"I know, honey. He told me too." He whispered, as he held her close and kissed her tenderly. He quickly fixed her makeup for her. This time she didn't even think about what he was doing.

As they got ready to leave their room, she quickly fell to her knees and bowed before him. "Master, it would mean a lot to me if you would bind my hands behind me before we leave. I am yours, and I want everyone to know."

He quickly retrieved the leather cuffs from their toy bag and fastened her wrists together behind her. Then he added a leather strap that pulled her elbows together, and helped her to her feet.

"There is one other thing we need to add as well." He dangled a small pair of nipple clips in front of her. Her lips trembled in anticipation as she looked at them. He pulled her dress up and unfastened her bra. He gently attached one clip to each nipple, tightening them down just the right amount so that she would feel the pain, but at a level where she would be able to wear them all afternoon. Then he surprised her again. Instead of fastening her bra again, he cut the shoulder straps and took it off entirely. As he pulled down her dress again, he also removed her panties. As they left their hotel room and walked to the elevator, all she could think of was her joy at being able to please him.

The humiliation of publicly walking with her arms bound combined with the pain on her nipples was mixing with her pure joy of serving him. Her mind was traveling to that place where there was nothing in it but her urgent need to please him. To show the world that she wanted to serve him. Once again, she so happy that she wanted to cry. But she knew that it would displease him if she did and ruined her makeup once again.

They entered the meeting room a short ten minutes before the ceremony would begin. The two sister slaves that she had chosen to stand with her were there with their Masters. The three men had become fast friends over the last year as she had with her fellow slaves. Only another such as herself could understand where her mind was right now. She couldn't speak, she couldn't even meet their eyes. She was in that place where she could do nothing without his permission. The Masters greeted each other with a warm brotherly hug; each Master asking his permission for himself and his slave to greet her as well. She knew that without that permission, neither her sisters nor their Masters would speak to her out of respect for her and her Master. Her Master granted his permission and asked the other Masters to have their slaves help her prepare for the ceremony.

Each Master and his slave greeted her and congratulated her on her pending new status. As her sisters began to lead her over to where the ceremony was to be held, she began to panic. They were taking her away from her Master. This can't be happening! Suddenly, she heard her Master's voice whisper in her ear: "Go with them, they are to help you make the final preparations." Her joy returned! He was there! He was making sure that she was ready!

Her sisters led her to a white silk pillow on the floor at one end of the room, and had her kneel down. They unbound her arms and wrists. She whispered to them about the nipple clamps, but asked them to leave them on. Her Master had put them there, and she would keep them on until he took them off himself. Her sisters knelt with her there on the floor. Each knowing what she was feeling. Tears of shared joy were streaming down their faces too. Each wore her Master's collar, and each had gone through exactly what she was going through right now.

Shelly, you have to come out of your special place now for a little while. You cannot take this vow while you are there. It is too important, and it must be your choice, not your Master's.

"But I don't want to come out. He is all that matters to me in the world. I exist only to serve him."

"I know, sis, and you can be his forevermore. But, right now you can't. This is what he asked our Masters to tell us to do for you. He said that this must be a choice that you make of your own free will."

Her world was spinning. She couldn't believe that he would let her choose not to give herself to him. She knew how much it meant to him, and he knew that she had given her self to him long before this. This ceremony was just a formality to her.

Suddenly his face was before her. He took her hands in his. He gently kissed her and said: "Honey, what they are telling you is true. You must feel free to make this choice without any coercion what so ever. You are my wife, nothing can change that. I will protect you in any way that I am able. Nothing can change that either. But, the choice to legally become my property must be yours and yours alone."

Then he was gone. Had she just imagined it? Was he really there?

Her sisters knew what she was thinking… "Relax sis. Yes, he was here. He said what needed to be said, and then he left you in our care." Come, let us pray with you.

They knelt there and prayed together for fifteen minutes. Finally, she put her arms around her sisters and told them that she was ready, and that she was more certain than ever before that this was what she wanted.

"Then all that is left is for you to stand up."

As the three slaves stood, the three Masters approached. That had been the signal that they had agreed would mean that she was ready.

She stood facing her Master with her attendants behind her. He stood facing her with their Masters attending him. The minister from their church had agreed to officiate at the ceremony. (Although he had been against it at the beginning.)

"Friends, we are gathered here for a rather unusual ceremony. I have to admit that initially I was totally against this. But, over the months since Shelly and her Master approached me, I have prayerfully considered it. I have studied everything that I could find both in scripture and from secular sources on the concept of a true Master / slave relationship. To this date, I have found nothing that says that Shelly cannot enter into a Contract Of Legal Ownership with her Master, if that is her choice. I have discussed this matter with Shelly's lawyer. I have discussed it with her Master. And I have had extensive discussions with her about it.

"She is determined to go through with this whether I officiate or not. There is no requirement that a minister preside over such a ceremony. But, these two are members of my church. They are entering into a contract that takes their relationship as husband and wife to another level. It is their desire that God be represented here as well as the law. I have prayed about this for a number of weeks, and God has given me no peace about it until I agreed in my heart to support this couple's commitment to each other.

"For those of you who do not understand, let me give a few words of explanation. A Master / slave relationship is one where one member of the couple surrenders all of their rights and privileges to the other person. A slave will literally do anything that her master tells her to. The Master assumes full responsibility for the care and protection of his slave. The six people on this platform all practice this type of relationship. As an example of what this means to them, you may have noticed that when Shelly and her Master entered, the others did not speak to her without asking permission from her Master first. This is customary for those in this lifestyle, particularly in a formal setting such as this one. After the many conversations that I have had with Shelly, I promise you that she would not have spoken to any of you without permission.

"In these types of relationships, there are varying levels of control that a Master exercises over his slave. Some Masters forbid their slaves from doing anything that they have not given express permission for. Shelly's Master has said that she can still communicate with friends just as she has since their marriage a year ago. Except in a formal setting, such as this one. She has asked me to ask each of you to honor this desire today, and not to speak to her without asking permission from her Master.

"The last comment that I would like to share with you is that you will probably have noticed that I have not used Shelly's Master's name once during my comments. Nor will I use it during the rest of the ceremony. I am doing this at Shelly's request. For her, he is 'Master' and no other name is needed."

(Minister faces Shelly.)

"Shelly, you have come here today to enter into a Contract Of Legal Ownership with this man who stands before you. Is that correct?"

"Yes."

"I hold here a legal document that your lawyer prepared for you that is titled: 'Contract Of Legal Ownership'. You have read this contract and signed it. Is this your signature?"

"Yes."

"Now I ask you before these witnesses, do you wish this contract to be legally registered with the court in this state, or do you wish for it to be destroyed?"

"I wish for it to be registered."

"Do you understand that this contract will make you the legal property of your Master, and that he will have the legal right to do anything to you that he wishes?"

"Yes, I understand."

(Minister faces Shelly's Master.)

"I hold here a legal document that Shelly's lawyer prepared for her that is titled: 'Contract Of Legal Ownership'. You have read this contract and signed it. Is this your signature?"

"Yes."

"Now I ask you before these witnesses, do you wish this contract to be legally registered with the court in this state, or do you wish for it to be destroyed?"

"I wish for it to be registered."

"Do you understand that this contract will make her your the legal property. That you will have the legal right to do anything to you that you wish, and that you will be responsible for caring for and protecting her to the extent that you are able?"

"Yes, I understand."

(Minister faces Shelly.)

"Shelly, bow before your Master and repeat after me. I Shelly, ask you of my own free will and with all of my heart to become your slave for the rest of my natural life."

She repeated, bowing with her head to the floor: "I Shelly, ask you of my own free will and with all of my heart to become your slave for the rest of my natural life."

(Minister faces Shelly's Master.)

"Master, Shelly has presented herself before you to become your property. I charge you here before these witnesses to treat her as a most valued possession. To care for her and to protect her to the best of your ability for the remainder of your natural life. If you accept this responsibility, say: 'I will'."

"I will."

"Do you have the collar?"

"Yes."

"Repeat after me: 'Shelly, I present to you this collar as an outward symbol of the commitment that we have each made in out hearts and I command you to wear it always except for such times where it is medically necessary to remove it'."

"Shelly, I present to you this collar as an outward symbol of the commitment that we have each made in out hearts and I command you to wear it always except for such times where it is medically necessary to remove it."

(Minister takes the collar and faces Shelly.)

"Shelly, this collar is an outward symbol of the commitment that you have made in your heart and of the contract that you have signed. Fasten the collar around your neck and repeat after me: 'Master, I accept your collar, and wear it as a token of the fact that you own me now and forever'."

Taking the collar and putting it on. She repeated: "Master, I accept your collar, and wear it as a token of the fact that you own me now and forever."

(Minister) "I give my word as your slave that I will never remove this collar except in situations where it is necessary for some medical procedure."

"I give my word as your slave that I will never remove this collar except in situations where it is necessary for some medical procedure."

"On the basis of the vows and contract that you have exchanged before me today, I pronounce that all has been appropriately fulfilled, and you are now bound as Master and slave now and forever."

Her Master took her in his arms and kissed her passionately. The kiss was the most magical kiss that she had ever felt. Even their first kiss as husband and wife hadn't had this effect on her. She was his. Forever. He slowly led her down the aisle using a silver leash attached to her collar, as their guests looked on. Her sisters and their Masters following, as the minister asked the guests to form a receiving line to greet the new Master and his slave.

As the guests queued up to congratulate them, she knelt before her Master and said: "I love you, Master. Thank you for making me your slave."

"I love you too. Thank you for giving me all that you are and all that you have to give."

Her parents were the first in the receiving line. She almost fainted when her father and mother congratulated her Master and then asked: "May we have your permission to congratulate your slave?" (Her Master said that it was okay as she knew he would.)

"Daughter, we have to admit that we do not understand why you wanted to do what you have just done. But, we hope it makes you happy, and we promise that we will do our best to honor your relationship with your Master."

She didn't remember anyone else who went through the receiving line. So complete was the shock and amazement at her parents' support of her decision. She was back in her special place where only her Master mattered.

Chapter 3: Collars

In our last story, we saw a hypothetical collaring ceremony. You will hear a lot of talk about collars in the community, at least among newcomers. A collar essentially means: "Taken"… "Keep-a-you-filthy-hands-off"… etc. Well, most of the time they do, anyway. There are times when a person just likes to wear a collar. Perhaps they are into goth-style clothing, for example. Or maybe they just want to go to a lifestyle event or party and not get hit on by every dominant in the place. In cases where a submissive likes to wear the collar, but IS available, I recommend simply hanging an open lock from the collar. The open lock signifies that the person is available, even though they are wearing a collar.

Types of collars

If you want to start a debate on a BDSM discussion group, one of the fastest ways if to ask about a "training collar" or about a "collar of consideration". There are dominants on both sides of the fence on this one. Before we talk about what and why, let me talk about what the different types of collars are. But, keep in mind that some dominants don't differentiate between one and the other.

In some cases, a submissive will have several different collars that are worn depending on the circumstances. In other cases, they will have a single collar that is never taken off. It doesn't really matter as long as it works for you. It is the symbolism that matters. As my girl said when she begged to wear my collar: "Wearing the collar around my neck is just a symbol of the one that already existed around my heart."

Collar of Ownership

The most common type of collar is a permanent collar of ownership. It signifies to all that a given submissive is "owned" by someone else for the rest of her life, or until she is released. The term "owned" follows the paradigm of consensual slavery that we discussed earlier. The intent of this type of collar is that it be worn 24/7, so comfort and durability are considerations. You also need to be aware of the fact that the collar will be worn in all kinds of situations.

For a collared submissive to remove their collar without explicit permission is generally considered a breech of protocol. Effectively, that person is saying: "I no longer wish for you to own me." There is quite often a very negative stigma in the community associated with a submissive removing a collar without being released. I know of dominants who would never trust a submissive who has done that.

A Collar of Ownership, it is often secured in place with a padlock. (The psychological effect of having a collar locked on can be significant.) If you choose to do so, you must make sure that there is an emergency key available so that it can be unlocked if needed. (Emergencies do happen some times.) One Master in a group that I belonged to wanted to find a way to actually weld a collar closed. I responded that I wouldn't recommend that for just this reason.

Collar of Consideration

This collar signifies that the submissive is considering a Collar of Ownership from a given Master, and that said Master is considering owning the submissive. Essentially, this is like an engagement ring. It is an announcement of a specific arrangement between two people. Unlike the negative associations of removing a Collar of Ownership, removing a Collar of Consideration is just a matter of saying: "This isn't going to work; I'm going to move on with my life." There is obviously a lot of emotional trauma if a relationship ends, but the stigma of breaking a collar isn't there. Traditionally, a Collar of Consideration is colored blue. But, even among those who believe in the various types of collars, that convention is only loosely held at best.

Training Collar

In a training situation, a submissive asks to have a given dominant train her to be a proper submissive. There are usually specific terms to the agreement identifying what that training involves. In most cases, the training collar is only worn when in the presence of the training Master. It doesn't imply any long-term plan, and most often is not a 24/7 thing.

Bridal / Wedding Collar

Sometimes a special white collar will be worn for a wedding or collaring ceremony. It is usually not worn after that. This is much like a wedding dress. It could be passed down to another if that is appropriate, or is could be framed with a copy of the certificate from the marriage or photos from the ceremony.

Collar of Protection

Sometimes an unowned submissive will feel like a guppy in the shark tank at Sea World, and they want some kind of protection from the jerks. Other times, they have tried to find an owner, and failed miserably due to poor choices. In such cases, that submissive may approach a dominant that they respect and ask to be put under a Collar of Protection. This type of collar normally goes away when the submissive finds the One he/she is seeking. If a submissive is approached by a dominant, he/she simply says: "I am under a collar of protection from Master X. I need his permission to talk to you. Could you contact him, please?" This gives the submissive a "way out" of an awkward situation. Many submissives are not comfortable telling a dominant to go away, and some are under the mistaken belief that they are not allowed to do so. If the suitor in question is serious, they will seek out Master X and talk to him about the submissive. (Most of the time they don't.) Then the protector can size up the person, and advise the submissive on what to do. This is mostly a mentor-type role. The submissive is still free to do whatever they want.

A word of caution is needed here too. Dominants can be very strong-willed individuals, with a dash of arrogance thrown in. There are some dominants who have the attitude: "Screw you. I don't have to get permission from anybody to do anything." If you choose to have a protector/mentor, you must be aware that these kinds of people will not honor that relationship, no matter how attracted to you they are.

Play Collar

A play collar is just that. It is a collar that is worn for the purpose of some play scenario, and is removed after the scene is over. It usually has no emotional significance at all.

Offered or Begged

There are essentially two schools of thought on how a submissive acquires a collar. The first is that the submissive must wait until the dominant feels that they have earned the collar. In this case, there may be specific tasks that the submissive must learn to do. Once the tasks are completed, the dominant may choose to offer a collar to the submissive, and the submissive then must decide whether to accept it or not. This most closely parallels the giving of an engagement ring.

The second school of thought is that the submissive must beg to wear the dominant's collar. In this case too, there may be tasks to learn first. Many who hold the more severe Master / slave beliefs are of this school of thought. The reasoning goes like this: "This is the last decision that the slave will make. After putting the collar on, all decisions will be made for him/her." It also accentuates the consensual nature of the relationship.

Like everything else we have talked about, there is no right or wrong here. It is simply a matter of what works for you.

Slave Petitions and Contracts

Some Masters use a formal proposal from the slave, called a slave petition, as a slave's way of asking to be owned by that Master. Many others do not want something that formal. A slave petition is a document in which the slave details what services she can (and will) provide for the Master. In a very real sense, it is a job application.

A slave contract is a document that details the conditions (including limits) of the slave's bond to the Master. It also details the Master's obligations to the slave. One other important part of the contract is that it details the disposition of any assets that the slave has rights to should she be released from ownership.

Obviously, since even consensual slavery is not recognized in a court of law, it would be difficult to make them the basis of a law suit. On the other hand, such written documents could cause a lot of legal problems for the Master.

Our Story

Our next story is about a Master getting a birthday present for His 50th birthday. In general, it is unusual for a submissive to try to surprise a Master. Most Masters don't like surprises! There is also the problem with trying to hide something from Him. Dominants tend to be very observant people, and will often catch details that others would miss. One of the key events in the story centers on the submissive being collared.

Story: "Birthday Present"

He was confused as they drove to the party. It was his fiftieth birthday. Half a century gone by. In fact, this party was all her doing. She had planned everything, the cake and decorations, the guest list, everything. The only reason that she had even told him it was a birthday party for him in advance was because he wasn't going to go otherwise. But now, as they drove to the party, she seemed nervous and pensive.

"Hey, Sugar, you seem upset tonight. What's wrong? The party will be a success. You've worked hard on it. Everything will be fine."

"I know, Sir. The party will be okay. Please, Sir, please don't ask me what's wrong; I can't tell you right now. But, I promise I will tell you before the evening ends. I just can't tell you right now. Please, sir, don't make me!"

"Okay, Sugar. I trust your instincts, and I won't push you… for the moment. But, once the party is over, I will have an explanation. Understood?"

She knew he wouldn't budge from that attitude. That was part of the strength she needed from him. She had seen him demonstrate over and over that he would do whatever he saw she needed in order to care for and protect her. Her heart was his. She wanted nothing in life except to hear him say: "Thank you, Sugar, you have pleased me." She simply looked at him, and said: "Yes, Sir, I understand." It was all she could do to keep from crying. She had secret plans for tonight that she couldn't tell him… not yet. And those secrets were what worried her. She had never kept secrets from him… never.

On the way to the party they had to stop and pick up a few last-minute things. She asked him to wait in the car for her. She had never done that before, but she didn't want him to see the cake. Perhaps he knew it was something special, perhaps he was just reacting to her mood, she didn't know. But, she was positively relieved when he agreed to wait there. She had purchased a very special cake for him! So embarrassing and yet exhilarating too. The local supermarket had a process where they would take a photograph and "print" it in icing on a cake. She had taken a picture of herself, totally naked, to the store to have it put on his cake. She had to talk to the store manager for nearly an hour before he finally agreed to do it for her… at twice the price of a regular photo cake! She knew he would love it, and their guests would as well.

While he waited, he checked the toy bag to make sure everything he brought was still there. He had a big surprise for her tonight. He was going to offer her his collar of consideration, asking her to begin the formal process of becoming his kajira; his property to love and care for. He didn't think she suspected anything. But, maybe she did, and that was why she was upset he was pretty certain that it wasn't just the party. He was sure that she would accept his collar… But what if she didn't? He had come to love her over the months that they had been together. He knew she loved him as well, but was she ready to take this step? He wasn't sure.

Kelly returned to the car with the cake and other party supplies. She had peeked at the cake in the store to make sure it had turned out the way she wanted. From the look on the bakery clerk's face, she liked it too, and was imagining having a look at the real thing.

Her sir reached over to peek at the cake as she put it on the back seat of his car.

"Sir, please don't look. It is a surprise."

Surprise? Surprise? Hmmm… He wasn't so sure about this. It wasn't like her to be secretive. In fact, the way she was behaving was totally out of character for what he had come to expect from her.

"Sugar? Are you okay? I mean, are you *really* okay? You are acting very strangely this evening."

"Sir, I'm fine. It is just my nerves. Please, Sir, can we leave and go to the party?" She couldn't tell him what she planned, and she didn't know for sure how he would react. He was such a complicated man sometimes.

He sat there for a few minutes looking at her; trying to decide if she was really "okay" or if he needed to take her home. Where her emotional well-being was concerned, he didn't give her a choice; he did what he thought was best for her. She wouldn't look at him. He could see that her hands were shaking and her eyes were tearing up… she was about to cry.

"*PLEASE*, Sir, can we go?"

He looked at her one moment more. Not at all sure what was going on.

"Yes, Sugar. But, if you get upset at the party, we are out of there. You are more important to me than cake and ice cream with our friends."

The rest of the trip to the party was pretty uneventful. Still, he was very worried about her. Maybe tonight wasn't a good time to offer her a collar. He would just have to play that by ear. It would be a disappointment, of course. But, her well-being was more important.

They got to the hall that she had rented for the party, and he was surprised at the number of cars in the parking lot. There were even one or two cars with out of state license plates. He didn't know anyone who would come that far for cake and ice cream.

"This looks like a bigger event than I thought you were planning. No wonder you are a little nervous."

They walked to the door with arms around each other's waists. As they entered, Joe and Jennifer, Sam and Sally met them.

"Jen, Sal, there are some things still in the car. Can you help me get them?"

"Sure thing, Kel." Both women answered in unison with a smile and a knowing wink.

Joe and Sam looked at Ed and simply said: "Follow us, please."

They ushered him to a small coat room off the side of the entry hall. Both dropped to one knee in front of him.

"Your majesty, tonight you are the King of the party. We kneel to honor you. Every dominant and submissive here has agreed to this. On the hanger to your right is a jeweled cape suitable for royalty. *(Obviously, not 'real' jewels, we were on a budget, and it is a rental, so please don't spill anything on it.)*"

Thinking: "This is just flat-out strange.", Ed donned the crimson cape and allowed his friends to lead him into the main hall. At his entry, every dominant dropped to one knee with head bowed, and every submissive in the room bowed in homage with their forehead to the floor.

In a rather loud voice, Joe said: "Loyal subjects of the 'House of Ed', I present your King!"

Nobody made a sound as King Ed was ushered to a raised dais and a "throne" that had been set up at one end of the room.

He stood in front of his chair in stunned silence. This was the most unexpected and absolutely wonderful thing that anyone had ever done for him. He looked for Kelly. This had to be all her idea. She really had a gift for finding the most unexpected things to please him. He was mildly amazed when he couldn't find her.

"My loyal subjects, I can't tell you how this makes me feel. I am not worthy of the honor that you have given me, and I thank you with every fiber of my being. Arise and be welcome in our presence."

As he seated himself, his guests began to come to greet him personally. Each one bowed to him respectfully. Each dominant presented their submissive's bottom to receive King Ed's birthday spanking. He still hadn't found Kelly though, and given her state of mind, he was beginning to be very concerned that she was okay.

Suddenly, the lights were turned out and the only light in the room came from a few candles lit near the dais. He could see some shadowy movement, but couldn't really tell what was going on.

When the lights were turned on, he could see a trio of women before him. He recognized Jen and Sal immediately, and it only took a second to recognize the raven black hair of the woman bowing with her head to the floor before him… "Kelly?"

Sally cleared her throat and began to speak. "Your majesty, your humble subject bears greetings from the woman bowing before you. What I read to you now are her words, not my own.

"Majesty, on the celebration of your birth, I bring several gifts to you. The first is…" (Kelly straightened to a kneeling position and removed her robe to reveal a large red ribbon taped between her breasts. She knelt naked before him and the assembled guests and Sally continued to read.) "… Sir, you have won my heart and my mind just by being who you are. As of this moment, I give you all that I am, for I can do no less than that. You deserve far more than I can give; I give you all that

I am."

Jennifer approached the dais with a small box and handed it to him. He opened it in astonishment to stare down at a shiny collar and lock.

Sal resumed reading: "… I present to you this collar of consideration as your second birthday gift. It is yours to give to anyone you select. I humbly offer myself to become your slave and your property for a trial period in the sincere hope that you will find me acceptable to become your slave for the rest of my natural life. If there is another more worthy, I beg you to cast me aside and take her instead. You deserve only the best."

Kelly knelt there before him. This is what the whole night was about. Was she worthy of him? She was shaking uncontrollably. Tears were streaming down her face. She knew that from this moment onward, she was his, whether he collared her or not, and if he sent her away, she didn't know what she would do.

He spoke to Sam briefly, who handed him his toy bag. He removed a small object that she didn't recognize, and then walked to stand before her. Through her tears she couldn't see it clearly.

He gently took her face in his strong hand until her eyes met his and whispered: "How did you know?" It was only then that she saw that he was holding two collars.

In a louder voice, he addressed the room. "My dear friends, I call upon you now to witness this next step in the life that Kelly and I share. I charge you all with responsibility to support this covenant to the best of your ability. This is understood to be a trial of the Master / slave relationship between Kelly and myself. Before each of you now I accept responsibility for her care, protection, and training until such time as she is released from this bond."

"Kelly. You have become kajira to my house. You understand that by this request you are committing yourself to total obedience no matter what, and that you will consider yourself to be my property from this point forward. If this is your intention, take this collar from my hand, fasten it around your neck, and secure it with the padlock. From the point that lock has clicked closed, you will refer to me only as 'Master' and you shall have no name other than 'kajira to the House of Ed' until such time as you have earned the right to have a name of your own."

With trembling hands she took the collar that he had selected for her from his hands and examined it. It was a light aluminum collar with a blue colored coating. On both sides of the padlock hasp, he had inscribed her new name in a fancy script: "*I am kajira of the House of Ed, by my own choice property of my Master.*" Finally, with her heart soaring, she fastened it around her neck and snapped the lock shut. With her eyes locked on his face and with a trembling voice, she said: "Master, all that I am is your property. I have seen in you the way that you care for all of your possessions, and I trust you without question. I am, from this day forward, until such time as you release me, kajira to the House of Ed." And handing him the key to the lock, she said: "Master, may I never remove this collar without your knowledge and approval.

All of the friends began to clap and cheer.

In a loud voice, trying to overcome the noise, Sally called for their attention one more time as King Ed returned to his throne. "There is one last gift that the kajira wishes to give her Master. She requests that all assembled here who would like to give her Master a 'birthday spanking' give it to her in his place. He is too kind and gentle to be spanked, and she is just a humble slave girl who deserves nothing more. She wants only to serve him in this way."

Everyone lined up to do as she asked. Each of the seventy-five invited guests proceeded to give her five hard swats on her naked bottom. Each of the seventy-five guests knew what was in her heart. Knew what she was feeling. Knew that she needed to serve Him. Not one of them held back. After the first ten guests spanked her, her bottom was starting to get sore. By the time all were finished, she was crying uncontrollably.

After the last person finished, King Ed sent Joe to fetch a cold wash cloth and some oil. He then went down to lift his kajira off the floor. Between her sobs, he could hear her soft words: "I-it... i-is... m-m-my... pl-pl-pleasure... t-to... s-serve... y-you,... M-m-master." He held her in his arms and whispered: "You did well, my kajira. You have pleased me more than you can know." As he began to minister to her sore bottom, and to hold her and comfort her, all she could do was to cry tears of joy that he was willing to own someone as worthless as her. It didn't make sense to her; any sub who really got to know him would have died to become owned by him. But, he chose her, and it just didn't make sense.

They spent the next hour together like that while their guests ate finger sandwiches and partied. Someone fired up a stereo and couples began to dance.

When she had recovered from her spanking, they rejoined their guests. For no reason other than the fact that he liked her that way, she stayed naked the rest of the evening. She didn't see that it mattered, they had each seen her body and had had their hands on her bottom; and it would please Him. Nothing else mattered in her world.

A few of the other subs doffed their clothing as well and joined her. All gave her congratulations, but she didn't even hear them... he said he was greatly pleased with her, and that was all that mattered.

At last it was time to serve the cake. She had kept it covered until then... "All right, who wants to eat my tits?" she shouted. The sheer comic relief of that moment released all of her stress, and she was crying again. But, tears of joy, not pain. She was his, and he was pleased!

As the party came to an end, and it was time to leave, she looked at her Master and said: "Master, is this one going home with you tonight?"

"Yes, kajira, you are. And tomorrow we will go collect your clothes and other belongings and you will come live with me."

"M-m-master, y-you w-want th-this g-girl to l-l-live with y-you??!!!" Her heart sang with a joy that she had never felt before. Nothing mattered but Him, and His happiness.

"Master, is this one required to put clothing on to go home, or may this one remain naked to please you?"

"Kajira, it is dark enough outside, and there won't be anyone around. I do not require this of you, but it would please me if you remained naked. If this is your choice, I will go out and check that it is safe for you to do so."

"That is this one's choice, Master. Thank you for keeping this girl safe."

Like the ride to the party, the ride home was uneventful. She couldn't stop smiling because she was so happy. She didn't care if she ever wore clothes again, as long as He was pleased.

When they arrived home, he parked the car in the garage and they went into the house. Once inside the house, she remained standing quietly by the door waiting for him to tell her what to do next. She ached to just hear the sound of his voice.

"Master?"

"Yes?"

"Did you know that this one has never been spanked in public like that before?"

"Yes. You told me that back when we first met. Remember?"

"This girl is sorry Master. This girl does not remember. Would you please punish her to help her remember better the next time?"

"Excuse me? I have never punished you for forgetting what you have told me before, have I?"

"No."

"'No.' what?!!"

"No, Master. This girl is sorry Master."

"That's better.... If I haven't punished you for things like that before, why would I start now?"

"B-b-but, Master," (she began crying again) "... A slave must be **PERFECT** for her Master."

"No, kajira, you won't ever be perfect, you can't; and neither can I. That is just a fact of life. A wise Master learns when his kajira is being lax or disobedient and when she just simply made a mistake. Disobedience or carelessness is a problem. Making a mistake happens. It is a question of intent."

"This one does not understand, Master."

"It doesn't matter whether you understand at this point. All you need to know is that I will not punish you for things that you have no power over."

"This girl understands, thank you, Master."

"Master? May this one ask where she is to sleep?"

"You are to sleep on the floor beside my bed tonight. In the future, you will earn the right to sleep in the bed with me. But you will always sleep in the room where I am."

"Thank you, Master. This girl is honored to breathe the same air that you have breathed."

"How may this one serve you, Master?"

"Go draw yourself a hot relaxing bath. Do not get in the tub until I get there. I will bathe you myself tonight."

"MASTER!!! NO!!! This girl is not worthy of you serving her like that! You can't be serious!"

He reached across and gave her a gentle but firm slap across the mouth. "That is our first rule. 'You will NEVER in thought or word consider yourself worthless.' You are the most valuable thing that I own. I will not allow others to talk about you that way, I will not talk about you that way, and you are not permitted to talk about yourself that way."

Her mouth stung from the slap, but that pain was just a nuisance compared to the pain in her heart. She had displeased him. She couldn't even go one day! She was a failure!

Suddenly his face was mere inches from hers. He laced his fingers into her hair pulling it tight. She couldn't more her head. "I know what you are thinking. STOP IT! Didn't you hear the words I just spoke to you? Now get that filth out of your mind, and go draw your bath. You will find bath oils in the linen closet."

She opened her mouth to speak; to make him understand. Before she could say a word, he raised his hand in warning. "This subject is not open to discussion. This is one area where you will simply obey. You are NOT worthless. There is NO justification for saying so. Go!"

As much as she needed the steel in his character, there were times she wished he would bend just a little. All she could do was to kneel before him and say: "Yes, Master. This one will obey you. She will not think of herself as worthless. Please help this girl, Master. She does not know how to do as you have commanded."

"I know kajira. This is something you have believed all of your life. I will help you learn, but it will take time and more than a few back-hands across the mouth. But, you will learn." He gently took her hands and helped her stand. He held her in his strong arms and kissed her. Then he whispered in her ear: "I love you kajira. Now go do as you were told."

All she could say was: "Yes, Master."

As she walked down the hallway to the bathroom, all she could think was that they had reached a new depth. Her feelings were deeper than she had imagined possible. "Love" was such a bland, dimensionless word to use for what she felt. She felt wonderful… more than wonderful… and had no words that she could use to tell someone about it. As she turned on the bath water she was crying again…

Chapter 4: Limits

There is much talk on BDSM discussion groups about limits. Both dominants and submissives have limits. A limit is simply something that you won't do, for whatever reason. There are a group of "standard" limits that most people have. I will discuss those toward the end of the chapter. However, keep in mind that what is a limit for you may be a real turn-on for someone else. No matter what activity you want to do, if you look hard enough, you will find someone that does it. There are four combinations of how the limits can work.

- ☐ X is a limit for both dominant and submissive.
- ☐ X is NOT a limit neither the dominant nor the submissive.
- ☐ X is a limit for the dominant, but not for the submissive. ("dominant limit")
- ☐ X is a not a limit for the dominant, but is a limit for the submissive ("submissive limit")

Obviously, the first two combinations are not a problem. Usually, the focus of discussion of limits is on the submissive's limits, this is generally appropriate. So, I will discuss Dominant limits first.

Dominant Limits

In a BDSM relationship, the dominant's limits usually don't become an issue since the dominant is the one deciding what is being done, and simply doesn't do anything that violates His/Her limits. This only becomes an issue if the submissive absolutely needs activity X to be part of their relationship and the Dominant will not do X because that is a limit.

For example, Sammi (a submissive) is interested in Fred (a strong Dominant). One of Sammi's requirements is that her Dom select what clothing she wears every day, and that He select what food she eats. Fred, on the other hand, is of the opinion that she is an adult and can choose her own wardrobe. He refuses to "dress her" every day. This is an example where the submissive has a need that the dominant refuses to meet. This is, in fact, a rare situation, but it does happen.

In reality, what it comes down to is that Sammi wants to be controlled more rigidly than Fred is willing to do. The level of control / submission desired in a relationship has to be a relatively close match. If the dominant tries to take more control than the submissive is willing to give, the submissive will rebel and claim that he/she is being smothered. If the reverse is true, the submissive wants / needs more control then the dominant gives, then the dominant "just doesn't care" about the submissive or what he/she does.

Submissive Limits

A submissive's limits, on the other hand, can be an issue. Let's use Sammi and Fred again. Sammi has a limit of performing oral sex. Fred likes a good blow job once in a while. Since they really clicked in other areas, Fred accepts Sammi's limit and things are good for a while. Then one night Fred forgets and asks Sammi to perform oral sex on Him. That leaves Sammi between a rock and a hard place emotionally. As a submissive, she has a strong desire to do what her dominant tells her to. But, this is something that she doesn't want to do. In addition, since He asked for a blow job, she can feel that He violated her trust that He would honor her limits.

This becomes a no win situation for everyone involved. Either she gives Fred the blow job or she doesn't. If she does, the trust is broken because He "forced" her to violate one of her limits. Or, if she doesn't do as she is asked, she feels bad about herself for not obeying her dominant and her self esteem suffers. There is a lot of danger in making sweeping generalizations. But, in this case I will. (Keep in mind that you might be the exception!) In general, emotionally, submissives are much more fragile than dominants are. So, breaking a submissive's limit will be more traumatic than breaking a dominant's limit. It is very bad for the dominant to adopt an attitude of: "I don't see what the big deal is." The fact is that to the submissive it IS a big deal.

Hard or soft limits

Often a person will try to classify their limits as either "hard" or "soft". A hard limit is one that they are firm about, whereas a soft limit is something they don't like and don't want to do, but that they are willing to do, however reluctantly. Taking our couple Sammi and Fred again. Let's say that Sammi is willing to suck Fred's cock if He wants her to. But she doesn't like it, and doesn't want to do it very often. That would be a soft limit. However, as part of the deal, Sammi says that Fred can't cum in her mouth. On her face is okay (another soft limit) but not inside of her mouth. That would be a hard limit.

Changing limits

Over time, what a person will / won't do changes. That is just the nature of things. Similarly, what a person wants will change too. You should expect this and plan for it. Periodically, you should review each other's limits and see if anything has changed. Perhaps a hard limit became a soft limit or not a limit at all. Or, perhaps you discovered that you have a limit that you didn't know anything about. Along the same lines, a dominant will sometimes "push" a submissive's limits. For example,

Fred might talk about wanting to cum in Sammi's mouth. You have to be careful not to make it a demand, and to be judicious about when you do it. But, as I say, limits do change.

"No limits"

Well, there's another hot button discussion topic! From time to time a submissive will announce that they are available, and have "no limits". Of course, that's a load of bull. Everyone has limits. I have never encountered someone who would allow their fingers to be cut off, just because someone wanted to do it.

So, what does "no limits" really mean? First choice: "No *unreasonable* limits." This interpretation has a basic flaw. It assumes that what I feel is unreasonable is the same thing that you feel is unreasonable. (Like cutting fingers off.) Second choice: "No limits other than those that a sane person would expect." (So, now you're calling me crazy too?) This comes down to the same argument. My definition of "sanity" must be the same as yours. The third choice: "No limits in addition to what my dominant's limits already are." This is typically what is meant when a person says: "No limits."

"Standard" limits

As I mentioned above, there are some limits that are almost universal. That is, almost every submissive has them. That list is:

- ☐ No children. No play, sexual or otherwise, that involves persons under the legal age of majority.
- ☐ No scat. Scat, also sometimes called "shit play", is using fecal matter in the course of play. I know of slaves that routinely consume Master's shit. As in, he goes in their mouth and they swallow it. I know of another Master who uses the toilet for a bowel movement, but uses His slave's tongue instead of toilet paper. There is another area of play called "anal lingus" which involves sticking your tongue up another person's asshole. This may or may not be "scat" depending on your definition.
- ☐ No body mutilation. No cutting off fingers. No making cuts that draw blood and leave a scar behind. Some would even include getting a tattoo in this group.

Conclusion

The whole area of limits is one that needs to be discussed frequently. You also may find that you discover limits that you never knew you had that need to be added to the list, or you might find that some things that you thought were limits really are not limits any more. For example, I am sure that more than one reader of this book has never considered that someone might ask them to drink piss or eat shit. As such, it wasn't on their list of limits before. (I bet it is now!) Yes, before you ask, there are submissives that do both of these to please their owner.

Another good thing to do is to fill out a BDSM checklist. Typically, these checklists have several columns. The first column is an activity name, the second column would be a check box that says whether you have actually tried the activity or not, and the final column is an indicator of how much you like the activity (if you have done it before) or how much interest you have in trying it (if you have not done it before). There are a number of sites where you can find these lists. They can be a mechanism for starting a dialog with a dominant, and determining the interests you have in common.

Our Story

The story for this chapter is about a first date. As you will see, the couple in the story cross into quite a few areas that you would probably find as limits on a first date. In fact, the woman who inspired the story itself had quite a few limits that would have been crossed by the events in the story.

Story: "First Date"

[Author's note: I dedicate this story to the wonderful young woman who inspired it... She knows who she is]

"Dear Diary..."

Tonight had been their first date. Sharon didn't remember what she expected from Him, but she knew that what she expected wasn't what she got. She got more than she had dreamed possible. Even now, in the afterglow of a wonderful evening, she could still feel the warmth of His touch and the strength in His hands, all under control.

"Oh my goodness, diary, where do I begin?... I guess a good beginning is: 'Holy Shit!' because that's what I am feeling."

She had been watching Him for months. They belonged to the same discussion list. She didn't post much; preferring to stay in the background and just watch. But, He was fairly active there. She had never met Him in person until a few weeks ago at a club meeting. From His posts on the list, she could tell that He was different. He was usually one of the first to welcome newcomers and make them feel at ease. Even in His personal chats to her He was warm and caring... even when she thought she was being a royal bitch.

"... I have so much I want to write. But, I am afraid that writing the words won't capture what I felt. Somehow, it will 'pop the bubble' and make the evening less than it was. I don't even know if I can put into words what He did to me..."

The evening began the way she planned it. He arrived at her apartment promptly at 7:00. He had told her that one of the things He liked to do was to select clothing for His sub and dress her. She had thought seriously about answering the door naked and leading Him to the bedroom. But, her roommate would have objected. So, she decided on just wearing a bathrobe.

There was a knock on the door. It had to be Him. She was nervous; really nervous. What if He didn't like her? For that matter, what if He DID like her? She felt "something" when she met Him in person. Even writing about that, she couldn't find words to tell her diary what she felt. She opened the door. A little more quickly than she thought she should have. If He noticed, He never said anything.

He was standing there before her with six long-stemmed red roses. He smiled as he handed them to her and said: "I picked the ones with the longest thorns." She just stood there and stared at Him struck dumb by such a simple thing. Nobody had ever gotten her flowers before... nobody.

"If you would back up a few steps, I could come in and you could close the door. I know that the draft of the wind blowing up your robe feels good and all that, but I doubt that the neighbors are interested."

She shook herself and came back to reality. She had completely forgotten that she was almost naked. "Oh… Of course, Sir … Please some in."

As He entered, she gently closed the door, still slightly dazed. "I'll put these in a vase." (If we have one, that is.) "Hey Jan." (She paused a minute.) "I'm sorry Sir, where are my manners. Sir Stephen, this is my roommate Jan. Jan, this is Sir Stephen."

He faced Jan, and with a slight bow said: "Pleased to meet you."

Jan responded: "Nice to meet you too." And gave Him a penetrating stare that almost withered the flowers Sharon had in her hand.

"Jan, do we have a vase for these?"

"I think there is one in the kitchen. Let me help you find it. Excuse us for a moment, Sir Stephen."

"Of course."

As they entered the kitchen, Jan turned suddenly on her roommate. "Are you out of you frigging mind? You take these flowers, and he will expect you to spread your legs for him. No man ever gives flowers without expecting you to 'pay' for them!"

"I don't care. If He wants to fuck, I'll do it and He can wake me up when it's over." (Now, as she thought back on the evening, she was so embarrassed to have even thought that about Him!)

"Okay. Okay. It's your business. The vase is under the sink. Don't forget to put an aspirin in the water to keep the flowers fresh longer. At least they'll outlast what you'll have to do to earn them."

Sharon put the flowers in the vase, added water and the recommended aspirin and returned. She put the vase in the middle of the dining room table, and motioned to Sir Stephen… "C'mon, I need your help picking out clothes to wear. Hell, I don't even know where we are going."

He laughed as he followed her down the hall to her bedroom. "That's easy. I thought maybe we would go to the Steak House that I saw driving in."

She closed the door and then in a single graceful motion she shed her robe so that she was totally naked before Him, and knelt at His feet. "Please dress me as you will, Sir."

He stepped to her side and gently rolled her backward onto His waiting arm. He slipped His other arm under her knees and lifted her up to the bed. He tenderly laid her down and locked His steel-grey eyes onto hers.

All she could think was: "*Holy shit, Jan was right. And I don't even get dinner first!*"

As He stared into her eyes, he simply said: "The beginning of anything is a very delicate time. I want you to remember forever your first moments with me." (And, she had to admit that she would… forever.)

He continued: "This is an exercise in 'trust'. Right now, you don't know a lot about me; and I don't know a lot about you. We have no reason to trust each other, other than our shared need to trust and to be trusted. You have no way of knowing if what I have told you is true, or a carefully crafted lie to get you right where you are now.

"Before I dress you, I want you to lay there on the bed and relax. Close your eyes and breathe deeply. Don't open your eyes until I tell you to. I am going to touch you; all I want you to focus on is the warmth of that touch."

She closed her eyes; expecting the worst. Her only thought was: "*Well, it will be over and I can fake cramps or a headache or something. This can't be the Dom who wrote all of those tender, empathetic posts to the discussion lists. He's just another asshole control-freak like the other Doms I've met.*"

Tenderly His lips touched hers. Lightly. Not the strong, forceful touch of animal lust, but a soft, tender caress that she wasn't sure was real or imagined. She felt his hands run through her long hair. Felt his hot breath on the side of her neck, just below her ear. She heard Him whisper: "You are safe. This is about your needs, not mine."

He began to lick her neck where His breath had been only seconds before. It was a light touch with just the tip of His tongue. His arm lay on her chest in the hollow between her breasts. His hand reached up to lightly touch her neck on the side opposite from his tongue. The sensation was starting to warm her, and she was beginning to genuinely relax. Ever so slowly He began moving His tongue and hand down to the hollow of her shoulders. He moved to stand above her head, and slowly, methodically, He massaged her neck and shoulders with both hands. He used alternating patterns of pressure; rubbing both the surface and the sides of the muscles that supported her head. He was in constant contact with her body, but the nature of His touch, for some reason, didn't feel alien to her. It felt like He was reaching into her and pulling out the bad parts… stress and tension… and leaving in their place only warmth.

Next He massaged each of her arms, servicing each individually. She was proud of those arms. She went to the gym three times a week to work out, and thought that the effect on her arms and legs was worth it. True, she was no Amazon. But, then again, she didn't want to be. He seemed to know exactly how to touch her arms to relax the muscles. He spoke quietly, continuing to set the mood for her: "You have nice, firm triceps and biceps. I can feel the strength in them even in this reclined position."

He moved on to her pectoral muscle group. She almost didn't notice when His hands caressed her breasts; rubbing and relaxing the muscles around her chest. He avoided her nipples. Although, she had to admit to herself, she wanted Him to grab them and pinch them like nobody had ever done before. (Wait a minute, where did that thought come from? Shit! They were only some damn flowers. But, what He was doing DID feel good.) She could feel the effect His ministrations were having on her. Not only was she becoming very relaxed, she could feel her nipples hardening slightly and

65

sensations between her legs that had been gone far too long…. *"Well, maybe fucking Him wouldn't be as bad as she had thought at first."*

He repositioned her on the bed so that her legs were bent at the knee and hanging over the edge of the mattress. Easier access to what He wanted, she assumed. *"Damn! I'm as jaded as Jan is. I've had the assholes like she has. But, why am I assuming Sir Stephen is one of them?"* As He massaged her abdominal muscles, the stress that had crept back into her began fading again. As He moved toward her hips and pelvis, he seemed to be keeping the same pace he had been using all alone. He wasn't in a hurry to just grab her pussy and ram his fingers into her. He was taking his time. Her time. He seemed to know that she needed longer than He did to get ready.

Finally! He slid His hand across her pussy, running His fingers through the hair He found there. Gently He slipped His finger between her lips and found her moist clit there. He rubbed it for a little while, and then returned to massaging her furry mound. He had an odd expression on His face. She had no idea what she was thinking.

Abandoning her pussy, He massaged the muscles of her ass. He was a bit firmer there. It seemed like a contradiction to her that the same hands that had been soft and gentle were now digging fingertips into her body. But, now that she thought of it, she loved feeling the pain in her ass. Her last "Dom" had a flexible pine switch that he had beaten her with over and over. She loved that. But, she had never told Sir Stephen about it. How could He know?

Still keeping His hands on her skin, he sat down on the bed beside her. He lifted her right leg so that it was straight up. He cradled it in His arms, holding it against His chest. He arranged it so that the back of His left arm rested against her pussy so that as He kneaded her thigh muscles, she would still feel the movement there. He finally stood up again, but kept her leg embraced against His body. He moved around so that His hip was against her groin, so that she would continue to be stimulated while he massaged her right calf, ankle, and foot.

Slowly, patiently, He repeated the same sequence with her left leg. After finishing both legs, He stood before her with both legs held together against His chest, He continued to stroke them. She could feel his pants rub against her ass as she laid there waiting, anticipating Him entering her.

Slowly he changed her position on the bed. When He could do so, He laid down next to her. He slid His hand between the lips of her pussy. Rubbing her clit and the opening of her vagina with His palm, He watched her face to see what she was feeling. His hand was wet from the fluids flowing out of her. To her surprise, He lifted His hand to her face to wipe it across her mouth. She opened her mouth and tasted herself on His hand. It was amazing the effect this had on her.

His hand returned to the moist area between her legs, and she felt his fingers enter her. She was past the point of stopping. She could smell her feminine perfume and taste the saltiness on her tongue. She begged Him: "Please make me cum. I can't stop. Please, Sir, Please." As He rubbed her faster and faster, he whispered into her ear: "It's all about what you need." With the last syllable of

His whisper, her body exploded. She was totally lost in the hedonistic pleasure of the moment. At that moment, He could have done anything to her. She didn't care. All that mattered was her need for release. She screamed. She moaned. She cried. She wrapped her arms around Him, and pulled His mouth to hers. She kissed Him greedily, pouring into that kiss all of the passion and pure animal lust that she was feeling. As the spasms began to recede, her kisses became more tender. More like the ones He began with.

Sir Stephen smiled down at her: "That's part one. I'll be back in a moment. Just relax."

He needed to go back out to his car to get his razor. Sharon definitely needed a "hair cut" before part two.

As he opened the door, Jan called from the living room: "You got what you wanted and now you're leaving?… You could have at least bought her dinner, you shit."

"No, Jan, I'm not leaving. But, I do need something out of my car. Maybe while I'm there I'll get some duct tape for your mouth too."

When he walked back in, Jan just glared at him. He walked past her without seeming to notice. He returned to Sharon's bedroom. She was still drifting in the glow of her released need. He gently spread her legs apart, and sat down between them. To His left, He sat her garbage can. Beginning by using the mustache trimmer on His razor, He clipped all of her pubic hair as short as possible. She watched silently as tuft after tuft of her black fur made its journey to the garbage can. Then He switched to using the shaver to get rid of the remaining stubble to make her smooth. As he put the garbage can away, she reached down and felt the smooth void that had been a hairy bush just moments before. Somehow, the sensations felt more intense. She didn't know if it was the shaving, or the fact that she had just had the most incredible orgasm she had had since leaving college. (Granted, there hadn't been many since college.) But, right now, she didn't give a damn either.

When He returned to her bed, He smiled and said: "Now for part two. Roll over."

She rolled over. If part two was as good as part one, she didn't give a damn what he did.

He knelt down and began massaging her back. She couldn't imagine being more relaxed. He seemed to be able to feel the tension in her muscles. He flawlessly found and kneaded each one. His touch was amazing. He skipped over her ass, and went straight to her legs. When he was finished with her legs, He returned to her ass. He kneaded her ass, sometimes reaching between her legs to rub her hairless pussy. He would slide fingers inside of her. Sometimes into her pussy, sometimes up her ass. She didn't care.

Finally, He moved back to speak softly in her ear: "Kitten, you are very dirty, and you need a bath."

She started to roll over and look at Him… "I took a shower just…" He gently pushed her back down on the bed and softly said: "Not that kind of a bath."

To her surprise, He began licking her body. Using His tongue to "clean" her, He washed every inch of her back, ass, and legs. It did give her a moment's pause to feel His tongue move in and out of her asshole. Even though nobody had done that before, she found the sensation of doing the "ultimate forbidden act" was quite a turn-on in itself.

He had her roll over on her back once again and proceeded to "clean" the rest of her body. It gave her a real rush when He kissed her, putting His tongue, the tongue that had just been in her ass just moments ago, deep into her mouth. He licked all of her body. He paid particular attention to her nipples. He sucked on them hard and then He grabbed them with His teeth and pulled on them. She didn't know how He could bite them that hard and not draw blood.

He stood above her... "Well, I guess you're almost clean enough."

Having said that, He put His head between her legs and began licking her clit in earnest. She hadn't realized just how much she wanted that. She reached down and grabbed His hair to pull Him closer. She couldn't talk, but she needed Him to feel her need. She wanted to savor what He was doing to her. But, when He put two fingers in her asshole and began to finger-fuck her there, it was too much to control. She was once again out of control. She pulled His face into her and clamped her legs down in uncontrolled response to Him. Her back arched. She screamed in ecstasy as wave after wave of her orgasm wracked her body.

Without speaking, He stood up. She whispered faintly: "Fuck me please."

He looked down at her glistening body and said: "Not tonight. You are not ready for that yet, and tonight was all about you, and your needs."

Saying that, he left the room and returned with a wash cloth.

"Tongue baths are all well and good, but to go to dinner, we probably need to clean you up a little."

With that, He washed her and dried her off. Then He dressed her in low-rider jeans and a halter top.

As he carried her out to His car, she smiled at Jan and said: "You were wrong about this one."

Chapter 5: Relationships

A relationship is simply an interaction between two or more people. They range from the very simple: "Do you want fries with that?" to extremely intricate. In most modern relationships today, the people in the relationship will generally claim that it is a relationship of "equals." But, in reality, that isn't totally true. For example, let's say your boss says: "I need that report finished by the end of the day." There isn't any equality there! Or is there?

The founding fathers of the United States wrote in the Declaration of Independence: ***"We hold these truths to be self-evident, that all men are created equal, that they are endowed by their Creator with certain unalienable Rights…"*** But, that was an era of non-consensual slavery and indentured servants. It was a time when women had virtually no rights at all. So, clearly our forefathers didn't see everyone as equal. Perhaps there is another meaning.

What does it mean? Equal?… Not equal in height, weight, or even hair color…. It means equal "personhood." But, even equal persons can be placed in unequal roles. We see this many times each and every day of our lives. The teenage girl asking: "Do you want fries with that?" is serving you by taking your order for food. You are the customer. Nobody would believe that those are equal roles. But, it is equally true that everyone views the two of them as equal persons.

In the BDSM lifestyle, relationships generally follow the Dominant/submissive model. That is, one person is in the dominant role and makes the decisions, and the other is in the submissive role and accepts having decisions made for them. They are equal as persons, but they are filling unequal roles. The biggest problem I encounter in talking about my relationship is when people say: "Ask your girlfriend what she wants." Or "Does your girlfriend let you…?" Generally, I reply: "She doesn't get a vote." and brush the matter aside. Many people in the "vanilla world" (vanilla meaning not in the BDSM lifestyle) have a fundamental problem with my slave not being allowed to select what food she eats or what she spends money on, even who she chats with on the computer. Even if I explain that she doesn't want to make the decisions, they still have a hard time accepting that.

Scales of Dominance/submission

There is a wide spectrum of variation in just how Dominant/submissive a person is. There is no right or wrong here, as long as it works for you. For some submissives, they want their Master to control everything, even down to whether they are allowed to use the toilet or not. It is all a matter of how much or how little control one person wants to give to the other. For other couples, they are mostly "vanilla", but they like to add some kink into their sex lives. You can think of it as a line with "Master" (or "Mistress") on one end and "slave" on the other. Using this scale, "vanilla" is somewhere in the middle.

One of Murphy's Laws that I saw once said: "Nothing is always, everything is sometimes." (Of course, this law doesn't apply to itself, since the law is ALWAYS in effect.) Do not make the assumption that if a person is ultra-dominant in one area, that they will be dominant in all areas, all of the time. It doesn't work that way; that would be far too easy. The level of Dominance/submission will fluctuate from day-to-day, sometimes from moment-to-moment. I will give you an example. I know a submissive who is owned by a Master. Her Master doesn't view on-line activities as "real." Therefore, He exercises no control over her on-line activities. Subsequently, she can do whatever she pleases in on-line groups. In fact, I know that she has said things on-line that would have gotten her into deep trouble in real life.

Switches

There are people in the BDSM lifestyle who call themselves "a switch." At first glance, this is confusing. (Sometimes at second glance too!) A switch is a person who is sometimes dominant, and sometimes submissive. Typically, this person has one particular orientation most of the time, and can switch into the other orientation under certain circumstances. I know a person who is a strong female dominant most of the time. However, with one person, and one person only, she chooses to be submissive. This is not an act that she puts on. It is not play acting. It is a fundamental shift in primary mental attitudes.

Of course, like almost everything that we have discussed, this isn't always clear. Let's say, for the sake of example, that I owned two slaves. I could tell one of the slaves to flog the other one. That would seem to put her in a dominant position over her sister slave. However, it doesn't. In reality, she is flogging the second slave as an act of submission to my wishes, not from any desire to exert control. It comes down to motives and mental attitude, not actions.

TPE and APE

The terms TPE and APE stand for "Total Power Exchange" and "Absolute Power Exchange" respectively. I will talk about the distinction shortly, but let's start with the common attributes. The phrase "Power Exchange" is actually a quite good one to express what goes on in a D/s relationship. The submissive gives the Dominant power over him/her to some degree in exchange for the Dominant giving the submissive something that they need. Sometimes, that need is simply the freedom from having to make a certain decision. My girl does not like to make decisions. She CAN make decisions if she has to, but she doesn't like it. She has a fundamental need to be cared for, to be taken care of.

Even in the vanilla world we see this principle at work. Most experts in relationships will state that the man's number one need in a relationship is sexual fulfillment. However, for most women, the number one need is for security. So, he wants to get laid, and she wants to be reassured that he isn't going to replace her. In fact, most divorces happen because one of these isn't happening. In modern US culture, women are taught that they can get whatever they want by giving or withholding sex to/from the man who can give it to her. We see this in the modern media repeated time after time. Similarly, men are portrayed as salivating idiots who will do anything to get a woman to take her clothes off. This interaction is a subtext to almost everything that happens in our daily lives. In a sense, D/s relationships are more honest in the sense that they at least admit that an exchange of power is happening.

The other focus that needs to be stressed is that in a "power exchange" the submissive GIVES the power of control to the dominant. In reality, it can't be taken. To take by force something that isn't given is simply rape. There are a lot of forms of emotional rape, and none of them are healthy. Rape is simply a matter of taking something that belongs to another without exchanging something that is of equal value to them. All forms of rape leave deep emotional scars that will last a long time. This also ties back into the notion of consent that we talked about in chapter one of this text.

Okay, that leaves us with the words "total" and "absolute". The basic reason there are two words here is that some group of people decided that "total" doesn't mean "total". Conventionally, TPE means that the slave (submissive) grants the Master (Dominant) blanket control over him/her. The Master is given the right to do anything he wants to with/to the slave. There is no asking permission. There is no requirement to say "Honey, please…". There are commands and obedience. The difference between TPE and APE comes from the issue of "limits" as we discussed earlier. In general, the practitioners of TPE will accept that at the time the slave becomes owned, a set of limits is negotiated that the Master agrees to. In APE, the convention is that there are NO limits other than those limits that the Master imposes on himself. Quite literally, the slave accepts that if Master wants, He can even kill her. (Don't try it… the law would **NOT** see it that way!)

Old Guard Slavery

This phrase is usually used in one of a few limited contexts. (1.) Just a statement of how long a person has been in the lifestyle… "I'm an old timer, been around since before the internet." (2.) My version of BDSM is "better" than your new-fangled version. (3.) You can't just proclaim yourself as Master (or slave); you need to be mentored and have the title conferred on you. (4.) I am a strict hard-ass Master, and I don't take any shit from anyone.

In Old Guard Slavery the community was comprised of scattered small cells of people who were tightly bonded together. In this community, each prospective Master or slave had to meet standards set by that community before they were accepted in the community as "Master" or "slave". This strict code of training was kind of a rite of passage, and, in a sense, was a mechanism for protecting the community from wannabes. Because the community had some standards, there are those who view old guard as being stricter than other forms of BDSM.

Gor or Gorean

The Gorean lifestyle is based on a series of science fiction novels by John Norman published over the last forty years. In the novels, the planet "Gor" is a counter-earth. It orbits our sun in the exact orbit of the earth, with the exact same orbital characteristics as earth. This is the reason it cannot be empirically observed; the sun is always between the two worlds. On Gor, real non-consensual slavery exists literally as an organized institution. There are many categories of slaves and various rankings among them. Here on earth, strict adherence to Gorean philosophy isn't possible. There are many, many web resources that will tell you about Gor, so I won't try to do that here.

You will often see various heated discussions about Gorean slavery verses TPE (or, as they typically call it, "BDSM"). Most Goreans will adamantly assert that Gorean slavery is NOT BDSM, and most non-goreans will assert that a lifestyle based on a collection of second-rate sci-fi novels is a farce, and those who believe in it are, at best, delusional. The fact is, that Gorean slavery does work for some, once the rules are adapted for our world. It can be very viable and fulfilling for those who follow it. But, it isn't for everyone, and it isn't "better" than other forms of BDSM, nor is it worse.

You will hear the assertion: "Gor isn't BDSM, because pain is only used for punishment." But that is as ridiculous as the assertion that "Gor isn't real because it is based on fictional novels." The truth is neither or both. Gor does not use pain as pleasure. That is a fact. However, there are a number of people in the BDSM lifestyle who don't use pain that way either. In terms of how I define BDSM, Gor fits in that category. Gorean slavery had its origins in a set of fictional novels. That is also true. However the fact if that it has evolved into a codified lifestyle that many people live their lives by each and every day.

Gorean slavery involves a very hierarchical society. Rituals are very important to the Gorean way of thinking. There are a number of positions that a slave on Gor must memorize, just as there are rigid protocols that must be followed. I find some elements of these quite attractive myself. However, in my opinion, the single biggest advantage to Gorean slavery is that its believers try to stick to a common philosophy. There aren't a bunch of small cells each making their own rules.

Poly or Polyamory

In BDSM there are a significant number of relationships that involve more than two people. There are submissive married women who have a Master who is not their husband, for example. I know of a triad of one woman and two men who are quite happy together. All three share a house, and all three raise their two kids. There are many forms of poly relationships. The bottom line is: "Does it work for you?!!"

Poly is not swinging. Swinging is a weekend or one-night-stand with someone who is not your spouse. Poly relationships are intended to be long term, perhaps as long as all parties involved are alive. It denotes a commitment to having a relationship with the other people involved. Swinging is just about sex. I do not mean that as a condemnation of swinging if that is your thing. Just don't call it "poly" because it isn't.

Poly is not cheating. Cheating is a clandestine secretive relationship where one (or more) of the parties involved knows nothing of the others. In a true poly relationship, all parties involved know about the others, and accept them as part of the dynamic.

There is a question that comes up from time to time. "My husband has another lover in addition to me. But, the other person and I are monogamous, since we don't have any other partners except my husband." You are splitting hairs. I recommend that you figure out why. For some reason it is okay for your husband to have more than one sexual partner, but it is important for you to be able to say that you don't have anyone else. That is a double standard. In essence, you are stating that you are a better person than he is because you are satisfied with just him, but he needs more than you. I am not saying that there is anything wrong with the relationship. Simply that you need to face facts and admit that you are in a poly relationship, and that it is okay.

MOTSS (Members of the Same Sex)

This is a sweeping generalization of course, but those in the lifestyle tend to be more accepting of same-gender couples than the general public is. (There are exceptions to every rule.) I attribute this to the fact that we all know that we don't fit into the norm of society; so we are in a very good position to know what it feels like. Making a second sweeping generalization, on a per-capita basis, the BDSM community has a higher percentage of bi-sexual persons. There is absolutely no requirement that you be interested in members of the same sex, I simply observe that the percentages are skewed.

It also needs to be mentioned that there are a number of trans-gendered people in the lifestyle. There are people who are biologically (genetically) one gender, but who identify as the other one. This is not simply cross-dressing (we have some of that too). It is the person's fundamental psychological composition. Often these individuals will identify that they are "pre-op trans-gendered." This simply means that they have the "wrong" genitalia, and that they expect to undergo gender-reassignment surgery. If you encounter such persons, treat them as they wish to be treated. So, the woman has a penis. What does it matter unless you are the one going to bed with them!!!

Others

I may not have covered your particular form of D/s relationship in this chapter. That doesn't make it any less valid. It probably just means that I didn't have a name for it. Labels don't matter. All that matters is that the relationship works for you and your partner.

I will mention that I have encountered some Dom-Domme and sub-sub relationships. These can be hard ones to manage. In a D/D relationship, there is a constant struggle for control. Both people want to be the boss. In a s/s relationship, neither wants to!!! These relationships CAN work, but it is very difficult.

Does "love" have a part to play?

I once heard a Master speak who made the assertion: "I love my slaves, but I am not IN love with my slaves." There is a lot of discussion about the place of love in a D/s relationship. Some feel that it is absolutely essential, whereas others feel that it gets in the way. Some are even of the opinion that it is okay for submissives, but not for dominants.

The argument down-playing love goes something like this: "Sometimes a Master must make hard choices; decisions about dealing with a slave's failure to obey. The emotion of love interferes with the Master's ability to control His property effectively." I have seen this happen. In another form, this belief appeared in the original Star Trek series: "Command and compassion is a fool's mixture, and you're a fool if you don't see it." In the military we all know that a commander must sometimes choose to send soldiers on a mission knowing full well that some, or even most, will not survive that mission. A wise commander cares for his troops, but doesn't allow that concern hinder him from doing what needs to be done. I assert that this is exactly how a Master must incorporate love in His side of a D/s relationship.

So, where does that leave the submissive? Is it okay for the slave to be in love with the Master? Those who say that it is not okay reason like this: "Emotions are fickle. They cannot be trusted. And a broken heart will undermine a submissive's service and devotion. However, a submissive who is serving because it is her choice to do so, does not have this liability." It is easy to make emotional decisions that you will regret later. That is the reason the divorce rate for vanilla marriages is over fifty percent! I assert that as long as the emotions are tempered with a voice of reason, they do no harm for either dominant or submissive, and I know for a fact, that for my slave girl, the element of love is a crucial one. She loves me, and I love her. However, she knows full well that my love for her requires that I discipline her when it is needed.

Our Story

The story in this chapter is our first one with a female dominant (called a "Domme", but still pronounced "Dom"). In fact, the story has a double-domme scene in it. Double-domme refers to a scenario where there are two female dominants involved in torturing or playing with a given submissive. In this story, the submissive is supposed to be dieting, but fell off the wagon. The punishment that the Mistress uses is somewhat creative. But, it does need a warning. In no way should you do this in real life. There are serious health risks, risks of infection, associated with what she does. This story is just a work of fiction!

Story: "The Diet"

"… and that concludes our lecture tonight. I hope we were able to give you some suggestions to building incentive to keep losing weight…"

Incentive? Incentive? The hell you say! When I get home, Mistress is going to give me "incentive" like you have never dreamed of! It wasn't a good week, and She was going to be disappointed and angry. Not only did he not lose weight this week, which would have been bad enough, but he had actually gained five pounds…. FIVE FREAKING POUNDS!!!… Mistress was not going to be happy at all.

"Does anyone have some suggestions for incentives that work for them?"

"Yes, Gloria?"

"Well, as you know, I have the kids and a hubby to worry about at home. So, I can't just not have the 'bad' foods in the house."

The lecturer jumped on that sentence immediately. "Remember, Gloria, there are no 'bad' foods. Just foods that we abuse. The first step to losing weight is putting a proper name to the problem. We can't blame the food for our problems."

I don't care what she claims, this witch hasn't had to live through having food in the house that she wasn't allowed to eat. She was just another pompous holier-than-thou cow.

"Oh, okay, sorry about that. Anyway, what I did was I went out and bought a bikini that I want to wear on vacation next month and hung it on the refrigerator. Every time I see it, it makes me want to get the extra twelve pounds off. I only have three more to lose!"

That woman could have worn the bikini to the first 'Debbie's Dumpers' meeting she came to. He remembered her; they had started on the same week. She was all worried about how she could lose twelve pounds to get down to 110 in three months. It was people like that who had no concept of what it meant to have to lose a hundred and fifty pounds like he did. No concept at all.

"That is a good suggestion Gloria." [brief applause]

"As a group, we had a lot of pounds lost this week. The whole group lost 92.3 pounds! [wild applause] Let's see if we can make one hundred pounds next week! Next week's lecture will be: 'Surviving the holidays. Remember that any new people need to stay for the orientation."

He left the meeting a little disheartened. He had known that there was a good chance he was going to gain this week. It must have been the half of the coconut crème pie that he ate last Monday. George brought dessert to work, and it wasn't polite to not have some. And then George kept saying that he didn't want to take it back home. Somehow, he had eaten half of the damn thing before the day was over. As he looked around for Her car, he saw the Biscuit Ribbons store next Debbie's Dumpers.

Why in the world Debbie put her weight loss center next to an ice cream parlor was totally beyond him!

He spotted Mistress's car and quickly climbed in.

"Well?"

"Mistress,… I-I-I…" he stuttered "… I-I-I d-didn't lose this week."

"How much?"

"Please, Mistress. Does it really matter?"

"How much? Don't make me ask again."

"Yes, Mistress, I gained five pounds, Mistress."

"Damn it! How could you do this to me? You know that I have to work tomorrow, and I have that lecture to give at the TESS meeting in the evening. I don't have the time to stay up all night punishing you."

"Yes, Mistress. I'm sorry Mistress."

"You will be… let me promise you that… you will be!"

"Alright, what did you eat?"

"George brought a coconut crème pie in to work."

"One piece of pie seems to not account for five pounds."

"Mistress, it wasn't just one piece."

She gave him a piercing stare… "How many?"

"Four."

"FOUR FREAKING PIECES OF PIE!!! It took that long for you to remember that YOU ARE ON A DIET!!!"

"It was all George's fault."

"George's fault? Well, I assume that he tied you up and forced you to swallow it?"

"No Mistress."

"Good. That's my right, and I am very jealous about who binds and tortures you."

"Yes, Mistress. I understand, Mistress. I would never allow anyone else take what is rightfully Yours."

She stopped the car in front of the Hardway grocery store at the end of the shopping center. "Since you like coconut crème pie so much, go in and buy another one."

"Yes, Mistress." He got out of the car and started walking toward the store.

She called him back… "I also need you to buy me something."

"Yes, Mistress, what is Your desire?"

"I want you to buy the largest hand of ginger that they have in the produce aisle."

"NOOOO!!!… MISTRESS… PLEASE, NOOOO!!!"

"Go! And be quick about it. I need to have time to sleep after punishing you."

"Yes, Mistress."

As he went into the store, his thoughts were centered on her intentions. He had heard of it before. It was called "figging". There was a great write-up on the internet about it, in fact. But, he hadn't experienced it himself. Clearly, if Mistress wasn't going to sleep, he was going to pay the price. She had warned him that if he gained weight, he would be punished. Maybe it wouldn't have been as bad if he hadn't been so disobedient. But, She was his "Mistress," and disobedience couldn't be accepted. He had earned whatever She did to him. He hurried to complete his task so that She wouldn't become more upset.

When he got out of the store and climbed back into the car the sun had set and it was dark outside. He must have gotten the slowest cashier in the history of retail marketing.

"Took you long enough."

She started the car and pulled out of the shopping center. He was mildly surprised when She turned and drove around behind of the shopping center instead of getting back onto the highway toward home.

When they reached the relative seclusion of the loading dock, She stopped the car.

"You are to get out and stand in front of the car where I can see you. You are to strip totally naked. Then you are to stimulate yourself until you have an erection. You may not get back into the car without one. Have I made myself clear?"

"You are clear, mistress. B-b-but h-here???... What if someone sees me?"

"This is a secluded spot. Nobody should be able to see. But, if I want you on display, then you will be on display. Get your butt out of the car. You already wasted enough of my time waiting for you to get done in the store."

"Mistress, it wasn't my fault. The cashier..."

"Enough! You could have picked another cashier. Besides, you are my property, and I don't need a reason to do with it as I please. Now get my property out of the car and do with it as I instructed."

"Yes, Mistress."

He got out of the car and in the glare of the headlights removed his clothes. He kept looking around to make sure that they were alone. He could feel a response beginning in his groin; a response born of the combined thrill of being caught and that of pleasing his Mistress. That, and an urgent need to obey and get back in the safety of the car.

Finally he got the erection as ordered. He hadn't known before just how stimulating the risk of being caught could be. As he began to pick up his clothes and get dressed again, She opened the car door and said: "No. Do not put your clothes on. Get in the car."

As he got into the car, She pointed to his swollen cock and said: "It is your responsibility to keep that thing hard until we get home.... And you are not allowed to cum. The upholstery was just cleaned and I don't want to have to clean it again because of you. You already screwed up my week enough."

"Yes, Mistress. I understand, Mistress."

As they drove home he focused on doing as She had commanded. It was like walking a balance beam. Too little effort and he would lose his erection and make Her mad. Too much attention and he would lose it and cum and make Her mad. He knew that the people they passed could look into the car. Fortunately, there weren't many people around. He assumed that because it was dark that they wouldn't see anything. Either way, as long as Mistress was pleased, he didn't care about anyone else.

They drove the rest of the way home in silence. He tried not to think about how mad she was at him. That would make it even harder to focus on what he was doing.

As they pulled into the garage at home, he breathed a silent sigh. He had made it home without disobeying her. She turned and looked at him. "Don't speak. Go down to the dungeon and clamp yourself to the bench. Leave the clothes here."

"The Bench" was a piece of their dungeon furniture that he had built for Her. It was designed to Her exacting standards. It started off as a simple spanking bench with a padded knee rest and a padded center support. She had specified that the height of the center be such that his knees just barely touched the kneeling rails. Each of the knee rails had a leather strap to restrain his ankles. On one end of the center support She had him build a penis clamp. It was a clamp that would hold his lower half immovable. Depending on how tightly She made the screws, it was either ecstasy or agony. Tonight he rather expected the latter. On the opposite end She designed a pillory that She used to restrain his wrists and head. Using all of the restraints, She could do anything that She wanted to him, and he could do nothing to stop her.

He knelt down and fastened his cock into the penis clamp. He tightened the clamp down to a "pleasure" level, and hoped that she wouldn't tighten it further. He then fastened the leather straps on his ankles. He looked at the pillory. He had designed it with a self-securing mechanism. He could put himself into it, but She had to release him. With a resigned sigh, he lifted the top bar and lowered his neck and right wrist into position. He closed his eyes as he put the left wrist into the groove and felt the top snap closed. He knew that the size of the wrist holes had been very carefully measured. If he worked at it, and made his hand as narrow as possible, he could force his hands out of the pillory and release himself. She had forced him to do exactly that when he had first built The Bench. She had to see for herself that he could free himself, albeit with great effort, if there was a problem. It had taken two weeks for the scrapes and scratches from that effort to heal.

As he knelt there waiting for her, his stomach rumbled. He hadn't eaten before the meeting like he usually did. He had been trying minimize the weight on the scale. With Mistress's attitude right now, he knew that there wouldn't be anything to eat this evening, and maybe not in the morning.

He then heard her on the phone… "Okay, Amy, I'll see you in ten minutes. He did it this time. He is already strapped down on The Bench." (Spoken in a slightly louder voice to be sure that he overheard her.) "Or at least he damn well better be strapped down. I want you to double-Domme him with me. No, you don't need to bring anything along. I have lots of toys to use on him. Besides, I have another plan for you. You don't mind having your pussy eaten, do you?… I thought that would be okay."

While she waited for Amy to get there, She finished Her preparations. She sliced the pie into six pieces and made coffee. She peeled the hand of ginger and shaped it unto a form that could be used as an anal plug. She put the ginger root into a bowl of ice water to chill it, and also to increase the moisture level in the root. She also knew that this would make the initial juices from the root be a little milder. The evening would last longer that way. She had every intention that this would be a punishment that he would remember for a very long time indeed. She knew that he would think long and hard before going off his diet again, and She had Her doubts that he would ever enjoy a piece of coconut crème pie again.

Amy got there on schedule, and they grabbed the dessert, coffee and ginger and headed to the dungeon. She sat the pie down on the floor in front of him where he could see it and smell it. Then they both sat down on the floor in front of him. Mistress served Her friend and herself pie and coffee. She took particular care to make sure that the pie brushed against his mouth just to tease him all the more. They sat there enjoying their dessert and totally ignoring him. After dessert was finished…

"Well, Amy, I have enjoyed your company, but we have business to take care of."

"Yes, dessert was quite nice. How can I help with business?"

"Well, I was going to start with the mild stuff first. While I get the enema bag ready, could you lick his cock and balls. He looks entirely too relaxed, and I want him hard."

Just the thought of his Mistress' friend licking him had him getting hard. And 'hard' wasn't necessarily a good thing with his cock in the penis clamp like that. But, Amy was relentless. She was licking him like her life depended on it.

Just as his Mistress returned with a filled enema bag, Amy had him almost ready to cum. He almost didn't care whether Mistress would be pleased about him cumming, he was that far gone.… Well, almost that far.

"Amy, that's enough for the moment. We can't have him cumming. He hasn't earned that yet." Holding up the enema bag, She said: "I need to empty this into him. Climb up on his back facing me so that you can help."

Amy climbed up on his back and reached between the cheeks of his ass to insert her finger into his ass. Just to tease him, she rubbed his prostate gland to turn him on that much more.

"Amy, I can do that, dear. Just spread his cheeks apart."

His Mistress put the spout of the hose into his exposed asshole and started feeding the liquid into him. He could feel his colon filling up. It was a sensation that he could never describe to anyone. It felt really good, and yet strange at the same time. He thought that she was filling him fuller than she ever had before when he felt the hose slide out of his asshole. Almost immediately, he felt something a bit larger inserted where the hose had just exited.

"You can let go of his ass now, Amy."

His mistress bent down and whispered in his ear. "So far, other than the teasing with dessert, this is just been the normal weight loss enema that you have been having me do every day for several months. As you probably suspect, what was just inserted into your ass is peeled ginger root. I suspect that you are beginning to feel a little warmth already."

"Yes, Mistress. It is not as bad as I expected, actually."

Smiling She said: "I can fix that."

"Amy, I need your help." With that She pulled two paddles down off a hook on the wall, and handed one to Amy. "We alternate strokes. The strokes are to come as quickly as we can manage at first. Our goal is to create enough pain so that he has to clench his ass cheeks together in an automatic response. This will squeeze the juices out of the ginger root."

When his Mistress had finished speaking, he felt the first paddle strike his ass. Then, almost immediately, a second, and a third. The pain in his ass was building so sharply that he completely forgot about the ginger root. That is, until the burning in his rectum and the pressure in his colon began building. He found himself automatically jerking sideways with a response to each stroke. With each spasm, he jerked his cock in the clamp, and shifted the ginger root in his ass. Too late he realized that moving wasn't a good idea either. He was in such discomfort by now that he didn't even notice when the spanking stopped until Her mouth was beside his ear.

"Is that coconut crème pie sounding good now?"

"No, Mistress." He responded. And, to his surprise, he found that he really didn't want it right now. All he wanted was to have the ginger removed and his colon emptied.

"I'm going to remove the ginger root now. You are not allowed to empty your colon until I give you permission."

Having said that, she removed the ginger from his ass. It was all he could do to hold his anus closed to keep the liquid inside. Even with the ginger gone, the burning sensation continued. He hoped that all of the liquid inside of him would cool it as it exited.

Mistress loosened the clamp on his cock and moved the liter box into position. They had built a containment to control the mess when he released the liquid some months back. It was essentially an empty litter box with a three-sided vertical sheet of plastic. Once the containment was in place, She told him it was okay.

When he released the liquid from inside his body, it was an explosive uncontrollable sensation. He felt the usual urge to climax on the spot, but knew that Mistress wouldn't be pleased, so he held it in. He was pleased that some of the burning from the ginger subsided… but there was still a reminder. She cleaned him up and came again and sat in front of him.

"Now it is time for you to have your dessert."

"Amy, there is a mechanic's creeper over there in the corner. Could you go get it please?"

When Amy returned with the creeper as requested, his Mistress continued: "Okay Amy, it is time for his dessert. Please remove your clothes and lay down on the creeper. It is time for him to eat his pie and your pie at the same time."

Amy did as requested. Once she was situated on the mechanic's creeper, his Mistress cut a very small slice of pie and smeared it between the lips of Her friend's pussy. She put a pillow under Her friend's bottom to elevate it to the correct height. Once She was satisfied that he would be able to service Her friend, She grabbed a hand full of his hair and pulled his face up so he could look into Her eyes. "You damn well better make her happy, slave." Having said that, she picked up the pie plate with the rest of the pie and pushed the creeper into position. Still holding his hair, She pushed his face into Her friend's pussy. Amy hooked her knees over the pillory to keep the creeper from sliding out of position.

After a minute or two, he felt his Mistress playing with his asshole again. He felt something hard penetrate him.

"Slave boy, while you eat your pie out of Amy's pussy, I'm going to shove the rest of this pie up your ass. Since it seems that you think that a half of a pie is a single serving, here is the rest of it." With that final word she began shoving spoonful after spoonful of coconut crème pie into his gaping asshole.

As he felt his colon begin to fill again, he ate Amy's pussy. He suddenly had a fear of what would happen to him if he didn't please her.

After the last of the pie was inside of him, his Mistress left to fill the enema bag again.

She returned and removed the funnel from his ass, and inserted the enema hose into him. The shock of the unexpected change of what was happening to his ass, he almost forgot about pleasing Amy. That is, until Mistress grabbed his balls and sternly reminded him: "Did you forget what you were doing?"

He returned to eating Amy; using all of his skills to please her. Just as the enema bag finished filling him, Amy reached the point of no return. She began to push into his face until she achieved orgasm. Her orgasm was so powerful that she legs were locked around his head and she was pushing his head into the pillory. He knew that he would have bruises on the back of his head for a week.

His Mistress moved the litter box back into position, and asked him if he was finished with the rest of his dessert. His only answer to her question was to once again evacuate his bowels.

She cleaned him once again and removed him from the bench. She commanded him to lay down on the floor on his back.

She fastened his arms out from his sides to hooks in the dungeon floor. Next She pulled his legs up and fastened them to the same hooks so that they were spread wide, giving her full access to him.

She left the area where he was for a moment. When she returned, she too was naked. Naked that is if you didn't count the eight-inch dildo that she had strapped around her middle.

"Amy, would you resume your position with your pussy over his face and his cock in your mouth, while I fuck his ass?"

All he could think was "Holy shit!"

Amy stood up and looked at her friend. "I'd love to, but I could use a bathroom first."

"Oh, that's no problem. Just piss in his mouth. He won't mind. Isn't that right, slave boy?"

"Mistress, I will do whatever you ask of me."

With that encouragement, Amy pushed her pussy down over his open mouth and let go. Once she filled his mouth, her fluids ran down the side of his face. When she was finished, all he could do was swallow what she had given him. He knew what Mistress wanted, and he had to give it to her. The one thing that he knew beyond all else was that he would lose weight next week, no matter what it took.

Chapter 6: The Internet

It is a truism that The Internet has changed the world as we know it. That is a fact that cannot be refuted. Is a matter of opinion as to whether the change was good or bad, and I won't even try to make a guess at that! Of course, The Internet has had an impact on the BDSM lifestyle as well, and here I will pronounce that the impact was both good and bad. First the bad news…

There is a LOT of bad information on the internet. Perhaps that isn't a fair statement. Perhaps "inaccurate information" would be a more appropriate description. To be sure, the author of the information believes what they are saying. Maybe even it is not so much inaccurate, as it is contradictory information.

If I have learned anything since I've been in the lifestyle, it is that there is great diversity in what is commonly called BDSM. In this book I have tried to communicate the basic principle that whatever works for you and your partner is okay. Unfortunately, there are many people who believe that what is right for me is, by definition, right for everyone. Furthermore, they assert that their way is the ONLY true way. Even those who admit that theirs is just one way out of many will rarely discuss any options other than their own. Now, before we go too far off the deep end here, in defense of those providing information, (a.) they may not know about anything else or (b.) they don't have an interest in anything else. The bottom line it that you should not take any single article as the only possible way to view a given topic.

Anonymity

Perhaps the single biggest advantage of the on-line world is that you can hide your identity. At least you can mostly hide. I doubt that anyone in this day and age fails to have an awareness of identity theft or stalking behavior. In that light, having some level of anonymity is a good thing. One expert put it this way: "On the internet, nobody knows you're a dog."

The down-side is that the person you are talking to, or that you *think* you are talking to, may have no resemblance to reality at all. I personally had an encounter a few years back with a "woman" who wanted me to show off naked on cam. Now, I am a nudist, so being naked in front of others it not a big deal. After showing off, I requested that "she" reciprocate. I mean fair is fair. It was one of the ugliest men I have had the misfortune to meet. I "dated" a woman for a while (internet dating) who had a dozen different on-line identities. She trained and encouraged her teen-age daughters to do the same; including training them to claim to be adults.

So, initially, I urge you to be careful. There are predators out there. Make up a screen name that is NOT personally identifiable. The first screen name that I used was my amateur radio call sign. You can't get much more identifiable than that! It wasn't a good choice. Many people make a specific name that they use only for lifestyle activities. They go so far as to create a separate e-mail account for it. That has the effect of compartmentalizing that part of your life until you are ready to share it. Perhaps the number one fear of most people in the lifestyle is that of being "outted" (having someone find out about their kinkyness who they were hiding it from). Keeping yourself anonymous helps. One word of warning…

> *Do not EVER meet up with someone in real life that you met on the internet unless you get real, verifiable, information about them. Also do not EVER meet up for the first time without a trusted friend knowing EXACTLY where you are going, and with whom. (See also "Safe Calls" discussed later in this chapter.)*

So, now you have an on-line persona that you will be using. You may have found a chat group or two that you want to join. Suddenly you meet "Mr. Right", how do you tell if He is faking it? Have lots of conversations. I recommend using instant messenger programs, e-mail, and real live phone conversations. If "Mr. Right" is lying to you, after enough conversations you will find inconsistencies in what he is telling you. It addition, you will probably find that his personality is very shallow. Obviously, there is still risk involved. But, you want to be as sure as you can be. Talk to this person's friends.

Take your time. There are really only a couple of reasons that people are seriously looking for a relationship on-line. First, they have "special requirements" that are hard to encounter in real life. For example, I required a woman who wanted to be an owned slave. One who accepted (or preferably enjoyed) being totally naked, even around others. One who enjoyed sexual variety. And, finally, one who was willing to entertain the possibility of a poly relationship. I didn't have any luck finding her in real life. Those topics just don't come up in general conversation. People with these special needs have probably been through a number of failed relationships trying to find the right person in the real world.

Secondly, there are people out there who do this for "fun". They don't want a real relationship. They want someone that they can toy with. Those of us who are desperately seeking the one we need become easy marks for these people. This type of person does not care about what emotional trauma they cause. You have no value other than the entertainment you provide. The more deeply you are hurt, the more entertainment you provide. I know of some submissives who are in active real-time relationships where their partner doesn't care at all what they do on-line. The attitude is: "It isn't 'real' so who cares if you hurt someone. It is their own fault for living in a fantasy world."

Finally, there really are predators out there. They are not in this for a real relationship, and they are not in it for fun. They are in it to get their hands on you and do some real physical harm. This harm could be rape or other physical injury, even death.

Now, it might sound as if all of this anonymity is negative. But, there is a silver lining. For those people who are not playing games, they have the ability to be their true selves. In a sense, people are free to express their real desires and dispositions. More than that, they are free to explore and find out about themselves in a way that doesn't risk compromising their real world day-to-day existence for something that they might not like anyway!

Safe Calls

A "safe call" is simply a call that you make to a trusted friend to say: "I am safe and having a good time." BEFORE you meet a stranger for the first time, you tell a trusted friend exactly where you are going and who you are meeting. You give them contact information, and you set up schedule of when you are going to call them. If they do not hear from you, they are to call the police and report the information that you have given them and say that they suspect that you are in trouble. Whatever you do, do not forget to make the call, or you could have an embarrassing situation.

Screen Names

There are no "rules" for picking a name to use on-line. However, there are some assumptions that will be made in most lifestyle chat rooms. The following bullets summarize these assumptions. Of course, you are at liberty to totally disregard them.

- Doms or Dommes begin their nicks with a capital letter (like "MasterIvoree") subs begin theirs with a lower case letter (like "gentle^spirit[SG]").
- If you are "owned" you can add a collar designation to your nick. Some people are owned on the net only and not in real life, others are real time. To indicate a real time collar, you use the square brackets, and some short representation of your master. For example, gentle^spirit's master is Sir_Gardener, so she added "[SG]" to her nick. Less commonly, it is done like this: "[gentle^spirit]SG" but you will see it that way some times. To indicate an on-line only collar, you use braces (also called "curly brackets") instead of the square brackets.
- I don't really recommend that you use your real life name in your nick. There are too many weirdos out there. But, you will see some people that do.
- If you use mIRC to chat on IRC, you will want a second nickname to use in case mIRC can't log in with the first one ... (I use "SirIvoree_AlterEgo" for mine.)

Is it "real" or not?

Another hotly debated topic in discussion groups is: "Can an on-line relationship be 'real' or is it just playing a game?" Of course, the correct answer is: "It is as real as the two people involved want it to be." Of course, there are just some things that you can't do in an on-line relationship. But, you might be surprised what you really can do at a distance.

Much of the power exchange in a D/s relationship is psychological in nature. If there is adequate communication, and genuine willingness to do so, this psychological bonding can take place at a distance. Willingness is the key to a successful D/s relationship whether it is real time or on-line. At a certain level, this comes back to the consent issue that I discussed earlier. But, it goes much deeper than that. In order for a submissive to bond to a dominant the submissive must be willing, even have a strong desire, to mold herself to His wishes. This desire springs from the submissive's mind. In reality, a dominant cannot create it. The best He can do is to foster it and encourage it to grow. With care and patience, this can be done quite effectively on-line. In fact, some aspects are easier to do when you are not in the physical presence of each other.

What can't you do on-line that you can do in person? Mostly all of that physical stuff. But, in terms of building the relationship, the physical activities are just icing on the cake. Marriage counselors have preached that mantra about "sex" for many decades. Religious leaders for centuries have preached at length on the virtues of waiting until you are married. I have had vanilla relationships built on just sexual activities. To be sure, I enjoyed the sex. However, there was also something very fundamental missing from those relationships.

So, I maintain that an on-line relationship CAN be real, and CAN be satisfying. But don't confuse that with "It WILL be satisfying."

How can long distance relationships (LDRs) be made to work?

The key to making a relationship work is communication. This is true for all relationships. With the advent of the internet, this communication is easier… and also harder. It takes a lot of effort to make a relationship a successful and satisfying one.

My second wife and I went through marriage counseling for a while. One of the things that the counselor discussed with me is that there is an inherent problem with internet relationships. Or, to be more precise, those who typically seek internet relationships have a problem with communicating at a deep level. The internet facilitates this because if it begins to get uncomfortable, they can just have "computer problems" until they think that the subject has calmed down. Just like the anonymity we discussed earlier, this issue is a double-edged sword. The ability to go off-line makes on-line relationships safer for those who have been badly burned in relationships before. Initially, this safety valve is a good thing. At the beginning of the relationship, a person who has been hurt before is naturally afraid of being hurt again. Such hurts tend to be very deep, and don't heal without a lot of work by someone who cares.

Most submissives want contact from their dominant several times a week, at a minimum. Although many need the reassurance of contact several times each day. (I have a Master friend who believes that this kind of sub is "high maintenance," and he has no use for that type of sub.) It is up to the dominant to set the tone of the conversation. Not all communication can be the surface level "how was your day?" type. But, it can't all be the deep and insightful "why were you thinking that?" type either. The dominant needs to find a balance.

Now before you get all upset, the submissive carries responsibility too. But, as I have told a number of people over the years: "You have to stop 'thinking vanilla'." The submissive is depending on the dominant to lead the relationship. Most dominants are just fine with that. What often gets overlooked is that the submissive expects the dominant to keep them accountable too. The logic goes something like this: "If you really care that I do X, then if I 'forget' you will notice and at least remind me of it." Most submissives need to know that there are consequences for inappropriate behavior.

Some practical things about on-line activities

There are a lot of diverse resources on the internet that can not only be used for learning, but can also be used for communicating long distances. In this section of the chapter, I will discuss a few of them. This list is by no means comprehensive.

Daily Journal

Many dominants ask their submissives to keep a daily journal. I know that I do. I use it as a tool to communicate. On IM or on the phone, the communication is conversational in nature. In her journal it is more of a narrative. Sometimes the journal entry is just: "This is how my day was." But, occasionally she will make a comment that brings up a topic that I want to delve deeper into. On occasion I will assign her a topic to write on.

It is my opinion that the slave needs a "safety valve" for her emotions. I have told my girl that she can say anything that she wants in her journal without fear of punishment. Sometimes she just vents: "Master told me to do X. I did it, but I didn't want to do it and here is why." The journal mechanism has worked well for us. (Your actual mileage may vary.)

There are a number of on-line sites where a journal can be entered. The one that we use is called "Live Journal" (http://www.LiveJournal.com) there are others. If you just do a search for "blog" sites, you will find quite a few.

Lifestyle-Themed Web Sites

On the internet, there are a LOT of web sites that discuss various aspects of BDSM. You could try doing a search using your search engine of choice, but that will give you a couple million hits. It could be daunting to filter through them to find the material that you want. It is probably better to start with known sites. Two good sites to begin with are "Bondage" (http://www.bondage. com) and "Castle Realm (http://www.castlerealm.com). Many of the discussion groups (see the next subsection) will have a "Links" area that will point you to other web sites as well. Remember, you can spend hundreds of hours reading "everything" you can find. So, don't try to learn it all in the first week.

The other thing that I will mention is that there are "personals" sites that are dedicated to connecting people who are looking. The three most popular are: "Bondage" (http://www.bondage. com), "ALT" which stands for "alternate lifestyles" (http://www.alt.com), and "Collar Me" (http:// www.collarme.com). These sites allow you to create a profile with your likes and dislikes so that people can find you. If you choose to use these personals sites, be prepared to receive messages from people who are jerks as well as those who are sincere. I know of people who have gotten extremely rude comments from them.

Discussion Groups

Yahoo and Google each operate BDSM-themed discussion groups. You will also find "forum" sections on many of the major lifestyle web sites. These groups can be a great source of information. They are also frequently good places to ask your questions and get honest answers / opinions. (All of the disclaimers I gave earlier apply double to discussion groups.) In each and every group you will find occasional disagreements (sometimes called "flame wars" because flaming arrows get zinged back and forth). If you are in the group any amount of time, and are an active participant, you will no doubt be the target of some of these arrows.

The other thing that you need to be aware of is that some groups are "high protocol" (some higher than others). I am going to discuss protocol and honorifics in the next chapter, so I won't repeat that material here.

Chat Rooms and Internet Relay Chat (IRC)

A chat room is simply a communication channel on a central server where conversations happen. In a chat room there can literally be hundreds of people logged into that room. When you type a message to the room, the chat server sends that message to everyone who is signed into that room. You can have some quite nice group discussions this way. There are various chat resources around the net, including Yahoo's chat rooms.

Internet Relay Chat (IRC) is a communication language on the internet (computer geeks call it a "protocol") that actually existed before the world wide web. There are tens of thousands of chat rooms on the main IRC chat servers. You can pretty much find a channel for any topic you are interested in. For those interested in BDSM, there is an IRC server hosted by bondage.com ("irc. bondage.com") that has many chat channels that are specific to our lifestyle. You will need special software to talk to the IRC server. There are some web sites that have a Java chat client that will work. Typically these have minimal features. You may want a special program on your computer so that you don't need to use a web interface. There are a number of chat clients that you can download. One of the most popular is "mIRC".

Chat rooms can be very high protocol as well. Again, I won't delve into that here.

Instant Messaging

Instant messaging is simply a point-to-point tool that allows two computers to exchange messages back and forth. There are several popular ones in use: MSN Messenger (comes with Microsoft Windows), AOL Instant Messenger (AIM), and Yahoo Messenger (YM) are the three most popular at the time of this writing. The biggest problem with instant messenger programs is that you, and the person you want to chat with must be using the same chat program. There is also a program named: "Trillian" that does know how to chat using multiple communications protocols. Some of the chat programs allow voice chat, and also sharing of video via web cameras.

Cell Phones and Voice over IP (VoIP) Phones

Over the last few years there have been a lot of changes in telephone capabilities. If you have a high-speed internet connection (DSL or cable) you can get a phone service like Vonage or SunRocket that uses the internet for phone conversations. Generally these Voice-over-IP providers allow unlimited long distance phone calls for free as part of the service.

The other option is to use your cell phone. Most cellular carriers give "free" long distance as part of the service (air time charges might apply). For my carrier, I can add a "family" line that doesn't use my air time quota for about ten bucks a month. This has allowed my slave and I to talk approximately 14,000-18,000 minutes each month for more than a year. This is a great solution, and I recommend it highly!

Our Story

In the story that follows there are examples of several things that are common in BDSM relationships.

- ☐ Master and slave do not eat together. Slave serves Master, and then eats her own food once given permission.
- ☐ Nudity. (As we have mentioned previously.)
- ☐ Objectification. (Use of the slave's body as an object. In this case, a dinner plate.)
- ☐ Verbal humiliation. (We will talk more about this in a later chapter.)
- ☐ Animal play. (Slave acting like / being treated like they are an animal.)

This last is the primary focus of this story. There are submissives who enjoy acting in the role of a kitten, a dog, a cow (including having their breasts milked), or a horse. I talked to one slave a few years back who is a "working pony" on a farm in the western United States. She pulls a cart to move garden tools and supplies around the farm. At night she sleeps naked in the barn with the other animals. And, most importantly, she could not be happier in her life than she is while behaving as a pony. There are other pony girls who pull a cart for people to ride in. There are others who have a bit put in their mouth and a saddle strapped on their back and carry riders around the room at clubs. These pony girls get so deeply into their role that they will literally walk into a wall if their rider doesn't stop them.

Story: "Kitten"

"Master, dinner is ready."

She had planned this dinner to please Him, it was one of His favorites. It wasn't fancy, just a garden salad with Balsamic Vinaigrette dressing (no tomatoes!), baked chicken, rice, and steamed cauliflower. But, He favored simpler meals.

"Then why am I not eating it, slut?"

Shivers ran down her spine. She loved it when he used terms like that to describe her.... "Slut." "Whore." "Bitch." "Cunt."... She loved them all, and He knew it! Her friends and co-workers, at least those who knew about her lifestyle, all thought she was "out of her freaking mind." But, just thinking about it made the moisture build between her legs. She didn't know why it turned her on so, but, damn it felt good!

He was sitting in His favorite chair in the living room. She brought His dinner and knelt before Him with her head bowed respectfully waiting on His pleasure.

"'Slave plate.' Now!"

"Yes, Master. At once, Sir."

She quickly stood and moved the coffee table close to Him. She removed her clothes and lay down on the table. She handed Him a fork and, holding her legs tightly together, she poured His salad on her pussy and said: "Master, your salad is ready."

"It's about time, whore. It took you long enough."

As He ate His salad, she could feel the salad dressing seeping into her pussy. She could feel the points on the tines of His fork as He speared the lettuce. She knew He was careful with her body, but the fork poking her felt so delicious.

When He finished the salad, He bent forward and licked His "plate" clean. She was so glad that she had shaved that morning. Master didn't like stubble on His plate. His tongue touched her clit as he cleaned there. She almost cried out and begged for Him to take her then and there. She wanted Him. She needed Him. She knew she would get what she wanted... later. But, she didn't want to wait.

As she waited for Him to tell her that He was ready for the main course, she thought back to last weekend. They had planned a dinner with several of their friends who were also Master / slave couples. As was their custom, the Masters were served dinner, and the slaves were allowed to eat after the Masters were finished. Just as she was putting the last of the food on the table, He smiled at her and said: "Go shower and return with the leg bands. Do not dress, you are to be the serving platter tonight." It had been wonderful. The four Masters sitting at table serving their food from her naked body. She really did enjoy serving her Master this way, and she was glad He relished it too.

"Main course." He commanded.

She dumped the chicken, rice, and cauliflower onto her pussy. She couldn't avoid a sharp intake of breath as the hot juices from the chicken hit her skin.

She handed Him a knife to go with the fork that He still held. "Enjoy your dinner, Master."

He didn't speak to her again until He was finished eating. "Thank you, slave for a very enjoyable dinner. You have pleased me."

Shivers ran down her spine again... pleasing Him was what she lived for. To hear Him say "Well done" was the highest praise she had ever received.

"Slave, You have earned the right to have dinner yourself."

She started to get up from her position as His plate.

"However, tonight I wish you to do something I have never asked of you before. Tonight you will be your own dinner plate. Go, cut your food up in bite-sized pieces and return here with it. Lay down on the table in front of me and pour your dinner on your pussy. You may then eat. Are my instructions clear?"

"Yes, Master. Your instructions are clear and I will gladly obey You."

She stood up and went into the kitchen and prepared her own dinner. She felt happy, she had pleased Him. She knew that the dinner she had prepared was one of His favorites, but to hear Him say He was pleased with her was important to her. In her experience, few Masters really understood a slave's genuine need to hear that she has pleased Him. Her Master did, and it made serving Him that much more important and satisfying to her.

She returned to the living room and lay down on the coffee table again. She dumped her food on her pussy and picked up her fork to start eating. By now, she was absolutely famished and couldn't wait to eat. She didn't mind waiting for Him to eat dinner first, and then to wait for Him to give her permission to eat. She was a slave; she had no right to expect anything else. She was glad that He didn't often punish her by not allowing her to have dinner.

She stabbed the first cauliflower with her fork. If felt strange to eat food from off her own body; strange, but also exciting. She extended the fork for the next bite. This wasn't as easy as she thought it would be. She was having difficulty aiming the fork. Her position didn't allow her to keep her legs together and get a good view of the dinner plate at the same time. Noticing her problem, her Master took the fork from her hand and fed her.

This wasn't the first time that He had fed her. But, it still amazed and humbled her that He would do such a menial thing to care for her.

He speared the last bite of chicken. He showed her what was on the fork. Then He spread her legs apart and inserted the chicken into her dripping vagina. He removed the fork, and removed the chicken from the fork with His teeth. He then bent over and kissed her. She could smell the pussy juices mingled in with the chicken juice as he placed it into her mouth. As His mouth covered hers, He reached between her legs to explore what he found there.

She was excited by what was happening, and she just let herself go in the ecstasy of the moment. He kissed her and played with her pussy until she finally climaxed. It felt so wonderful to cum. She wanted it… needed it… and He was giving her His full attention to see that she got what she needed.

As the spasms of her orgasm subsided, He looked into her eyes. "You have pleased me greatly. Go wash the dishes." He patted her pussy and added: "Including this one."

"After your shower, do not put your clothes on and return here. We need to talk about the weekend. I have special plans."

"Yes, Master."

She reflected as she stood naked in the kitchen doing the dishes… it had been a rather nice dinner. Even she knew that she had outdone herself, and she could tell that Master was genuinely pleased. Although, He had never told her that He was pleased with her if He wasn't. So, she didn't doubt His words.

After her shower, she returned to the living room and lay down on her back at His feet. She reached down and grabbed her feet and spread her legs as wide as she could so that He could access any part of her body that He wanted to explore (this is what He called "inspection position", and then she smiled at Him and said: "Master, Your slave is ready for inspection."

He was watching the late news on TV. She knew that He heard her, and that she was required to hold that position until he completed His inspection. The first time He had made her hold that position and wait for Him, it had hurt like hell. She got muscle cramps in places where she didn't even know she had muscles. That had been many, many months ago. The nightly inspections had loosened the muscles and she had practiced during the day as well. In her practice, she would hold that position until she couldn't hold it any longer. She knew that her limit was about an hour-and-a-half now. But, He had never waited that long to inspect her… yet. Her personal goal was to be able to hold the "inspection position" for four hours. Then she knew that she would be able to do anything that he asked of her. She could hear that the sports report was on the news, so the newscast would be ending soon.

At the commercial break he knelt down beside her. He checked her arm pits first… He frowned at her… a frown wasn't good…

"Holy shit! Did you use soap?"

Nope, not good at all. "Yes, Master." Was all she could whisper.

Everything else seemed to pass inspection until he stuck His fingers up her ass.

"Damn it, slut" (It didn't feel good for Him to call her that now. He was angry at her.) "Go get a rag, soap, and the bottle brush. I don't know why I have to do everything myself!!!" He slapped her ass hard. "MOVE!"

She ran down the hall crying to do as she was told. The bottle brush wouldn't be fun, but it was better than steel wool.

She returned with the required items and again resumed inspection position.

He ignored her. He was watching the weather forecast.

The newscast ended, and He silently picked up the wash cloth and the brush. He wrapped the cloth around the brush, and then shoved it into her tight asshole. She screamed, but only once. She knew she should have cleaned herself better. He worked the brush back and forth a couple of times and then removed it. As He folded the rag so that he had a clean surface to wash her arm pits and put soap on it, he said.

"As punishment for not cleaning yourself adequately, you will use the brush on your asshole Monday through Friday next week while I watch you do it to make sure you clean yourself correctly."

She looked at Him through her tears. She had been so happy only moments ago because she had pleased Him. Now she was in tears because she had disappointed Him. "I understand, Master. I am sorry I did not take proper care of Your property." She never understood how her emotions could shift so rapidly.

"You are forgiven, and the punishment will help you to remember in the future. Now go rinse yourself off and get back here, I have things to talk over with you."

"Yes, Master." She was "forgiven." Such a simple word; but, oh, what a grand concept. For her Master, she knew, it was far more than just a word. In His world, "forgiven" also meant "forgotten." Other than the assigned punishment, He wouldn't ever mention the incident again. In fact early in their relationship, before she had accepted His collar, He had made it clear to her that she would be punished for bringing up past offences when He considered the matter closed. It was a wonderful feeling to know that an issue was closed. That she could truly put it in the past and forget it. Even now, as she reflected on that simple phrase… "you are forgiven"… her heart was happy again. Her asshole was a bit tender, but her heart was happy. She quickly rinsed off and returned to Him, assuming inspection position one last time.

"Sit on my lap. I don't need to inspect my own work, and I have things to tell you before we go to bed tonight."

She quickly climbed up on His lap. She felt protected and loved. It was her favorite place in the world. Her second favorite place being at His feet, of course.

He reached over to the coffee table and picked up a box.

Where did that come from? I KNOW it wasn't there while I was serving as the dinner plate!

"Slave, I have an assignment for you for tomorrow. We have talked about 'pony girls' in the past. If you will recall, we went to that exhibition at 'The Black Caldron' a few months back."

"Yes, Master, I remember. How could I forget? The ponys seemed so happy in their role as animals, and You seemed to enjoy it too. It is too bad there is no room in our apartment for me to be a pony too."

"That is true. I have been thinking about that problem, and I have come up with a solution."

He opened the box, and what she saw inside was a long furry tale. It was a sandy blond to match her own hair.

"This is your tail, kitten. Put it on."

As she quickly inserted the anal plug at the end of the tail into her asshole, she thought: "'Kitten'??? He's never called me that before." The fur sticking out from her ass and rubbing her legs felt fantastic. She showed it to Him.

He said: "It suits you quite nicely, kitten." Then He patted His knee indicating that she should return to His lap.

"Tomorrow is Friday. Your normal Friday tasks are rescheduled to next week or are cancelled. Your single task for tomorrow while I am at work is to surf the internet and read everything that you can find on how cats behave. Particularly, you are to focus on kittens. Beginning when I return home tomorrow evening, you are to behave in totality as a kitten. That includes being playful... I bought you a ball to play with... eating out of a food dish on the floor, and using a litter box as a toilet. He pointed to the corner at the litter box that He had placed there while she had showered earlier.

She could only stare. Where did THAT come from? "Master, I..."

"This is not something you can change. You WILL be a kitten for the weekend. Arguing about it will only get you punished."

She was crying again. "No, Master, th-th-that's not it. This is unexpected, that's all. I am just overwhelmed. This tail is absolutely gorgeous, and I love it. B-b-but, I don't know HOW to be a kitten!"

"You are intelligent and obedient. You know that this is what I wish of you. And you have all day tomorrow to study and learn how. Perhaps I can find another kitten to help you learn." (He knew already that another kitten would be there, and her Master too. This had been in the planning stages for several months.)

As He swatted her bottom playfully, He said: "Now, it is time for bed."

"Master, may I wear my tail to my place on the floor beside Your bed, please?"

"Yes, you may wear your tail. But, tonight you will sleep in the bed with me. Before that, I am going to spank you and then use your body for my pleasure."

"Yes, Master. May I know why I am being punished?"

"Yes. You are not being punished. It pleases me to have your ass red and hot before I make love to you. So, I will spank you."

"Thank you, Master. It is my joy to serve You, Sir."

He swatted her bare bottom again and simply said: "Go!"

She ran down the hallway before Him so that she would be in position when He got there, wondering how the spanking would feel with the tail sticking out of her ass. He generally preferred to use "inspection position" for spanking her too. That position gave Him access to all of her… ass cheeks, pussy, inner thighs, tits, and even her face if he wanted. She had also noted His use of the phrase "make love" instead of the cruder "fuck." That was one of His subtle ways of telling her that He was more concerned about her pleasure than His own tonight. And she had to admit that feeling His hands on her ass made her seriously hot and bothered in more ways than just where He was hitting.

He threaded her tail between the lips of her pussy and up over her stomach. He started her spanking with one hard swat directly on the plug sticking up her ass. The plug poking inside of her made her jump in surprise as he hit it. Then He gave her a good sound spanking in the style He usually used for His pleasure. Twenty nice solid swats on each cheek of her ass, and none on her pussy tonight. (Whew! She hated those pussy spankings… but, He owned her, and He could do as He pleased!) It was His rule that she had to count each stroke otherwise it didn't count toward the total. She had to count each cheek separately, and her pussy and tits too if he spanked her there. He didn't always alternate where he hit her, so that required her to concentrate that much harder on what he was doing to her. She couldn't just zone out and just endure it. She had made that mistake once… just once… he had told her later that it had taken thirty-five extra strokes to get her to remember that she was supposed to be counting. She didn't know how many strokes He would have given her if she hadn't remembered… and she didn't ever want to find out!!! But, she had to admit, that was a spanking she would remember forever!

Her ass stung and throbbed, but she was loving it. She almost asked him to give her an extra five on each side. But, she knew that a request like that might also get her ten on the pussy too. Every time His hand hit her ass she felt the plug in her ass move, and she felt the fur tail rubbing her clit and stomach. It was one of the oddest sensations that she had felt in quite a while.

After His pleasure, and before the rest of His pleasure, He chose to please her. She held inspection position because He had not told her she could move. He leaned forward to kiss her tenderly on the lips and to suck on her nipples. As she laid there with her legs spread wide for Him, He gently massaged her burning ass. Slowly, intentionally, he worked His way toward her pussy. He moved her tail aside and began flicking His tongue over her swollen clit and into her moist vagina. Faster and faster, deftly bringing her to orgasm as He had done so many times.

As she climaxed, she forgot to hold her legs apart. She let go and grabbed His hair. Wrapping her legs around His head, she pulled Him into her and held Him there. Time was suspended. She was lost in what He was doing to, and for, her. She even forgot her throbbing ass. This was better than it usually was, and it was usually very good indeed!

As her spasms began to fade, her eyes met His and she remembered, and she KNEW that He had noticed too! As quick as she could, she grabbed her ankles and spread her legs wider than she had ever done before. He stood up and swatted her once on the pussy and said: "Just a reminder."

And then He took her. She could tell He wanted her as much as she wanted him. She liked it when He penetrated her in this position. Sometimes it felt like he was so deep inside of her that she wouldn't be surprised to feel His cock shoot out of her mouth. Damn it felt good! He was building up to... Ah, there it was, the key thrust, deeper than all of the others. She knew that he was shooting cum inside of her, and she loved it!

"Thank you, slut. You are a great little whore! Now get the sleeping straps, you're sleeping on the bed tonight, so you have to be bound. You haven't earned the right to be free in my bed yet. Perhaps if you are a good kitten this weekend..." His voice trailed off as she got the straps to bind her arms and legs while she slept.

"Master, should I bring the gag and blindfold too?"

"No, not tonight."

He bound her legs together and bound her arms behind her back. It pleased her to note that he left her tail in place for the night.

In the morning He woke her as He normally did when she slept in His bed... By grabbing a fist full of her hair and pulling her to a standing position. Over the years of being His property, she had learned to awaken before Him so that she could prepare herself. Once she was vertical, He removed the binding straps.

"Coffee before bathroom unless you use the litter box."

It didn't matter, she couldn't wait. She ran to the living room with Him one step behind her. He stood there and watched her empty her bladder into the kitty litter. As she finished, before she could stand up, he walked over to her. While she crouched over the litter box, with her fluids dripping off her pussy, He pissed on her chest and stomach. She could feel His fluids running down her body and over her pussy before dripping into the litter box with hers. He held her in that position until her body stopped dripping.

"You did well, now go make the coffee."

She stood up, still wearing her tail, and walked to the kitchen. It was funny, the tail just seemed part of her now that she had worn it through the night. In fact, she found that she was swinging her hips more than usual, just to make her tail swing. She wasn't sure how it happened, but somehow it had gone from being just "a tail" to being "HER tail." She had heard how pony girls felt about their tails, but she never understood until that moment. In fact, she wasn't sure that she understood how it happened. She just knew that it was part of her like nothing ever had been before.

She brought Him coffee and croissant for breakfast.

Quietly setting His breakfast beside the newspaper He was reading, she softly asked: "Master, may I shower now?"

"Yes, pet, you may."

"Master, is my tail safe to wear in the shower?"

"Yes, pet, it is. Now, go shower and don't bother me until I call you again."

"Yes, Master. Thank you, Sir."

She went into the shower, leaving the door open as He required her to. (His "open door" bathroom policy had been hard to accept at first. Now that He had seen every bodily function that she did in there more times than she could remember, she couldn't think of not allowing Him access to those personal moments too.) She turned the water on, adjusting the temperature to meet His requirements. He had told her that she needed to have the water as hot as she could stand it without burning herself.

As she stepped into the shower, she could feel her tail get heavier as it got wet. The fur stuck to her skin as she washed. She removed the tail's plug to wash it and to wash her anus as well... She still remembered the bottle brush from last night... But, she felt a real need to have HER tail attached again, and quickly inserted the plug back into her ass. She shaved her arm pits and pussy and shampooed her hair... and her tail... and got out of the shower. She had to use the blow dryer on her tail. It made the fur all "poofy," and it was a real gymnastic trick to hold her ass cheeks apart to blow dry the fur that was between them! But, there was no way she was taking the tail out until she had to in order to go the bathroom, or because He told her to!

She went back to His bedroom and brushed her hair. Then she sat there on the bed brushing HER tail. It felt soooo good to feel her fur brush up against her pussy and her legs.

"Here kitty, kitty, kitty. Here kitty, kitty, kitty."

She assumed that was His way of telling her that He wanted her. She knew that she wasn't required to be a kitten yet, but she felt like it.

She got down on hands and knees and scrambled to where He was... and ran right by Him, just as kittens are wont to do.

He turned and scooped her up with a strong arm between her legs and across her shoulders.

"Mrrrreow!!!!!" She squirmed and tried to escape.

He held onto her tightly and petted her head. "Nice kitty."

"PUUURRRR !!!" she rumbled.

As a not-so-kitten-like reward, Master rubbed her clean pussy.

"Kitten, I need to go to work. When I get home, you will be a kitten. You will not stand up. You will be on all fours all weekend. You will not speak, other than normal cat sounds. In every way you will be a kitten. If you are very good, you will have another kitten to play with.

"Mrrrreowwww" she said in her best sultry kitten voice.

With that said, Master left for work.

As He had instructed her, she surfed the net all day reading about cats and kittens. To mentally get herself in the mode of being an animal, she stayed naked and wore her tail. She also only walked on hands-and-knees all day long. But, the real surprise came when she had to go to the bathroom for the first time after He left for work. She wanted, really wanted to go in the litter box instead of the toilet. She squatted in position, pulled her tail aside, and peed there in HER kitty litter. She could look between her legs and see her fluids seep into the litter as it absorbed her moisture.

As she crawled back to the computer, she purred contentedly to herself. She was enjoying doing as her Master wished.

When He returned home from work at His usual time, she ran to greet Him on all fours, her tail swinging happily between her legs. (Well, to say she "ran" is probably overstating the case, since she was on hands and knees.) She nuzzled her head up against Him to get His attention.

"Meow!"

He nudged her a little with His foot and chuckled. "Kitten, at least let me get in the door."

She responded to His nudging by moving only the minimum amount required. After all, cats don't give way easily. He reached down and petted her to reassure her that He was home and all was right in the world again. She went into the living room to play with her ball. He dropped His brief case on the desk and walked back to His bedroom to get out of His suit and into more casual clothing.

She looked up from her ball. Master was gone! She scampered to the kitchen… "Meow"… down the hallway to the bathroom… "Meow"… to the guest bedroom… "Meoooowww"… finally she found Him!

She jumped up on the bed. (As His slave, she wasn't allowed on the bed without permission… but kittens don't wait for permission from anyone!) She landed on His suit. But, that wasn't her problem. Cats don't much care what they walk on.

"Kitten!!! Bad kitty!" He chided her as he pulled the suit coat and pants out from under her and put them some place safer. She just rolled playfully as He pulled the suit out from under her; blissfully oblivious that she was in even the slightest bit of trouble.

He sat down on the edge of the bed to read the mail.

Seeing Master so close, kitten just had to be near Him. She crawled over and rubbed herself… head to tail… against His arm. (Although to tell the truth, the tail part wasn't EXACTLY cat-like… smile.)

"Purrrrr!"

He rubbed her tail, but she could tell that His concentration was on the mail, not on her. This just wouldn't do. Cats are always the center of whatever universe they live in. She wedged her head and body under His arm, knocked the mail on the floor, and rubbed against Him, kneading His leg with her paws.

"PURRRRR!"

He sighed a sigh of resignation. Sometimes He wondered why He liked cats so much. Since it seemed that kitty wasn't going anywhere without getting the attention she wanted, He held her close and she curled up on His lap in a ball. He sat there petting her and listening to her purr until the doorbell rang.

He knew who it was, but He waited a few minutes to see if she would step out of character and answer the door. She knew it was her job to answer the door and usher guests into the house.

She didn't budge.

The bell rang a second time. He shouted "Coming!" and then softer: "Get down, kitten."

She stretched leisurely, meowed at Him, and got down; giving the impression the whole time that it was her idea to move.

He stood up and took a step toward the hallway. He almost tripped over her. She was under foot, just like a cat. He hadn't figured on her picking up the annoying traits as well as the good ones. He used His foot to move her to the side and said: "Get out of the way, kitten." She moved and then followed Him down the hall.

As He opened the door, she rubbed up against His leg and strained to see who it was. It didn't even occur to her to worry that she was naked. Cats don't wear clothes, and cats don't care. Besides, she really wanted to show off her tail!

"Move, cat." He gently pushed her out of the way. Dave entered carrying a rather large bundle in a blanket.

"Good evening."

"Good evening. Enter and be welcome in my… ouch… home." She was scratching His leg, trying to climb up to the security of His arms. Strangers are outsiders. Invaders to her Master's home.

Dave sat his blanket on the floor. As he unwrapped the bundle, she could see that it was Donna, her best friend in the world. (Well, second best… Master came first, of course.) Donna was also naked and was wearing a long black tail to match her hair and Nubian skin.

"Ah! A black cat!" Her Master exclaimed. "Quite a beautiful animal, Dave."

"Thanks, I think she is."

"Come on into the kitchen for a minute. I was just going to order pizza and make us some coffee. Does your cat like fish?"

In the living room the two cats were nuzzling against each other in greeting. Donna noted the litter box and went over to relieve herself while kitten sat there and watched her. It was fascinating to watch someone else use her litter box. To her surprise, Donna reached down between her legs and scooped litter to cover up the wet spot she had just made. Belatedly she remembered that cats were supposed to do that.

Donna was just finishing as the Masters returned to the living room. She spotted the play ball and pounced on it. It skittered out from under her across the room. Kitten caught the idea and chased the ball batting it back toward Donna. Donna's return shot hit Kitten right in the butt…

"M'row!!!" she said as she jumped.

Then she ran after Donna and knocked her over playfully. The two of them just locked arms and legs onto each other and just rolled back and forth ignoring everything but themselves. Both Masters just sat and watched, enjoying the show. This was definitely worth the effort it had taken to pull it off.

The Pizza guy arrived with the Masters' pizza, and Dave went into the kitchen.

"Here kitty, kitty, kitty… " he called as he put a plate of tuna fish down on the floor for each of them next to where the bowl of water sat, and he filled up the bowl with fresh water. "Here kitty, kitty, kitty!"

They both ran into the kitchen to eat their dinner. They both purred in delight at getting fish instead of dry food, and began eating.

Her Master walked into the kitchen and took in the scene of two naked women on hands-and-knees with fur tails sticking out of their ass, eating tuna just like a cat would, and almost lost control of himself. He wanted to take one of them, and at the moment He wasn't sure if it mattered to Him which one He took!

Dave took the pizza from His hands and said: "C'mon, let's eat this before it gets cold. Do you have any beer to go with it?"

Her Master jerked himself back to reality. "Oh, yeah!… There is beer on the bottom shelf of the refrigerator that should be cold. Let me grab some plates. He leaned over, between the two cats to get two plates. He briefly sat the plates down on the counter and reached down and petted each of the big cats between their legs. They each wiggled against His hand, but didn't let what He was doing distract them from their dinner.

Once dinner was done, the Masters retired to the living room to watch a movie. Having finished their fish as well, the two cats also returned to the living room. Since eating fish that way can be somewhat messy, the cats proceeded to clean each other. Once their faces were clean, just for the fun of it, they moved on to other areas. Kitten knew that her Master liked to watch her eat other women's pussies, and from the way Donna was eating her, Dave must have too.

After the cats were done cleaning themselves, they returned to playing with the ball and wrestling, and the Masters watched their movie. She was just as happy that she didn't have to sit and pretend to enjoy another car chase movie. The movie they were watching was the latest James Bond movie. Car chases and gun fights, and not a lot of plot. Besides, her kitty friend's pussy was more interesting.

After they tired from playing, the two cats entwined themselves into a ball. They were both laying on their side, and had their friend's upper leg tucked under their upper arm, and their head resting on the thigh of their friend's bottom leg. Each had her face contentedly buried in her friend's pussy and had her friend's tail draped over her head.

After the movie ended, the cats were sound asleep. Kitten's Master turned to His friend and said: "They look happy. Why don't you spend the night? The guest room is made up, and you are welcome to use it. Those two can just sleep there."

"They do look happy, don't they? Yeah, that sounds like a good idea. I don't have anything scheduled in the morning. I have to change the oil in the car tomorrow, but I can do that any time."

With that decided, the two Masters headed off to bed, leaving their kittens sleeping together on the floor.

In the morning, the kittens were awake before the Masters. After each using the litter box, they went out to the kitchen to look for breakfast. Since the bowl was empty, they each went to wake up someone who could fix the problem. Just to be playful, Kitten went into the guest room to wake Dave, leaving Donna to wake her Master. Cats are such fickle animals!

Donna jumped up on His bed and began to lick his face. He didn't wake up, but he did roll over. With the covers shifted that way, she could see that he was naked too. She positioned herself so that her black tail was hanging in his face and began licking His cock to wake Him. She wanted breakfast, and she didn't care what (or who) she got to eat to get it. Slowly He began to wake up. To her delight, some parts of His body woke up faster than others! She took him into her mouth and gave Him a very un-cat-like blow job. He opened His eyes and saw Donna's pussy and tail in His face, and felt her ministrations to His swollen cock. His brain hadn't woken up yet. All He wanted to do was to bury His face in her pussy until he came in her mouth. And it didn't take long to get what He wanted.

In the guest room a similar sequence of events was taking place.

Dave and Kitten met her Master and Donna coming down the hall. All four had smiles on their faces.

"I think the cats are hungry."

"M'ROW!!!" said both cats urgently at the same time.

"Sounds like it." Dave said. "You make us coffee, I'll find something to feed them."

"Okay, no fish though. Not at breakfast. They need a balanced diet."

"Sure. No problem. C'Mon cat!"

The rest of the weekend followed a similar pattern. The oil in Dave's car didn't get changed that weekend, and each Master had fun with each of the kittens several times.

Sunday evening just before bed, her Master released her from being a cat. Told her to take off her tail and go take a shower. He reminded her to clean and dry her tail before putting it away.

"Thank you, Master, for the gift of this weekend. It was one of the best things you have ever given me. Now I think I understand ponys better. I will be your 'kitten' whenever you wish."

"You're welcome slave. Now get cleaned up and ready for bed."

She, once again, wore her tail in the shower. She washed it and washed herself and then took her tail off so that she could clean the plug and that part of her body. She dried off her tail and put it in the box to keep it safe. Her asshole felt empty and she started crying as she closed the box. She knew now that she would do absolutely anything He asked to be allowed to wear HER tail again.

Chapter 7: To "Sir" or not to "Sir" (Protocol)

At the simplest level, "protocol" is a set of rules for accepted behavior. There is no single defined set of rules. (Does this surprise anyone?) In general, if there is a universal rule, it is this: "Treat all with respect." For an owned submissive, the first rule is that you follow what your Master / Mistress says to do. If you are not owned, honor what other's wishes are. Having said that much, I'll discuss some general guidelines in the rest of this chapter.

Honoriffics

"Honoriffic" is a fancy word that simply means that it is something that is spoken to honor, or show respect to, another individual. There are many words that can be used for this purpose. However, there are really a handful that are in common usage. You could use these words to show honor or respect on your own, or you can be commanded to use them.

"Master" or "Mistress"

The word: "Master" is one of the common words used. By convention, "Master" alone is used only to address one's owner. Most see the use of the word alone to be an indicator of ownership. However, you may also see the word "Master" used in combination with a name; for example, "Master James". It is common in Gorean culture to address all dominants as "Master" followed by their name. This is intended to simply show respect, not to show ownership.

For other couples, the word "Master" is only used to refer to one's owner. All other dominants are addressed as "Sir" or "Ma'am". In general, for me personally, I have my slave use "Sir" or "Ma'am" for most dominants. For a few that I deem as deserving an extra measure of respect, I have told her to use the word "Master" and their name. There are also a few who request that they not be addressed as "Master", simply as "Sir".

Capitalization

As I'm sure you have noticed by now, in this book I have used unusual capitalization rules. Frequently, particularly on the internet, names and honorifics referring to dominants are capitalized, and submissive's names are not capitalized. This is not a universal rule, but it is a convention used by many people in the lifestyle.

"Elmo Speak"

Actually, it is called: "third-person speech". But for those of you who are familiar with Elmo from Sesame Street, you have heard third-person speech before. To use third-person speech, you take the words "I", "me", "my", etc. out of your vocabulary. So you will get sentences like: "This one slept well, Master." Or "One's boss was being an ass today. He was getting on one's case all day long."

The theory behind the use of third-person speech is that it constantly reminds the slave of her status as slave. It can be quite difficult to maintain this mode of speech consistently. It also has a side benefit in that it reminds those around the submissive of her status as well. I have thought of using it as a punishment for exactly these reasons. It really is quite difficult to get accustomed to.

Permission-Based Protocols

Some people in the lifestyle require a high degree of formality. Practitioners of the gorean philosophy tend to be very much into rituals like this. In this type of relationship, the submissive / slave must ask permission for virtually anything. This typically includes entering or leaving a room, using the toilet, sitting on the furniture, etc. This type of ritual formality is another tool used to re-enforce the role that the slave holds in the relationship.

Ritual Protocols

These are closely related to the permission-based protocols that we discussed in the last section of the chapter. But the difference is that the slave is to go through a specific sequence of actions. Once again, Goreans are very high on the list of those that make ritual part of their life. There are a list of "slave positions" that the Gorean slave must learn. (There are web sites that describe all of them in detail. Many include pictures.)

Rituals can take all forms. One of my rituals is that my slave is not generally permitted to open her own doors. The purpose of this ritual is to show my girl that even though she is property, she is treasured property.

It is common for couples to have a greeting ritual that the slave goes through when Master returns home from work. Perhaps the slave is to kneel naked with hands and arms stretched in front of her, and face to the floor. When Master enters the door, she says: "Master, the body of your slave is ready for your use." She then waits there in silence (for as long as it takes) until Master calls her, giving her permission to stand up. The rituals used are important because they, once again, re-enforce the slave's chosen role.

A word of caution is appropriate here. For some very religious persons this can be perceived as the slave worshiping the Master. I suppose that it can be seen that way. But, in some very real senses, it doesn't have to be. It is all about your thoughts and motivations.

Public Play and Dungeon Etiquette

This isn't a text on play activities there are already quite a number of those available. But, it would seem appropriate to talk about rules of playing in a public dungeon. The list below is typical of what you might find. If you have any questions, find a dungeon monitor (DM) and ask. Most events will have several DMs who try to make sure things stay safe.

- ☐ If the dungeon provides toys (floggers, paddles, etc.) for use, there should be cleaning supplies available to clean them after use. If you use them, you clean them. (This is a good job for the submissive after the scene is over.)
- ☐ If you are watching a scene, be careful to stay clear of the action. It wouldn't be good to get hit with a wayward back-swing of a flogger!
- ☐ If you are in a scene, try to be mindful of your surroundings.
- ☐ If you are watching a scene, be quiet. Even positive comments about technique welcomed after the scene can distract the participants and break the spell that the dominant is trying to weave. (This leads to a very frustrated and unhappy submissive.)
- ☐ If you believe a scene is going over the edge, get an experienced dungeon monitor and express your concerns, but do not interrupt the scene yourself. You may find that your concerns are completely unfounded.
- ☐ By all means, if you admired the scene, say so… AFTER the scene. Also remember that there may be several scenes going on at once in a given room.
- ☐ Honor the rules of the group that you are with. Many groups have rules about "no penetration". That includes fingers as well as anything else.

Aftercare

The term "aftercare" means to care for the submissive after a scene. I know of subs where the aftercare they want is to have a blanket thrown over them and to be left alone. I have known others that need cuddling and reassurance that they are okay and that they performed well in the scene. Aftercare is important whether the sub goes to subspace or not, but the needs might change. I know of some dominants that are of the opinion that aftercare is a myth. They believe that it is a way of the submissive manipulating the dominant.

Subspace

From time to time you will hear "subspace" discussed. This has absolutely nothing to do with faster-than-light space travel. The term "subspace" refers to a mental state that a sub reaches resulting from some kind of stimulus. I have taken a sub to subspace just through anal stimulation with a finger deep in her ass. This is a genuine physical sensation; it is not just in the sub's mind. It has to do with the release of chemicals into the bloodstream; chemicals that the body releases due to the stimulus. Primarily, these are endorphins. This chemical release triggers a sense of euphoria. Many subs call a trip to subspace "flying."

There are various levels to subspace, and you won't get to the deepest level every time. In all probability, you won't get there the first several "flights." But, you will enjoy the trip enough to make you want to do it again. I can't tell you what will take you to subspace, it is not the same with everyone. But, one thing I am sure of is that you can stop it from happening. You have to be in a frame of mind where you are willing to let go and let the dominant take you wherever He wants to. This level of trust is not always easy to achieve.

There are several myths about subspace that you need to be aware of.

"She is totally unaware of her surroundings. It doesn't matter what you do or say to her." There are, as I said, various levels to subspace. At the deepest levels, the sub does become nearly totally inner-directed and really doesn't know what is happening around her. She will not be able to talk or communicate in any way. In fact, with one sub I took on her first trip to subspace it looked like nothing so much as a seizure. I actually wrote a two-page letter for her to give to any dominant that she plays with so that He wouldn't panic and she would have to explain to the EMTs. But, the fact is that at some levels of subspace, the sub is generally aware of what is happening around them. Frequently they will not be able to speak coherently, but they are generally aware.

"You can't go into subspace over the phone." This is just not true. I wouldn't try to drive a sub into deep subspace over the phone, but you can most definitely take them on a nice flight.

"You can't go into subspace without pain." This one probably originated with a dominant that didn't know any other way. With my slave I can have her use her Hitachi Wand until she is begging wantonly to be allowed to climax. The first several times she asks, I tell her: "No, not yet." But when I do allow her that release, she flies higher than a kite. She becomes incoherent, and literally can't talk. (We have done this over the telephone more than once.)

Our Story

In the story for this chapter we have a very emotionally-charged situation. A slave has found out that she will not be physically able to care for her Master very much longer because of a terminal disease. She actively begins planning for someone else to care for Him. This is not an unheard of scenario in the lifestyle.

In the majority of cases, when one person in the relationship dies, the relationship will normally end. If the slave dies, most likely the Master will find another and life goes on. But, in some cases, if the Master dies, He will find another Master to take on His slave(s) so that they will not have to go through the trials of finding a suitable Master. The logic is two-fold. First, it is a way to provide for the slave after the Master passes. But, it also includes the notion of: "Who is better suited to find a new Master for a slave than the person who currently owns her?!!"

Story: "The Gift"

"Master?"

"Yes?"

"Can we talk about something that has been on my mind?"

"Of course we can. You know that. What is it you want to talk about that has you so nervous?"

"Well… ummm… I… ummm… I mean… Sir, I…"

"Out with it!"

"'Poly', Master Phillip, Sir."

"'Poly'?… Well, I assume that you are not talking about plastics or string cheese."

"No Sir, poly relationships, Sir. You know, more than two people in an intimate, long-term relationship." Why was He being so dense? He knew what she was talking about!

"Oh. Okay. What would you like to discuss about poly relationships? Have you found another Master or Mistress that you would like me to share you with?"

"NO!!! SIR!!! I am YOURS now and forever; until my life ends. I would never suggest that I be permitted someone else to be with. If I am to ever be with someone else, it would only be if you asked that of me and I would do so only to please You!"

"And if I were to ask you to be with another woman while I watched you?"

"I would obey you without question, Master."

"That's good. But let me ask you the same thing another way… Is that something that you would like me to ask you to do?"

"If that is Your pleasure, Sir, you may ask anything of me."

"Slave, you missed the point. Yes, I accept that I own you. I have owned you by your own choice, since you locked my collar around your neck.. That means that I may command anything of you that I wish. However, part of being your 'Master' means that I care for you, and that I desire you to be happy. So, I ask you again: 'Would you like to be commanded to be with another woman? Would this make you happy?"

"Master, I don't know if I would like it. I have never even kissed ANYONE, male or female, other than You. I want only to please You. Master, You complete me. You care for and protect me. I exist only for You! Please, Sir, this isn't what I want to talk about."

"Peg, don't get upset. Your needs are important to me. To meet your needs, I have to know what they are."

"Master, I have told you EVERYTHING." *Well, everything but what I learned today, she added mentally.*

"'Everything'?... Then what has changed that you ask me about 'poly' now? Are you not happy?"

She was frustrated. All she wanted to do was to see that His needs were met for the future.

"Master, I have a reason for bringing this up, and I will tell you in a moment. Do you remember back when you collared me? You immediately took steps to make sure that I was cared for in the event that something happened to you. You bought a life insurance policy to pay for my future should you be unable to, and you found another Master, whom I have come to love almost as much as You to own me should you become unable to do so. Over our time together, you have done everything possible to insure that my life and needs are secure and that I am protected no matter what for the rest of my life."

"Yes, Peg, I remember. That is part of the commitment I made to myself when I assumed responsibility for you. I don't understand why you are going on about this now, and how this relates to talking about a poly lifestyle."

"Master, I went to the doctor's office today, as You know."

"Yes."

"Sir, what You do not know yet is what the doctor told me."

"That is true. I was waiting until after dinner to discuss it."

"I can't wait any longer, Master." She dropped to her knees at His feet, and began sobbing uncontrollably. "Sir, I have terminal cancer, and it is in a very advanced stage. There is nothing that can be done about it. No drugs. No radiation. No chemo. Nothing."

He pulled her up on to His lap to hold her in His powerful arms. "Peg, we discussed this. I will not abandon you to someone else to save myself pain. You are mine, and my responsibility, until you leave this world."

"Yes, Master. I am more grateful than I can tell You for that. The doctor also said that I have, at most, six months to live, and probably less then three."

With that news, He began to cry as well. To lose her is pain beyond imagining.

"Sir, that is why I have asked you about 'poly'."

"You cannot be replaced."

"Nor can you, my Lord. You are my life, and it has been my joy to serve you with all that I am. But, just as you have taken extraordinary measures to provide for me in the event that something happened to you, I have begun a plan to see that you have someone else to do those things that I gladly do for you now. However, to go any further with my plan, I now must have your permission and agreement."

"Perhaps you need to tell me about this plan."

"Master, it will be easier to show You." She quietly stood and walked to the door of the guest bedroom and opened it.

He had noted that the door was closed when he got home, but had elected not to say anything about it.

Peg looked into the room and spoke one word: "Come!"

At her word of command two women, stripped naked, bound, and gagged walked out of the room and followed Peg back to the living room. All three naked women, with His Peg in the middle, knelt at His feet and bowed with their head to the floor to honor Him.

Peg sat up and looked directly into His eyes. "Master, I have acquired commitments from these two slaves to do anything that I command them. You have met each of them before."

"Yes, I recognize them."

"Master, I have not much life left. It is my desire that I spend my remaining days training these two to become yours. They are my final gift to you. I seek your permission to complete this task before I die."

"Peg, it is not that simple. These are free women who must speak for themselves in this matter. They wear no collar. Moreover, you cannot be replaced."

"Master, I know that I cannot be replaced, just as Master Bill couldn't have replaced You. Yet, You insisted that he agree to take me if something happened to you. I am your property, and it was and is your right to do with me as you please. I do not have the authority over You that You have over me. Nor do I seek such authority. I simply desire to give to You a gift such as that which you would have given me in the same circumstances. It is my most profound desire to know that You will be served and respected in a way that you deserve after I am no longer able to serve you myself.

"As far as them being 'free women' they are not wearing a collar, but they are no freer than I am. These two have sworn to me the same oaths that I swore to you. They have pledged their lives to me as I have pledged mine to You. That bond ends then I die, unless someone else will take them. Just as You asked Master Bill to take me in the event of Your death, I now ask you to take these slaves of mine when I die. I have no power to force you to do this, nor would I force you if I could. But, I beg you with all my heart, Master please let me do this for you as my final gift of service to you."

"What are their names?"

"Sir, they have not earned the right to have names. As you taught me when I became yours, the privilege to have a name must be earned. I simply call them 'slave'. If I need to distinguish between them, I call this one" she pointed to the brunette at her left "'slave one' and this one" pointing to the blond at her right "is 'slave two'. Their number designations have no meaning. They were simply a random roll of the dice, nothing more. I have given them basic instruction for serving you, but nothing more."

Oddly the words from some comedian he had seen years ago sprang to His mind completely unbidden. "… when I was young, 'number one' and 'number two' was not something that you wanted to be."

"Peg, please remove their gags and bindings at this time so that I may speak to them and inspect them."

"Yes, Master." She said as she released them.

Looking at the brunette, her Master said: "Slave one."

"Mistress, May I answer?"

"Yes you may. You will do anything that He asks immediately without question."

"Thanks you, Mistress."

"Yes, most respected Master of my Owner, how may I serve you, Sir?"

"Stand up."

She almost fell over in her haste to obey him such was her desire to please her Mistress and Her Master.

He continued: "Now display your self for my inspection."

She began at the top, pulling her long brown hair away from her shoulders and ears; turning her head from side to side to give Him full views of her head and face. Next she showed Him her supple arms. First the left and then the right. She displayed them to Him as a jeweler shows an engagement ring. Next came her shoulders and then her breasts. She knew that her nipples were a little hard because of His scrutiny. She grabbed each nipple between the thumb and forefinger of her hand and squeezed them hard and pulled them away from the areole, stretching them for His inspection. She cupped her hands under her breasts and jiggled them for Him. By stretching her neck as far as she could, she could just barely suck her own nipples. She did so now, in a desperate attempt to please Him. She knew that pleasing Him would please her Mistress. Mistress is all that mattered to her now; She was her reason for living. She continued her show with her abdomen and then spread her legs apart to show Him her bald pussy. (Mistress had told her that she was to keep her pussy as smooth as her face. It meant shaving twice a day, but she had to obey.) She leaned back to thrust her hips forward and ruthlessly grabbed her pussy lips and pulled them apart as far as possible until she couldn't stand the pain any longer.

"Mistress?"

"Yes?"

"Does Your Master want to inspect inside of my vagina?"

"Master?"

"Not at the moment, Peg. You may grant slave one permission to address me directly if you choose."

"Thank you Master. She is not always properly respectful, Sir."

"As you wish."

"Slave, Master does not require that He inspect your vagina. However, I require that you show Him that you can put your full fist inside."

"No!"

Peg's hand seemingly flew out of nowhere into the brunette's face. The backhand slap contacted her lip with a force she had never felt from her Mistress before. She could taste blood in her mouth.

With very real tears streaming down her face, in a soft voice she said: "I'm sorry, Mistress," as she bowed her head in shame and embarrassment.

Peg could see the blood marking her teeth, and viciously kissed her; biting down on the swelling lip.

"Now, slave, I will demonstrate since you refuse to." As she said the last word, she made her hand into a small, but solid, fist and rammed it into the slave's pussy.

Slave one screamed.

"PEG!!! STOP!!! NOW!!!" her Master shouted as he grabbed a fist full of His slave's hair.

Both women crumpled to the floor. Slave one curled up into a fetal ball and cried. Peg just lay there and shook in the trauma of what she had just done. She had never struck anyone before. She even carried the flies that got into the house outside so that they wouldn't get swatted and die.

"Peg, get up and take care of your slave. You know better than to let your anger control you like that. You will be punished later. Now get off your ass and TAKE CARE OF HER." (These last words were spoken in a roar that He had never used on her before.)

She got up.

Slave one scooted away from her in terror of what might happen next, and watched Master Philip. Her eyes were begging Him to protect her.

Peg reached her slave, who had backed herself into a corner and had no place to run.

With tears streaming down her face in sorrow for what she had done, Peg said: "My beautiful slave, I punished you in anger, and I was wrong. Please forgive me."

Her slave just stared at her shaking uncontrollably in fear and terror.

Peg stroked her hair and held her close, trying to calm her. She repeated reassurances to calm her; reassurances about how wrong she was to strike in anger, and her regret.

Once she seemed to calm down, Peg tried to get her to spread her legs so that she could determine if she had injured her slave. Slave one was having none of it. She held her knees close to her chest and held her legs squeezed tightly together and she was shaking in fear.

Peg knew that she needed to check for injury, and tried to force her way in with all her strength.

"MASTER!!!! HELP MEEEEEEE!!!!" slave one shouted at the top of her lungs with her arms reaching for Him.

Philip could tell that she was terrified and nearly hysterical; he was at her side faster than she could believe. He took her in His arms and whispered: "Slave, you have to be examined. This could have done serious injury, and we need to see if you must go to the hospital."

"M-M-Master Ph-Ph-Philip, S-S-Sir, W-W-Would Y-You d-do it s-s-sir, p-p-please?" she said through s sobbing voice.

"Slave, you are your Mistress's property by your own choice. I cannot examine you without her permission."

Slave one glanced at Her Mistress. Her eyes said what her mouth couldn't ask.

After staring into her slave's pleading eyes for what seemed like an eternity, seeing nothing but fear and terror there, she spoke softly: "Master Philip, Sir, I would be honored to have your help. I have broken her trust, and it will take time to rebuild it. But she needs to be checked now. Please examine her, Master."

He began His examination with her swollen lip. It looked worse than it was. Her front teeth had cut her lip on the inside. But, the cuts weren't deep, and didn't need any medical attention; although they would smart for a few days, they would heal.

Next He gently spread slave one's legs. She cried with each movement. He tenderly examined her both inside and out. There some bruises, but no cuts. Fortunately, not as much bruising as he expected. It didn't look like she needed a doctor, but she would be sore for a week or two. It seemed that the smallness of Peg's fist and slave one's prior experience had protected her. Still, that was no justification for what had happened. He looked at his slave:

"Get an ice pack."

Peg ran to the kitchen. She got out the ice bag and got ice out of the freezer. She was so upset that she dropped a third of the ice on the floor before getting it into the ice bag. The quickly returned to Her Master and to her slave.

Master took the ice bag and gently placed it between slave one's legs. "Hold this here. It will help with the swelling."

He looked at Peg, and sternly said: "Back to your place."

She returned to her place before His chair and knelt beside slave two with her face to the floor. She felt very strange. She knew that He was furious with her, and she deserved whatever punishment she got, she knew that. And, it was a relief to not have to look at the slave she had harmed, and to be able to hide her face in shame for her actions. But, at the same time, it was disconcerting that she couldn't be with her slave to comfort and care for her. She had never even suspected this part of owning someone. She knew that her Master felt pain when she was upset or hurting. But, she never understood. She wasn't entirely sure she understood now. But, as she knelt there, she reviewed every time, every act that had hurt Him. She loved Him more than she had ever thought possible. He never told her how much it hurt Him for her to rebel and disobey. She cried harder and louder as she began to understand what she had done to Him.

Master Philip carried slave one back to her place and helped her kneel as she was expected to.

Slave one looked up at Him. "Master, may I speak, please?"

"Yes."

"Sir, I apologize for my disobedience. My Mistress commanded me, and I refused. I have committed my life to Her, and I failed her. I am a disgrace to my Mistress. I beg you, Sir, please do not punish Her for my actions."

"She will be punished; but not for your actions. She will be punished for her own actions. I have made mistakes in the past when I had my first sub, long before I owned Peg. Other Masters in my circle of friends took me to task for what I had done. I won't tell you what they did to me, but suffice it to say that I will remember it forever. I deserved what I got, just like she does, for being irresponsible.

"I also want you to consider that your Mistress received very traumatic news today. It is hard to hear someone tell you that you won't have another birthday. To hear that you will be taken from all of those who love you. That they will have to go on with that void in their lives until they too die."

"Yes, Master, I have felt the loss of loved ones. It is a difficult thing to endure. Sir, I have one more thing to say."

"Yes?"

"Sir, I thank you for coming to my aid, and I ask that you refuse to take me. I am ashamed to have not trusted my Mistress. I don't deserve to be owned, particularly not by one such as you."

"That's just not going to happen. Deal with it."

"Yes, Master Philip, Sir."

"I will not tolerate disobedience any more than your Mistress did, and you may find that you like my punishments even less than what has just happened to you. But, I have never issued punishment to anyone while I was angry. You will note that I have not pronounced punishment on your Mistress… yet. My punishments are generally tailored to teach a lesson that needs to be learned."

"Thank you for sharing this with me, Master."

"You're welcome. Now resume your position. Be careful to keep your ice bag in place."

"Yes Sir." Slave one returned to kneeling before Him with her face bowed to the floor like the other two women.

"Peg, look at me."

She raised her head just enough to look at Him. "Y-Yes, M-Master?" She hadn't been so embarrassed… hadn't felt such shame… in all the time he had owned her.

"You are to direct slave two to interact directly with me for the moment, and then you will resume your position and be silent."

"Yes, Master." She was in deep shit, and she knew it.

"Slave two."

"Yes, Mistress?"

"You will address Master Philip directly and you will immediately do anything he commands."

"I understand, Mistress. I will obey."

Peg silently returned to kneeling with her face to the floor.

"Slave two."

"Yes, Master of my Owner?"

"Stand up and display yourself for me."

"Yes, Sir."

She stood slowly. He knew that she must have cramps in her muscles from kneeling. It had been much longer than it should have been. She endured the pain silently. Not so much as a whimper came from her mouth.

When she was fully erect, he stopped her. "Relax a moment. Let your muscles get used to moving again. When you are ready, you may proceed."

"Thank you, Master of my Owner. I do not need to rest, Sir."

She displayed her body for Him. Head. Breasts. Pussy. Legs. She turned around and showed Him her back and ass. She rubbed her hands over the penguin tattooed on her ass before bending over to spread her cheeks to show Him her asshole. She stood back up and turned to face Him once again.

"Slave one."

"Yes, Master of my Owner?"

"Slave two."

"Yes, Master of my Owner?"

"Slave one and slave two, you have heard what your Mistress intends. She has terminal cancer and is going to die soon. In the traditions of myself and my close friends, we take steps to ensure that our slaves are cared for in the event that we are not able to do so. We each take this responsibility very seriously." He paused.

Slave two spoke: "Master, we understand this."

"Good, I'm glad that you do. What you may or may not realize is that our tradition also allows the slave to choose. She is allowed to elect to become freed rather than to be transferred."

Slave two spoke again: "We understand this too, Master Philip, Sir."

He looked at slave one: "Does she speak for you too in this matter?"

"Yes, Master, We are of one mind in this. Our Mistress has explained that it is her wish that we serve You to the best of out ability just as she has served you. We know that neither of us can replace Her. But, we hope that You will find us acceptable, and that You allow us to ease the pain of Her passing.'

Slave two quickly added to what her sister slave had said: "Master Philip, Sir, if there is another that You find more desirable, one who will better serve and care for You as our Mistress wishes, we both beg that You choose her instead of us. This is the best way for us to fulfill our Mistress' wish. However, if You find accepting us to become yours is the best way to honor our Mistress, we beg that you accept us."

With the last word, both slave one and slave two knelt before Him. This time, they were not kneeling to simply respect and honor Him, this time they knelt with their backs upright, heads bowed, and arms outstretched toward Him in a posture of begging that He accept them.

"Peg."

"Yes, Master?"

"Stand up."

"Yes, Sir."

"Peg, this gift you have given me pleases me greatly. It is the kindest act of service that you have ever performed for me. I accept the responsibility for these two at such time as you cannot adequately care for and protect them."

"Thank You, Master Philip, Sir."

She addressed her slaves: "Slaves?"

"Yes Mistress?" They replied in unison.

"Return to the guest room and return with the two small boxes that you will find on the table there."

They each quickly performed the task She had requested.

When they returned to her side, each slave held a small box about a half inch high and about six inches on a side.

"Open it."

Upon opening their box, each slave found a blue anodized aluminum collar with a small silver pad lock and two keys.

"These are slave collars that you are to wear as a mark that I own you and later that my Master owns you. You must put these on of your own free will. At this moment, I release you. You are free women with the right to choose your own destiny. You know the full details of what your life will be if you choose to wear a collar and become my slaves for life. Now choose. Either leave here now and be released to become free again, or place my collar around your neck and become a slave for life."

The blond to her left immediately snapped the blue collar around her neck and secured it with the pad lock. She held the two keys in her hand, awaiting further instructions.

The brunette struggled for a moment, but only for a moment. She looked once at Master Philip and then with her head bowed, she knelt before her Mistress. "Mistress, please forgive my doubts. I want this with all my heart." She too snapped the collar shut and locked it.

Peg signaled Her blond slave to kneel too.

"Slaves, I accept the pledge you have given me. I desire that you remember this day for the rest of your life. To that end, I will no longer call you simply 'slave'." She turned to the brunette. "From this day forward, you will be known as: "alpha' or 'slave alpha'. I honor you with a name that means 'beginning' for this event began with me hurting you. It is a reminder that even Masters and Mistresses make mistakes. Mistakes have consequences. I know that I will have to face my consequences, just as you will."

"Thank you, Mistress. That name pleases me."

She turned to the blond. "From this day forward, you will be called 'omega' or 'slave omega'. For every beginning there must also be an ending. The two of you are now bound to the ending of my life. I give you this name to signify that binding."

"Thank you, Mistress. That name pleases me as well. I am also pleased that you have given my sister slave and I names that show that we are bound together. I am happy to be omega to her alpha."

"Alpha and omega, as my first command, I bind you into secondary ownership to Master Philip. As is fitting, you will obey every command that he gives you immediately without question."

"Yes, Mistress. We will obey."

She bowed before her Master. "Master, I have collared these two slaves named 'alpha' and 'omega'. I have bound them to secondary ownership to you. They will do anything that you command."

She took the keys for the pad locks. One key for each one she fastened to the ring on her own collar. The other she presented to her Master. "Master, this completes the beginning of my plan to provide for you after I am gone. How may I serve you further?"

"Peg, what you have done pleases me. For this gift, I could even forgive what you did to alpha earlier. However, as a Master, mentoring a Mistress, I can't. You acted irresponsibly as the owner of a slave, and I can't overlook that."

"Yes, Master, I will accept anything that you pronounce as punishment."

"Kneel."

"Yes, Master." She knelt before Him, waiting.

"Alpha, Omega?"

"Yes, Master of our Owner." They answered in unison.

"Stand up."

They stood and faced Him.

"Peg, the first part of your punishment is that your name will be taken away for the next week. For seven days you will simply be known as 'slave'."

She began to cry. How could He take her name away? The name that he had given her when she had put on His collar. She would have preferred that he simply cut her arm off.

"Alpha?"

"Yes, Master?"

"Go to the dungeon and you will find a royal blue flogger hanging on the wall. Bring it to me."

"Yes, Master. At once."

"Omega?"

"Yes, Master?"

"Go to the dungeon and you will find a cranberry red flogger hanging on the wall. Bring it to me."

"Yes, Master. At once."

As both of her slaves ran to do His bidding, all she could think about was losing her name. Belatedly she realized what He had told her slaves to do…. She almost begged Him…

Alpha and omega returned with the two floggers.

"Slave, sit up."

It hurt her to hear Him address her that way. "Yes, Master."

He took the two floggers from alpha and omega. "Do you recognize these?"

"Yes, Master."

"Alpha, omega, these two floggers were constructed by myself and this slave on the night she was collared. They were the first real toys we had…. To this day, they have never been used by anyone but myself, and have never been used on anyone but this slave. This means that they have a very special meaning and significance.

"In a very real sense, by putting on those collars, you each have become 'family'. As part of my family, we will build a unique flogger for each of you that will be used only on you."

"Thank you, Sir." They each answered.

"The second part of this slave's punishment is that you, her slaves, will each give her thirty lashes on the back with one of these floggers. If I even think that either of you are holding back and not giving her what she deserves, I will flog both of you myself. Am I clear?"

"Yes, Master."

"Yes, Master."

"Slave!… All fours."

She hurried to obey.

"Slave, you are to count the lashes."

"Alpha, omega, if she does not count the stroke, it does not count. Begin."

With His word of command, alpha and omega began whipping their Mistress. Each of them began crying as they saw welts begin to show on her back. When the required sixty lashes were completed, all three women huddled together and cried.

"Slave?"

"Y-Y-Yes, Master?"

"Have you learned your lesson?"

"Yes, M-Master, I have. But…"

"Yes?"

"B-B-But, Master, PLEASE can I have my name back? Please, Sir, I'm begging you!!!"

"Yes, slave. You may have your name back in…" (checking His watch) "… six days, twenty-two hours and fifty-three minutes. Until then, you are simply 'slave'."

She started crying anew for her loss. "Yes, Master. Your slave obeys."

"Alpha, omega, there is something that I want you to learn from this too. In each and every punishment that a Master of Mistress assigns, there is an element of pain that Master or Mistress must also endure. We endure this willingly because we know that it will make you a better slave."

"We understand that, Master." Omega said.

"Sir," alpha added, "I don't believe that I understood it before like I do now having felt it."

"I am glad. Alpha, take the two floggers and hang them in the dungeon. Omega, go out to the kitchen and get the bottle of olive oil. It is on the middle shelf of the upper cabinet between the sink and stove."

When each of the women returned, he poured a little olive oil into his hands and began rubbing it into His slave's tender back.

For the next ten weeks the house kind of had a standard routine to it. Peg got her name back, as promised, and with four extra hands to help, Peg could get her chores done that much quicker. That left time for training her slaves. There was one over-night hospital stay and Either alpha or omega were at their Mistress' side the whole time. It had been extremely difficult to get permission for one of them to stay outside of visiting hours. But, He had a friend in the lifestyle, Dr. Pill (odd name for a doctor), at that hospital who was able to pull a few strings and secure permission as long as there were no problems. Peg had forbidden them both from being there all of the time, so that one of them could care for her Master. Philip was secretly pleased to see their loyalty to their Mistress.

Near the end of the three-month window, Peg was getting very ill, and needed better care than could be provided at home. To make things better all around, they moved her into the local hospice unit. Philip spent as much time as possible there, and alpha and omega were also there as much as they could be, with one of them always being there. They all knew that she would never leave the hospice alive. But, she exuded peace. She was content. She had done what she set out to do.

Her Master had someone to serve and take care of Him, and He would care for them. Master was all that mattered. Her family was all that mattered.

One Tuesday evening a nurse stopped Him as He was arriving at the hospice.

"My name is: Karen, and I have been at this hospice for six years, and I have never seen a family like yours. Can I talk to you about it?"

"Yes."

"I don't understand the dynamics here. All three women are obviously in love with you. Actually, 'love' is a inadequate word to describe how they act.

"I have never seen a family so fiercely loyal to each other. With both alpha and omega there, if someone came to harm Peg I doubt that the person would leave the room alive."

He chuckled. "Yes, you're quite probably right."

"In all of my years, I have never had a hospice patient where someone was always at the patient's side. They leave to get something to eat while the patient eats or sleeps. They go home to their own lives and come here when they can. Those two don't even go to the bathroom unless there is someone to take over for them.

"You and those two women are different. I have never seen such loyalty before."

He smiled. "Yes, that is part of it to be sure. Each of the three of us have committed ourselves to Peg's care until she passes.

"But there is more to it than that. You have to understand that there is a unique bond of duty and responsibility here too. Quite some years ago, now, I assumed responsibility for Peg. By her own choice she became my slave."

"Slave?!!... For real?... You're not kidding?"

"No, I'm not kidding. I'm sure you've noticed other things that seemed unusual."

"Yes, like the locked collars that the three wear and how alpha and omega kneel and call you Master when you enter? Yes, I have noticed those things. Are they your slaves too then?"

"No, they are Peg's slaves. They will become my responsibility when she dies."

"Are they in love with her too, then?"

"Oh, most definitely."

"Well, I ummm... I mean this in the most sincere way ... Your relationship... the love and loyalty... the way you defend each other... I don't know how to put this... It just seems too good to be true, and I can't believe what I am seeing. If this is for real, sir, I would like to find out more about it. I know that now is not a good time, but, sir, after a decent time has passed, could I come see you?"

"I'll do better than that. Would you please come with me?"

She followed Him down the hall to His slave's room.

He opened the door and alpha and omega, who were both there, immediately dropped to their knees. In unison with their Mistress, they said: "Good afternoon, Master."

He opened the door wider and allowed Karen to enter.

Alpha and omega started to quickly get to their feet, not wanting to cause trouble with the hospice staff. But, He quickly motioned them to stay where they were as He closed the door.

Not knowing for sure what was going on, but seeing that Master intended to include this person in the circle of people who knew about their world, they continued… As they bowed with forehead to the floor, again in unison the three said: "How may we serve you, Master?"

Peg added: "Forgive me, Master, for not kneeling before you to honor you. Please know that my heart is bowed with my sisters before you."

She had said the same thing every time since she became unable to kneel.

He smiled at her and whispered: "Peg, when have I ever required you to do something that you were not physically capable of doing?"

With a tear rolling down her cheek, she whispered: "Never, Master."

"Stand up and be comfortable."

Alpha and omega stood.

For a moment, He ignored both Karen and Peg's two slaves.

As He sat down on the edge of her bed, He smiled at her and asked: "How are you feeling today?"

"I am not important, Master. Are my slaves caring for you and meeting your needs?"

It was the formula that she had been using since entering the hospice. He continued with the expected response: "Yes, Peg, they have performed well. I am satisfied. You have trained them well. Now answer my question. How are you feeling today?"

"Master, I am in a great deal of pain, but they dare not give me any more morphine. To do so would dull my mind, and I refuse to allow that. I must see that those I own are safe. You taught me that lesson well through the example of your life."

"Peg, I love you, you have been a wonderful addition to my life." He bent down and tenderly kissed her.

"I love you too, Master. You ARE my life."

"Alpha, have you been caring for your Mistress?"

"Yes, Master Philip, Sir. I have done all that She has asked of me."

"Good, you have pleased me, and I'm sure that you have pleased your Mistress as well."

"Master she pleases me by caring for you." Peg added quickly.

To hear that both Mistress and Master were pleased was joy beyond measure.

"Omega, have you been caring for your Mistress?"

"Master Philip. I have only just arrived. I was attending to your needs at the house as she commanded me."

"Good, you have pleased me, and I'm sure that you have pleased your Mistress as well."

"Master she pleases me by caring for you." Peg again added quickly.

Now that He had checked His family out to make sure all was as good as could be expected, He motioned His guest over.

"Peg, alpha, omega, you remember Karen?"

"Yes, Master." All three answered.

"On my way in tonight Karen was asking about us. She said that she didn't know what we had, but that she wanted it very much. When she asked about coming to visit in the future, but I thought that now was just as good a time as any. Besides, Peg, I wanted her to know you. She would like to talk about your life as a slave."

Karen walked over to the bed. "Thanks for inviting me in Master Philip." After witnessing the women interacting with Him, it just felt natural to use their honorific for Him too. She hoped it wasn't inappropriate. "What I just witnessed was amazing. I thought that slaves always resented being owned. These ones certainly don't."

Peg spoke up: "Master, with your permission, may I speak with Karen."

"Please do. That is what I brought her in here to do."

"Karen, this is the kindest, gentlest, most sensitive Man I have ever known in my life. As odd as it may sound, the day I put His collar around my neck and begged to become His slave was what I think of as the day I gained my freedom. I was suddenly free to serve without shame. I had friends who told me: 'You don't have to do that, let Him get His own coffee.' What they couldn't understand was that I needed someone to serve. It was my choice to get His coffee. My strongest desire to make it exactly the way He liked it. It is who I am……."

The four women talked for the better part of an hour.

Finally, Karen said: "I really must get back to work. I am so appreciative of you taking the time to talk to me. With all my heart I wish I could have what you four have."

As Karen left the room, Peg left a parting invitation that she should come back again.

When Philip left the room to go home that evening, Karen called Him over.

She looked to see that everyone was out of hearing range and said: "Master Philip, I loved talking to your slaves. But I have to also share something with you."

"Okay."

"Sir, I have been at this hospice for six years. I have seen thousands of patients go through these doors. I know the signs to look for. It will surprise me if she lives another forty-eight hours."

"I know, Karen. I've seen the signs too. But, let's keep this out little secret, shall we?"

"Okay. I just thought you needed to know."

"I know, it was kind of you. Good night."

"Good night, Master… I hope it doesn't bother you that I call you that."

"It doesn't. Why should it? It is who I am."

The next day was uneventful.

Thursday, when He entered her room, He could tell by looking as her that she would not be alive when he left that evening. When she saw Him, alpha began to cry. She ran to His arms and pushed Him back out into the hallway.

"Master, She's dying. I'm losing her. I can see it in Her face that She is only waiting for You to be here. Help me, Master. I'm lost and I don't know what to do."

"I know, alpha, I know. You know that this was only a matter of time."

"I know. M-M-Master, Pl-lease don't leave me."

"Alpha, I promised Peg that I would take you as my own. I did not make that promise lightly. I will not leave you. Now we must do what can be done to ease her passing."

They returned to the room for the greeting that had become a ritual with them.

However when they finally got down to talking about her, Peg started crying. "Master Philip, Sir, I know I only have a short measure of minutes left. I have done my best to serve you. You have brought joy to my life. Is my final gift acceptable, Master?"

"Yes, Peg. If I can't have you, they are what I would have in your place."

"Master, My work is finished. I can leave in peace."

"You may leave in peace."

"I have one final request, Sir."

"Yes?" He whispered as he stared into her eyes one last time.

"Will you take my final breath?"

Without a word, with tears streaming down His face, He placed His mouth over hers and inhaled the final breath to leave her body.

Alpha and omega were both in tears. He went out to tell Karen that Peg had died as expected.

Karen knew without Him saying a word and just motioned Him back into the room. With tears in her eyes she made the necessary calls to the morgue to collect the body that Peg no longer needed and to have it delivered to the funeral home. Although it wasn't her job, she made the calls to the newspaper and the funeral home itself.

Back inside of Peg's room, alpha and omega clung to Him. He was now the only Rock in their world. Without Him they would drown. Mistress wanted Him to have them. They were His now.

When the mortuary attendants came to remove Peg's body, all three of them formed an honor escort around the stretcher. Master Philip Himself insisted on pushing it down the hall as far as the hospital rules would permit.

The next several days brought several viewings at the funeral home and the funeral itself.

For every moment that they were able to, alpha and omega stood motionless, totally naked, shackled to their Mistress' casket. It was their final vigil to honor her memory. They spoke to no one. Said nothing. They simply stared at Her face and cried.

Some thought the graveside service was a bit strange with alpha and omega chained to the coffin. As the service ended, Master Bill symbolically removed the manacles from the coffin and fastened them to Master Philip's wrists, binding the naked women to Him as was their Mistress' final wish.

It took a while for things to settle down at Master Philip's house after Peg's death. But, they had known about it for three months and had been given time to really say good bye. Still, as He looked down to see alpha and omega sleeping on the floor where Peg used to sleep, a tear ran down His cheek in wonder that she would love Him enough to give Him this gift.

Chapter 8: What if something goes wrong?

There are actually two aspects that we want to discuss there things go wrong: in a play scene, or with the relationship itself. Both of these are potential risks that you need to be prepared for. It doesn't matter if you are dominant or submissive.

What if a scene goes wrong?

A wise man once said: "Shit happens."

Most play events in a public dungeon will have some sort of off-duty medical personnel in attendance. It isn't necessarily planned that way, it is just that there are a fair number of medical professionals involved in the lifestyle. In addition, the event will have experienced dungeon monitors around to keep things safe.

The first piece of advice is: "Get a first aid kit, put it in your toy bag, and make sure you know how to use it." You should also have EMT-style scissors for cutting bindings loose if the submissive gets into distress. The last piece of advice is: "If you have to call the EMTs, be honest about what you were doing." They have seen a lot, and can probably guess what you were doing anyway.

The other observation I will make is that there is a higher per-capita rate of people in law-enforcement, education, and healthcare involved in the lifestyle than from other professions. Obviously, there are no formal statistics; this assertion is based on my personal observations, and on the personal observations of others.

What if a relationship is having problems or ends?

"You have to kiss a lot of frogs before you meet your prince."

Well, it certainly seems that way. Many people entering the lifestyle do so at a later age after one or more failed relationships. More often than not, these failed relationships are a result of the person needing "something" that their vanilla partner was unable or unwilling to provide. Once these individuals find the lifestyle and that there really are people like them, they are often desperate to find "the One" who matches them and will finally meet their needs. This results in the person jumping into a relationship too quickly. Just because a person has needs that were not met until they entered the lifestyle, doesn't mean for a minute that their needs complement your needs. In other words, for a given submissive who needs a dominant, not just any dominant will do. Unfortunately, people learn this the hard way. I know that I did! So, what happens when a BDSM relationship ends?

Generally, a D/s relationship ends by the dominant "releasing" the submissive. Although that is not always the case. Sometimes the dominant releases the submissive because the submissive requests it. These are both usually amicable partings. But there are others. Particularly in long-distance relationships that are totally, or mostly, on-line, either the dominant or submissive can simply disappear. This happened to my slave in the past. She was collared by an on-line dominant who simply abandoned her after a short time. To her credit, she did not decide on her own to remove his collar. She went before three other Masters to petition to remove her collar on the grounds of abandonment. (Permission was granted.)

I had one sub that I was involved with who borrowed money and then disappeared. I have tried to contact her to get the money repaid as agreed, but she refuses to take my calls or answer e-mails. So, in a very real sense I was abandoned. Another sub I had collared asked for release because our needs were not the same. Another threw a temper tantrum and removed her collar.

When a relationship ends, everyone gets hurt. There are no winners. And, let's face it, there are players in our lifestyle just like everywhere else. There are also those who simply get into relationships that they never should have gotten into. In a discussion group that I belong to, a situation like this came up recently. The dominant involved announced to the group that he and the submissive were no longer a couple; she had been released. Now I have no problem with that since the group knew that they were a couple. However, this dominant went on to detail WHY they broke up. It was all her fault, of course. In my experience, it is rarely one-sided when a relationship ends. Furthermore, I think that to detail what happened to several thousand people on the list shows a lack of discretion, and doesn't show that the dominant was in any way caring for or protecting the submissive.

Doms as protectors

This is another hotly debated topic. I maintain that because the submissive is giving some measure of control over to the dominant, the dominant is responsible for protecting the submissive, at least to the extent possible. My belief in favor of this is that it is not right for the dominant to betray the trust that the submissive is putting in Him. Secondly, in some scenarios, the submissive is bound in a way that precludes taking any action whatsoever to protect themselves.

Opponents to this way of thinking are concerned that this way of thinking absolves the submissive of any responsibility for her own safety. In fact, nothing can be further from the truth. The submissive is ultimately responsible for calling a halt to a scene where she feels she is not safe. She is required to talk to the dominant to express all of her concerns BEFORE getting involved in some potentially unsafe situation.

Our Story

Once again we get a double-Domme story. In this case, it is more of a Mentor-student scenario. The mentoring Domme had actually owned the slave in question in the past. This gives her some insight into his behavior and how to best motivate him. One of the truisms in the story is that using pain to discipline a masochist (or, in this case, a "pain slut") doesn't work. It is like trying to convince a child to eat their dinner by forcing them to eat extra dessert if they don't. It doesn't work.

Story: "Bad Boys"

The two women sat talking at a secluded table at the coffee shop close to the office complex where Tina worked. Tina was wearing a tailored deep purple business suit, and Gina was dressed in a freshly pressed city police officer's uniform. They had each had coffee and dessert. Tina had a problem that she needed Gina's advice with. It wasn't easy to ask, and the coffee was cold by the time she got the courage to talk about it.

"Gina, you know that I am relatively new to the lifestyle, and I have a problem. Ted just got his third speeding ticket this month. I've told him that we can't afford to pay these tickets, and he knows that if he loses his license, he is screwed as far as work goes. You can't drive a delivery truck without a license. He just tells me that his boss hasn't given him enough time on Thursdays to make his deliveries."

"Okay, what have you done so far?"

"I assume that you mean, other than pay the tickets." She smiled at her friend in mild apology for the joke that flopped. "I did pay the tickets. But, other than that, I chained him up and flogged him with the braided flogger; one lash for each dollar of the fine."

Gina stared at her friend with a look of surprise on her face. "You what??? He is a 'pain slut'! You didn't 'punish' him, you 'REWARDED' him."

A look of comprehension crossed Tina's face. Gina continued: "I'm sorry, hon. I can see from the look on your face that nobody ever explained this to you. That is one of the problems in our world. Well, it isn't exactly a problem, just something that you need to know. In the vanilla world, 'pain' is a negative reinforcement, and you can use it as a punishment. For us, it doesn't always work that way. The Domme needs to find something that the sub doesn't like.

"Today's Thursday. Would you like some 'official' help?"

"Sure, what do you have in mind?"

For the next fifteen minutes the two Dommes plotted and planned.

Looking down at the coffee, that had grown cold while they talked, Tina finally pronounced: "Sounds good, it will take him a while to forget that."

Tina went back to her office to finish the day. The afternoon wouldn't be too bad, just three meetings preparing for her project's critical design review that would start on Monday. Being the project manager had its own set of problems, and there were days when she wanted to bring a flogger to work! But, mostly, she kept things under control.

Gina went off to finish her day of protecting the city. She was looking forward to seeing Ted later that day. It had been a while since she had a good punishment session! This was going to be a good one, and a double-Domme session at that.

It had been a long hot day, and the air conditioning in her patrol car wasn't working. So she wasn't in the mood to be particularly congenial. So much the better. Tina had told her the name of Ted's employer. Initially, they weren't too cooperative in telling her which truck Ted was driving and what the tag number was... But, a uniformed police officer isn't necessarily something that a company wants to have hanging around the office either. They gave her the tag number and his general schedule, just to get rid of her.

She had parked close to a couple of his afternoon stops. He was about twenty minutes early for the first one. ("Not enough time, indeed." She commented to herself.) For his remaining three deliveries, he was 20 minutes late. This was a puzzle that she didn't like to ponder. There weren't a lot of reasons that she could think of for a forty minute shift in his schedule in the middle of the day, and this was one explanation that she was going to hear before Tina got there, no matter what it took to get it out of him. She was waiting for him when he came around the corner at the end of the day. She pulled her patrol car in behind him and turned on the pretty blue lights. Blue lights to match her blue eyes. Eyes that could signal just as much trouble for the unwise as the lights on her cruiser did.

As he pulled over, she pulled in behind him.

As Gina got out of her cruiser and walked to the driver's door of Ted's truck, Ted looked in the mirror and muttered: "Holy shit! The ticket would have been bad enough!" He knew that his ass was in trouble. More trouble than he even wanted to think about. He had been in Gina's clutches before.

Trying to stay in character, Gina said: "License and Registra... Ted?!!"

He stammered: "Gina, please, don't give me a ticket. Tina is going to kill me."

She looked at him, her heart turning to stone over what he was doing behind her friend's back. She leaned forward and looked him square in the eyes and said in a low but menacing voice: "That's if you're still alive when I tell her." Standing up straight and resuming her official voice she said: "License and registration, please."

The look she gave him chilled him to the very marrow of his bones. He knew from very personal experience that Gina could be a royal bitch when she was pissed.... And she was definitely pissed! "Yes, officer." He politely replied as he handed her the required documents.

Gina returned to her cruiser and ran the documents through dispatch to keep up appearances for anyone looking on, even though she knew that there would be no official record of this traffic stop. Fortunately, there were no outstanding warrants that would have required that she take official actions. To continue with what she had started, she wrote out a standard warning notice, and returned to the driver side of Ted's truck.

"Okay, Ted. Here is your registration and a warning ticket."

Ted breathed a deep sigh of relief. "Thank you, Gina. Tina would have killed me if I got another ticket."

In an official voice, with no warmth in it at all, Gina continued: "I still have your driver's license. You may drive on my authority without it. Take your truck in and park it, sign out, and return here." In a quieter voice, dripping with venom, she said: "And you damn well, better make it quick."

"Yes, Mistress." He said, automatically responding to her tone, and then he reconsidered and said: "I'm sorry, yes, officer, I will be back as quickly as possible."

Gina returned to the cruiser to wait for Ted's return. A small smile of satisfaction turned the corners of her mouth. Not that she would have allowed Ted to see it, but she was pleased with how things were starting. He knew he was in trouble.

It took about fifteen minutes for Ted to turn in the truck and clock out. He didn't even chit chat with Shelly, the company dispatcher, as he usually did. Gina was pissed, and he knew it. He knew very well what she was capable of doing to him, and the prospect wasn't pleasant. No, not pleasant at all.

She saw him as he walked back to her cruiser. It had taken him less time than she had expected. Not that she would admit that to him either. She got out of the car and waited for him.

In a lowered voice she said: "I told you to be quick!" Then again in her official voice: "Here is your driver's license. Put your hands on the car and spread your legs. I need to check you for weapons."

She quickly frisked him and cuffed his hands behind his back. Then she helped him get into the back seat of her cruiser. As she buckled his seat belt, she said: "I'm off duty in a few minutes, and we're going to my house to have a little 'chat' about your schedule and your speeding tickets. Then I'll call Tina and see what she wants me to do with you."

From the tone of her voice, he knew that "chatting" meant far more than having peaceful conversation over a cup of coffee.

Gina got into the driver's seat and started the engine. Quietly and efficiently she drove to her house across town, and parked her cruiser in the driveway.

She crisply spoke into her police radio: "Dispatch... Baker 27... 10-7."

"10-4 Baker 27... 10-33 seventeen twenty-three" Dispatch responded.

She opened the back door and began undoing his seat belt.

"As you've probably guessed, I am more than a little pissed at you. And it isn't just the damn tickets. You are to keep you vile two-timing mouth shut until I give you permission to speak. Nod if you understand."

He nodded.

"When I give you permission to speak again, we're going to talk about the missing forty minutes in your Thursday schedule. And before that, I am going to make sure that you WANT to talk to me about it. Nod again if you understand."

Oh no! Shit! Nervously he nodded. This cesspool just got deeper than he had thought possible.

"Gina, I…"

She slammed a gloved fist into his mouth.

"You stupid asshole. What part of 'don't speak without permission' are you having a problem understanding? Now get your ass out of the car before you get blood all over the place."

He got out of the car.

She closed the door and secured the cruiser for the night. Without a second thought, she strode to the front door of her house. She didn't check to see that he followed her. She didn't need to. He now knew how deep the rabbit hole went, and he would follow her no matter what.

Her house was a nice little three-bedroom rancher with a two-car garage and a full basement. The front yard sported four large maple trees (which deposited great quantities of leaves in her yard in the fall each year). Gina had planted flower beds along the driveway and sidewalk, and around the base of each tree. She took a lot of pride in how her house looked both inside and out.

She opened the front door. He stepped into the small foyer and smelled the scent of honeysuckle. The thought occurred to him that there was almost a contradiction between the feminity of her house and the sheer power and dominance he knew from experience she was capable of, and that he was sure he was going to experience again in very short order. The thought was not a pleasant one. She closed the door, but left it unlocked so that Tina could just come in when she got there in two hours.

She removed her handcuffs from his wrists and said: "You know where the dungeon is. Get your ass down there and strip naked. After that, stand in the corner with your nose against the target. I'll be there after I change and make coffee. Now MOVE!!!"

He moved. In fact, he almost tripped going down the stairs. As he walked to the dungeon, hundreds of memories floated through his mind as he thought about the year that he had spent with her as his Mistress. Thinking about the day she released him still brought a lump to his throat. In retrospect, he knew that she was right in her reasons for releasing him.

He got to the door of the dungeon and opened it. Now he had a decision to make. Turn on the light, leave it off, or light a candle. He dismissed the candle almost immediately. He didn't like hot wax, and in her state of mind, he didn't need to give her any ideas. That left a fifty-fifty choice. Turn on the light and be punished for doing something that she had not told him to do, or leave the light off and be punished for being stupid…. Just flip a coin…. No matter what, there was a 99% chance that he would do the wrong thing. He turned on the light.

Oh no! She had painted it! Who in the world ever heard of a PINK dungeon?!! He looked around, recognizing some of the old furniture and taking in the additions. She had been busy!

Directly across the room from the door was a dungeon wheel... a PURPLE dungeon wheel! The person bound to it could be tilted at any angle, or even spun until they didn't know which direction they were. She had added a motor since he had last had been there, so she could spin the wheel by remote control for as long as she wanted to let it run.

In the corner to the left of the wheel was her toy cabinet. If his memory was correct, Top-Left held gags and hoods. Top-Middle held dildos, plugs, strap-ons, ropes, and cuffs. Top-Right held whips and floggers. Bottom-Left held assorted chains and her violet wand and TENS unit. Bottom-Middle held several spools of cling-film. The last time he was here, the Bottom-Right was empty.

To the left of the toy cabinet was a small refrigerator. It looked to be just large enough to have a small freezer compartment. It was new since he had last been here. He had no idea why she had it in the dungeon, and he was pretty sure that he didn't want to know! Beside the refrigerator was a white laundry tub, big enough that he could have sat down in it without a lot of discomfort.

He continued examining the room to the right of the dungeon wheel. Immediately to the right of the wheel was a Saint Andrew's Cross. But, to demonstrate her creativity, Gina hadn't fastened it to the wall, or left if free-standing. Instead, she had suspended it using chains connected to the floor joists above. Like the dungeon wheel, it was painted purple. It was designed with leather straps on either side so that two people could be attached to it at the same time.... Although that wouldn't be happening tonight.

In the corner, next to the cross, was a small "fucking machine" on a wheeled dolly. Judging from its appearance, it was intended to be used on someone bound to the cross. All he could think was: "Oh, my poor asshole!"

Along the right wall was a table that looked like nothing so much as a medieval rack. It too was purple. He thought to himself again: "Dungeons should not be painted pink and purple. It just seems so out of place!"

In the final corner of the room was a traditional spanking bench. Well, he *thought* it was traditional. On closer examination, he noted that it had a pillory attached to the end. Every time he saw one of those blasted things, all he could picture was Samantha Stevens from Bewitched in one of the episodes where she was sent back in time. He didn't know why he thought of that, because he didn't remember her even being bound in either stocks or pillory in the show.

His final glance of the dungeon decor was to note that the floor and ceiling were painted blood red. The ceiling had an array of hooks and chains embedded into the floor joists from above. The floor had recessed hooks as well.

The walls had dozens of toys hanging on the wall... mostly crops, paddles, and canes.

Gina, or rather Mistress Gina, to give her the title of honor indicating the respect she was due, would be down soon. He quickly removed his clothes and looked for the target in the corner. There it was, of course it was purple too, three feet off the floor! How in the hell did she expect him to keep his nose against it there?!!

He spread his feet apart as far as possible, bent his knees slightly, tilted his head back, and put his nose on the target. It felt so uninhibited to feel his cock and balls dangling freely there with his legs spread.

He had no idea how long it had been when Mistress Gina came into the room. But, his nose hurt and his legs had cramps. She didn't say anything. She walked over to the refrigerator and sat her coffee down. He heard her open the refrigerator and close it again. Suddenly, he felt her grab his cock in her fist. The pain was a stab of pleasure. He wasn't sure where she was headed with this, but it was a good start. His moment of pleasure lasted just that long... a moment. He felt rough hands shove two ice cubes up his ass, and followed that with a chilled anal plug. His ass felt like it was on fire from the cold.

With all of her considerable strength, she grabbed his cock tighter and lifted his feet off the ground using his cock as a handle. His nose came away from the wall, and he was on his back staring up at her.

She was wearing red leather... gloves, corset, and knee-high boots with four-inch heels. Her attire didn't hide anything. Her ample breasts hung out over the top, and the corset didn't cover her shaved pussy or her ass. Just the vision of looking at her dressed that way gave him an erection.

She looked between his legs and commandingly said: "That will be enough of that!" She walked over to her toy cabinet and got out a male chastity device. It was a metal cage that fit over his cock and balls and held the penis in a downward position with a small padlock to hold it locked in place. The cage fastened around his scrotum so that if he did get an erection that it would feel like the device was cutting off the circulation in his cock, and pulling his balls off at the same time.

She squatted down over him with her pussy almost touching his mouth and fastened the chastity device on him. He could feel the metal frame cut into him as the smell of her pussy filled his nostrils. He fought the erection that just wouldn't go away. As she stood up, she "accidentally" brushed against his mouth. He groaned as his cock strained. This was not "pleasant" pain at all. The damn thing was ripping his nuts off.

"MISTRESS PLEASE!!!"

She reached around and grabbed her cup of hot coffee and dumped the whole cup over his face. "You were not given permission to speak. Now stand up while I go get another cup of coffee."

He almost said "Yes, Mistress" but the stinging coffee reminded him that he shouldn't.

As she left to get coffee, his throbbing erection started to diminish and he was able to stand.

It took her a little longer than he expected to return with her coffee. She entered the room carrying a tray with her coffee... and, what looked like, the makings of her dinner... bacon, lettuce, tomato, bread... He was under no illusion that dinner included him being fed. She pulled out a small folding table and sat the tray on it.

"You don't mind if I have dinner do you, you trashy little whore?"

It wasn't a question. He lowered his eyes so that he wouldn't have to look at her and risk his anatomy getting out of control again.

"Look at me slut!!!"

He stood where she indicated. He tried to look at her without really *looking* at her. It wasn't easy! The situation gave new meaning to the expression: "having your balls in a sling."... "Sling hell," he thought "try putting them in a steel cage!"

"Come here."

He moved to the spot she indicated.

She went to the toy cabinet and returned with two ankle cuffs and secured his feet, separated about three feet apart. Next she retrieved suspension cuffs from the toy cabinet for his wrists. She stretched his arms tightly and hooked the wrist cuffs to chains hanging from the ceiling. His heels were no longer touching the floor.

He thought she would stop and eat dinner at that point, but she returned to the toy cabinet one last time. When she came back to where he was, she held a large red ball gag.

"Since you seem to have a hard time keeping your mouth shut as you were commanded to do, you are going to wear this." She put the gag in his mouth and fastened the buckle on the strap that held it in place. "I am not wasting another cup of coffee because of you! I made the coffee to drink, not to give you a bath."

The gag stung a little against his mouth where she had backhanded him earlier in the police cruiser. That pain had been quite nice at the time. Or, at least it would have been if he hadn't known how much real trouble he was in.

"One last thing before I eat dinner..." She walked over to the refrigerator and retrieved another ice cube. She stood behind him and pulled out the butt plug whispering in his ear as she did so: "Don't you let one drop of what's already in there out either!" She inserted the fresh ice cube.

He shivered as one more ice cube joined the two that were already there. Intellectually, he knew that the two she placed there earlier were mostly melted. But, emotionally, he knew he could feel all three cubes there now. He felt his whole body shiver as she put the plug back in.

She moved close against him so that he could feel her naked breasts and the leather of her corset against his back. It was all he could do to keep his erection from starting again. But, when she reached around and caressed his cock and balls through the cage, he lost it. He was straining against the cage again. It was not a pleasant feeling. She stroked the back of his neck with her tongue and said: "Good. You get that hard-on just like you did this afternoon. Maybe I'll give the cage to Tina so she can keep that thing out of action except when she wants it."

"Oh shit, not that. Gina would give Tina very explicit instructions on how to use it most effectively too," was all he could think as the metal of the cage dug into the flesh of the cock that seemed to have a mind of its own.

Gina moved the folding table directly in front of him, pulled out a folding chair and sat down. While he watched her arrange the bacon on the bread, his mouth began to water, and he heard his stomach growl. She carefully spread a bit of mayonnaise on the bread. She noticed his attention on her preparations and spread a little mayo on her nipples just to get to him once again. Noting the visible evidence of the effect that had on him, she smiled and picked up the tomato and knife. She sliced the tomato and put it over the bacon. Finally she sprinkled a bit of pepper on the tomato, added some lettuce and put the other piece of bread on the top.

To complete preparing him mentally for the next event in the evening, she pulled out a meat cleaver and violently chopped the sandwich in half. He cringed as the cleaver split the sandwich in half and slammed into the cutting board. Gina stood up with the cleaver in her hand and walked around behind Ted. She pushed her body up against him again and put the edge of the cleaver against his cock.

"When I finish my sandwich" she whispered in his ear "I will take off the gag and we'll talk about your additional stop this afternoon. And you had better make me believe that it will never happen again." She applied just the slightest pressure on the cleaver and added: "Or I will make sure that I KNOW that it will never happen again. I am sure that you understand me."

He was shaking by this point with tears running down his face. He knew that she would do as she said if he didn't tell her what she wanted to hear. He didn't want her to see how afraid he was right now. But he couldn't stop. He was genuinely terrified.

Gina returned to her chair and quietly ate her sandwich. She could tell that she had gotten his attention, and now it was time to allow him to contemplate the image she had just put in his mind. Right now he believed that she would do anything it took to get her way. She needed him to believe that… and he would. But first, she needed him to talk himself out of believing it.

She slowly finished the sandwich and her coffee. When she was done, she took the tray upstairs and fixed herself another cup of coffee. Tina would be there in half an hour. She put on a fresh pot of coffee and went back to the dungeon.

When she got there, one glance into his eyes told her that he was at the place she needed him to be. He believed that she wouldn't carry out the threat.

She put the folding table and chair away and walked behind him to get to the toy cabinet. As she passed behind him, she slapped his ass hard… "Wake up!"

She looked in the cabinet for her special knife. She had ordered it from a novelty site on the internet. The handle had a reservoir that held liquid. The blade was metal and had an opening that allowed the liquid to flow along the blade to make it feel like blood flowing from a cut. Gina kept the reservoir loaded with a substance that looked remarkable like blood (also from the same novelty store). The knife was so dull that it wouldn't cut warm butter. However, the point itself could be used to cut. She finally found the knife at the bottom of a drawer of dildos and butt plugs. "How in the world did it get there?" She asked herself.

She stood in front of Ted and used the tip of the blade to cut (well, not more than a scratch really) the letter W into his chest.

"'W' stands for 'whore', you little tramp."

She rubbed her hand in the blood from the cut and rubbed it onto the end of his nose and removed the gag from his mouth. She put the blade against his cock and said firmly: "Now what would you like to talk about?"

"Mistress, please!!!" He began.

"Enough!" She pressed the blade against his cock and made a cutting motion as she squeezed the handle to eject some of the liquid.

"Mistress! No, please… I'll talk, I'll talk."

Now he believed that she would really dismember him. She would get the truth in short order.

"Yes, Mistress Gina, it is true that I had an extra stop today."

"And the last three weeks too?" she quickly asked?

"Yes, Mistress."

"Explain… I want the truth and I want it now."

"M-M-Mistress… I-I-It wasn't s-sex… I-I k-know t-t-that was what you a-assumed…" He had no idea why he was so nervous that he was stuttering so.… Maybe it was the knife threatening his genitals… which he viewed as being in great danger at the moment.

"Go on." She prompted.

"Mistress, you know how I love the pain?"

"Yes."

"Well, Tina just doesn't get it. Mistress, she uses the flogger like she is afraid of it."

"Continue."

"Ummm… Well, I've been seeing Master Bob on Thursday afternoons, just for a short session to take the edge off."

"And you don't see this as being disloyal to the woman who has her collar around your neck?"

"Mistress, I didn't see it that way. I love her and I would never hurt her or be disloyal to her. Please tell me what I should have done."

"You should have talked to your Mistress and explained it to her. She cares about your needs, and would have at least talked to me about it. After she and I punish you for the speeding tickets tonight, I will give her a few 'lessons'."

"Thank you, Mistress." After a brief pause he added: "Mistress, these ice cubes are really getting unbearable."

Gina quickly released the cuffs restraining him and told him to go use the toilet and return.

He quickly made his way up to the toilet, removed the butt plug, and evacuated his bowels. Passing the ice cubes out was more painful than Gina shoving them in, in the first place! He knew that Gina required her subs to clean the toys, so he washed the plug thoroughly and then washed his hands. He couldn't help but notice the blood smearing his chest. He wasn't sure he wanted to check to see how badly she had cut his cock. With trembling hands he painfully pulled the chastity device forward to expose the base of his cock. He could see a great deal of blood there, but couldn't see of feel any sign of a cut. It was a mystery that he didn't have time to check further. He grabbed the clean butt plug and headed back to the dungeon.

"This is the last I want to hear about schedules and speeding tickets. Are we clear?"

"Yes, Mistress."

Gina looked at her watch… "Tina will be here shortly, I need to get you ready."

She removed the chastity device, and washed the blood from his chest and the fake blood from his genitals. After he was cleaned up, she fastened him to the cuffs again, like before, but this time with his feet flat on the floor, and without the gag.

Next she got a larger silver case, a smaller brown one, and a black object about six inches by two-and-a-half inches by about three quarters of an inch out of the bottom of the toy cabinet. She sat the two larger items on the rack, but kept the small black box in her hand.

"I don't know if you know what this is. It is called a 'Personal Security Device' or "PSD', and it can be very effective."

She held the PSD about a foot from his face and pressed the trigger switch on the side. Immediately streams of living electricity arced between the two contacts on the top. Ted strained in his restraints to try and get away. She could see that he was absolutely terrified of electricity.

"When Tina gets here, I'll bring out the other toys, but this is the newest one I have and I just wanted to show it off."

Without warning she pushed the PSD against his abdomen and pressed the contact for just a fraction of a second. Pain shot into the spot on his stomach between the contacts, and when the pain stopped, he felt nothing. Where the electricity had been, there was no sensation at all. She gently ran her hand over his stomach and he could feel it fine. Then it would contact the area where she had shocked him, and he couldn't feel anything at all. It was one of the oddest things he had ever felt. He was afraid to ask if the numbness would go away.

Gina smiled at him and patted his face. "Well, I'll let you savor that memory until your Mistress gets here." She turned and left the dungeon, turning off the light and closing the door as she exited to leave him totally in the dark with his fears.

Tina arrived a short ten minutes later. Gina invited her in and poured her a cup of coffee. The two women sat and talked about events since they had talked earlier that day.

"Well, the afternoon sucked." Tina began. "The lead software engineer is jerking me around trying to rationalize not meeting the development schedule. With the critical design review next week, I don't really need that."

"I know. But that isn't what you really wanted to talk about, is it?"

Tina grimaced. She assumed that since Gina was up here instead of in the dungeon beating the crap out of her slave that she had found out something. Now that she was face-to-face with it, she wasn't sure she wanted to know.

"No, Gina, it isn't. Tell me this first, did you find out what is going on with Ted?"

"Yes, he and I had a long 'talk'. I don't know how you are going to take what I have to say, so I'll just start at the beginning, and then we'll decide what to do next."

Tina nodded.

"Well after I left you this afternoon, I went to Ted's employer…"

For the next fifteen minutes, Gina detailed her whole afternoon, including the confession that she had gotten out of Ted just moments before. Tina sat in silence and listened.

"… I am convinced that he was genuine in his confessions to me, and that he didn't mean anything disloyal to you. However, he is your property, and you must decide what to do with him. I have set out the electrical toys as we discussed at lunch, and I will give you some tips on satisfying his desire for pain, if that is your wish."

"Thank you, Gina. You have been a good friend. Before we convince him that he isn't going to add to his schedule any more, I need to hear from his own lips that he doesn't want to just be released. I won't keep him against his will."

Ted's eyes hurt as the lights came on in the dark dungeon. He couldn't see, but he assumed that Tina had joined Gina now.

"Mistress…"

He felt Tina's fist slam into his abdominal muscles. The shock of it chased the air from his lungs.

"Okay, whore. I've just had a long talk with Gina, and she told me all about your visits with little Bobby. That asshole couldn't be a Master with honor if he had to."

"Please, Mistress…"

She hit him again.

"You are a slave. You will not speak until I tell you to." She paused. "Now this is the deal. In a moment I am going to ask you if you want to be released to go be with that slave-stealing dick of yours. If you want to be released, then we are through. You will have twelve hours to get your shit out of my house, and then I don't give a shit what you do. If you choose to continue to be my slave, then you will not meet with ANYONE without my knowledge. Nod if you understand the two options that I am giving you."

Ted nodded.

"Good. In that case, I ask you, do you want to be released? Yes or no?"

"No, Mistress, I wish to continue to be your slave."

"Good. That being the case, Gina and I are going to demonstrate to you just why you damn well better not cheat on me again."

Tina turned to Gina. "Mistress Gina, this is your home and your dungeon." Tina bowed slightly, a bow meant to show honor to an equal. "You are the more experienced of the two of us, and I yield to your leadership and instruction in correcting this slave."

Gina returned the bow and said: "Thank you." As she once again picked up the PSD, she said: "I suggest that we begin with the Personal Security Device since Ted is already acquainted with it."

"Nooo…." Ted whispered desperately, knowing he wasn't going to get a lot of sympathy.

Gina snapped at him: "Shut up or I'll zap your cock and balls just for the fun of it!"

"Yes, Mistress."

Gina ignored him as she continued. "This is essentially a battery, a capacitor, and a transformer. The transformer steps the battery's voltage up drastically; from about ten volts to over forty thousand volts. To keep the electrical laws functioning, this means that the current drops to one four thousandth of the current at ten volts. As you probably know, it is the current that kills and injures, not voltage. The effect is however…" She again pressed the trigger. "… is quite dramatic." She said as the crackle of the arcing electricity filled the silence in the room. Gina concluded: "As Ted is aware, allowing the electricity to arc through human flesh will result in a numbing sensation in that area. Follow me, and I'll show you."

Both women walked around behind Ted.

"Hey, slave." Gina asked. "Do you want to talk about traffic tickets?" With the last syllable, she pressed the contacts against his ass and pressed the button.

At the unexpected pain Ted simply cried out.

Handing the PSD to Tina, Gina said: "Here, you try, I'm not sure I'm getting through to him."

Tina found a different spot on his ass to shock. "Are you ready now slave?" Without pausing for him to answer, Tina zapped him a third and then a fourth time.

Gina signaled her to stop. "Give it a moment for his ass to talk him into it."

Ted was panting now, trying to catch his breath. His whole ass was numb from the PSD.

"Mistress,… please!!!… I'll… talk,… I'll… talk!"

Gina opened the large silver case that held her violet wand. "Oh, I'm sure you'll talk. In a minute you'll be BEGGING to talk!"

"MISTRESS TINA!!!! PLEASE!!!! NO!!!!"

Gina plugged in the mushroom attachment into the end of the wand and the wall outlet. The crackle of the electrical discharge from the Tesla coil that was the heart of the device filled the room. Gina approached Ted. He knew that she was headed for his groin...

"Mistress Gina... Mistress Tina... Somebody... Help Me!!!!! PLEASE!!!"

Gina bumped up the wand settings a few notches. The sounds got both louder and more frequent. Ted could see the violet lights flickering in her eyes. Eyes that held no compassion. Eyes that could passively watch as she did anything she wanted to him. He lost control first of his bowels and bladder, and then of his sanity. He was in hysterics from fear of the electricity coursing through his body. He couldn't breathe. He couldn't stop shaking. His terror ripped his sanity from him.

Gina touched the mushroom to Ted's stomach. He jumped, pulling against his bonds. His arms pulled his feet off the floor.

Tina touched Gina's shoulder and whispered: "Enough." She was no longer the novice learning from a senior Mistress. Now she was Mistress Tina, owner of the slave Ted, and she was required to protect him too.

Gina bowed in acknowledgment of Tina's control over what happened to Ted and turned the violet wand off.

"Help me get him to a chair." (It was not a request.)

Tina spoke to Ted, assuring him that he was safe now and that all was forgiven. This was the time for aftercare. Time to bind him closer to her.

Gradually, Ted recovered and became himself again.

"Mistress?" He whispered.

"Yes?"

"Please forgive me for not having trust in you. I betrayed you and I wouldn't blame you for abandoning me."

"Oh, my precious slave, I care for you and I won't release you... this time. But, the next time, I will allow Gina to continue."

"I understand, Mistress. There won't be a next time."

"I know. Now finish recovering so that Gina can show me some techniques to meet your needs as a pain slut."

After Ted recovered, Gina fixed dinner for the three of them and settled down to talk about the methods and techniques that she used when she had owned him.

Chapter 9: Dealing with the 'nillas

It is a fact that there are people that we encounter who simply cannot comprehend our lifestyle… those who see what we do as nothing more than abuse. For many of these people it is simply not possible to rationally discuss our lifestyle. They cannot conceive of a loving nurturing relationship that includes kinky activities. Sadly, many of these people come from fundamentalist religious backgrounds. Forcing us to take sides between what we know is right and what we believe in faith. In general, we call those who are not in the lifestyle: "vanilla."

You are going to have to decide for yourself just how much you want to tell who. Some slaves wear lifestyle fetish collars all the time. Others don't even tell their best friends. There is a certain amount of justification for secrecy. Much of what we do is a violation of state and federal law. Frankly, I disagree with those laws. I think that their enactment is a violation of personal freedoms. But, the fact is that the laws are there. Mostly, it is a don't ask, don't tell scenario… mostly. There are law enforcement personnel who are involved in the lifestyle. In fact, I know a few.

We call the event of some vanilla person finding out about your lifestyle being "outed." There can be dire consequences if the wrong person finds out. Personally, my slave and I are fairly open with people. But there are few who know the full truth of everything. Being open has two major advantages. First, you don't have to remember what lies you told to who. Second, if someone is curious and doesn't know how to ask, it can open the door to being able to share with them. My girl had a co-worker pull her aside and ask: "I hear you are into that stuff." My girl replied: "You'll have to be more specific than that. I'm into a lot of stuff." But it speaks volumes about my slave that this other person felt that it was safe enough that she could talk to her about it.

Family

This is the big one, so we'll talk about it first. If you have young children, hiding your lifestyle from them is probably your biggest concern. If not, hiding from your parents probably is.

Parents

As strange as it might seem, even adult children with children and grandchildren on their own have a strong need to receive approval from their parents. They will hide anything that they believe will garner displeasure. Even in cases where the parent says: "All I care about is that you are happy." The child will have the attitude: "That's only because you don't really know what makes me happy." They will usually say: "He (or she) makes me happier than I've ever been in my life."

That is well and good, as far as it goes. But, as I've said, honesty is a major issue in the BDSM lifestyle. Failing to tell all is a "lie of omission." Simply put, a lie of omission is allowing someone to believe something that you know is not true, it is a lie through inaction; but a lie none the less. We all do this every day of our lives. Most dominants and submissives hold the view that all lies are problematic, and will avoid lying if at all possible. Most often, this takes the form of a lie of omission.

Children

Young children present a special problem. Parents naturally want to protect their children from exposure to non-traditional activities for as long as they can. I can remember as a child trying to separate my parents when they were kissing. Even after a child learns about sex, it is often years before it actually occurs to him/her that their parents do that gross and disgusting thing… and like it! The second, and perhaps more dangerous, problem with young children is that they will talk to ANYONE about what happens at home. If you are not careful, you can find yourself having an interview with Child Protective Services. The third sad fact is that marriages end. Frequently, one disgruntled partner will do anything in their power to hurt the other partner. It is a very real possibility that the children will be pawns used in this battle.

Older or even adult children are often equipped to deal with your D/s relationship. But really just don't want to know about it. If you had a prior abusive relationship, the problem is even worse… "If you wanted to be whipped, I don't know why you didn't stay with dad!"…Once again we're back to the person not understanding the subtle differences between abuse and consensual kink. But, the kids don't understand, and frequently don't want to understand. Several times my slave has observed: "I wish I had hidden the nature of our relationship from the kids." But the flip side of that coin is that since the kids know some, they do get into the spirit of things. For example, I altered my slave's dietary habits. One of the rules is that slave can only have French Fries on Friday ("French Fry Day"). Her kids know this and on those occasions where I give her permission to have fries, they will frequently ask her: "It's not Friday, did you get permission for those?"

Work

This is another sensitive issue. For some, being outted at work means that they lose their job immediately, without discussion or a chance to defend themselves. There are others who can be more open with their co-workers. In general, you have to be very picky about who you tell. Some people can keep a secret, some can't. As I said, I am fairy open about my choices. So, if I mention going camping for the weekend and someone asks: "Where are you going?" I will usually respond: "Don't ask questions that you may not want the answer to." If they ask again, I tell them. In fact, I went to lunch with three co-workers last week and mentioned that My girlfriend and I are going camping for Memorial Day weekend. One of the people asked where, and I gave my standard reply. He said: "Okay." And then I told him that I was going to a nudist resort in Ohio. One of the other people said: "I thought it might be a leather event." I smiled and said: "No, that is in two weeks." (And it really was.) Part of the reason I am open it because for me it is an integrity thing. But, part of it is plain and simple that I can't lie with a straight face. Never have been able to.

Church

This is a tough one. I am a Christian. We are commanded to love one another. Yet, the most blindly judgmental people on the face of the earth are fundamentalist Christians. They will hold to what the church teaches no matter what. I have talked to devout believers in a number of faiths, and they all have one over-arching characteristic. They cling to what some man's interpretation of God's word is. I won't go deeper into this because we have already had a whole chapter on it. But, being outted to your church can mean being ostracized from that community. In fact, that is probably the single biggest factor in people in the lifestyle distancing themselves from religion. There are discussion groups for people of various faiths who practice the BDSM lifestyle. So, you can find a community of believers who do, in fact, share a lifestyle with you.

Friends

I have some long time friends who know about my choices, at least at a surface level. I was asked once by one of them: "Why would you want a woman who couldn't take care of herself if something happened to you?" I replied that I didn't. I want a woman who can care for herself if she HAS to, but who depends on me to make decisions when possible. But this sums up a lot of the confusion that the vanillas have. In general, they see dominants as bullies taking advantage of and abusing the weaker submissive, and they see the submissive as needing to grow up and learn to take care of herself. I have been generally fortunate in that most of my friends who know about the nature of our relationship have been very accepting.

So, what do you do when it happens?

Well, you only have a few choices:
- Tell the truth and put a positive spin on the facts.
- Act confused and deny everything.
- Tell them EVERYTHING and don't hold back.

How you handle it is purely a matter of what you personally are comfortable with. Obviously, I would recommend the first solution if possible. Here is an example. A number of weeks back I was visiting my mother, and she asked me: "Why does your girlfriend wear that collar? Does it have some special meaning?" I simply answered: "Yes, it has a special meaning." I was prepared to say more if she asked more. But, I only gave the information that she asked.

Our Story

In this story we have a poly trio (Master and two slaves). For some time the Master has been forced to choose which slave goes with him to family functions. This has resulted in the slave left at home alone feeling alone and excluded. He has concluded that this is unacceptable, and in an unfathomable act of commitment He risks being alienated from family in order to stop harm to His slaves. To be sure, this is a high-risk move, and not one that should be taken often, if at all in real life.

Story: "Christmas"

[Author's note: This is a work of fiction. It would take a VERY special slave for this approach to even have a chance of being moderately successful in real life. Most slaves will seek release before being "outed" to family.]

dee couldn't sleep. It was Christmas Eve, and that had been a problem for her since she was a little girl. Master had put both of His slaves in the cage to sleep tonight. He didn't make them sleep in the cage often, and she had to admit that tonight she delighted in the closeness of her sister slave.

She nudged kathy "You asleep?"

"I was." kathy mumbled in a drowsy voice. (she wasn't awake enough to be grouchy at being woke up.)

"sis, I am worried about tomorrow. What if…"

"honey, we've been through this. He is Master, He makes the rules. If this is what He decided is best for the three of us, I am going to push on and do my best to make it work."

Tomorrow, the three of them; Master and both slaves, were going to visit dee's family for Christmas dinner. Up to now, they had made due with simply stating that kathy was a live-in housekeeper. But, you don't bring the hired help to dinner with mom and dad. Master had pronounced that they were a family, and it was time for them to act like one. Master and kathy had spent Thanksgiving with kathy's family. It had nearly broken dee's heart to not be with the two people she loved the most on that special day. When Master saw the effects on the three of them for that short separation, He pronounced that it was the last time. From now on, no matter what, the three of them were a single unit, and if the friends and family couldn't accept it they could go screw themselves. At the time, dee and kathy were both elated. That was before dee found out that her family was to be the first to have to deal with a poly triad.

"sis, please don't put it that way. You know that I am as committed to the three of us as you are. It isn't that at all. I will do whatever it takes to support Master's decision. But I worry that it may cost me my family."

kathy wrapped her arms around her sister slave and pulled her close. (Well, closer, anyway. There wasn't much room in the cage.) As their naked bodies pressed together, she whispered. "honey, I know what you are worried about. I am concerned for your sake as well. I know that family is very important to you. But, we are your family now. It's like Master always says: 'The reason that the windshield of the car is bigger than the rear window is because that is what you are supposed to be concentrating on.' Sis, the three of us are the future. We each made vows to the others that this union is forever, until the three of us are dead. I meant that vow as much as either of you did."

"I know that you did. But, it's not your parents that we will be meeting tomorrow."

"He didn't tell you?"

"What?"

"I'm sorry, I thought you knew. Master is bringing all three families in tomorrow at the same time. They are all getting the explanation together."

"Holy shit! He can't do that!"

"He is Master, He can do as He pleases." dee buried her face in her sister's hair and started crying. "W-w-why d-did He t-tell you and n-not me?"

"Relax, sis. He didn't. I don't think that He knows that I know. Although, the way He figures things out, He might know that too. I don't even try to keep secrets from Him any more."

dee laughed. It was a deep laugh, one of shared understanding. "I gave up trying to keep secrets from Him long before you became part of our family. Ninety-nine times out of a hundred He knows what I am going to say before I do."

kathy returned the laugh of understanding that she and her sister slave shared. "Anyway, I overheard Him making the travel arrangements when I brought in His breakfast about three weeks ago."

All dee could do was hold onto kathy and cry all the more. "Then He knows that you know. There is no doubt of it. He NEVER risks us overhearing things that are really secret."

With that, the two women curled up in each other's arms and went to sleep.

"Wake up!!!" He called to them as the cage shook.

"Merry Christmas. I need coffee and toast."

"Yes, Master." The two women answered in unison and scurried out of the cage, as He swung the door open, to see that Master's needs were met. "Merry Christmas, Master." They said as they paused to kiss His feet, cock, and lips.

He caressed both of them to express His love for them both and playfully swatted their bottoms... "Get a move on it!"

They both ran to the kitchen giggling, their concerns from the last night forgotten. They never made it that far. They both came to a dead stop in the dining room. The table was set with Master's family silverware and their good china. Coffee and orange juice filled glasses at each place. Serving bowls held eggs and fried potatoes. The meat platter held sausages, bacon, and ham. He had even baked fresh biscuits! They both began to cry.

They turned to see Him standing there with a smile on His face. "Merry Christmas, my lovely slaves. You will have enough work preparing the meal today for our guests, and you need a good breakfast to get you ready. Sit down.'

They sat.

Only after sitting down did the two women notice the small box set at each of their places at the table. At His nod of approval they opened them. In each box was a "Story of O" ring done in solid gold with two small diamonds, one to each side of the slave ring in the middle. This was obviously not something purchased over the internet. On the inside of each band He had engraved their names.

"Oops, I have the wrong one." Said dee with surprise. (He never made mistakes like that!)

As she started to swap rings with kathy, He said: "No you don't. Look closer."

She looked. Written in script on the band were the words: "*The wearer of this band declares for all to know that the name on the inside of the band is that of her sister slave for the rest of her natural life.*" She almost couldn't read the end of it because tears were filling her eyes.

"These rings symbolize the bond the three of us share. You may put them on, but only if you mean what they symbolize. From this day on, there is no turning back."

kathy spoke as she quickly put her ring on. "Master, there has been no turning back for quite a long time now. Thank you for the beautiful gift."

"I know that. The rings are a symbol of what already exists. Nothing more. In a way, they are a parallel of the collar that you both wear. Your collar symbolizes your individual commitment to me personally as your Master, but I was your Master BEFORE you put the collar on. There are many types of relationships, and ours could have simply been a relationship that I have with each of you, and you don't have a real relationship with each other."

"Been there, done that, Master. I don't ever want THAT again." dee stated flatly.

"I know, girl. Besides, I won't allow it. The fact is that you two have bonded with each other as well, and that is what I required when we were considering bringing a third person in. These rings symbolize the triad that is the fact of our lives."

After the two slaves had put on their rings, He showed them that He also had a new ring. It was a gold band, like theirs, but it had a blue sapphire instead of the slave ring that their rings had. Beside each of the two diamonds a slave's name was engraved. They all joined hands. No words were needed. Indeed, no words were adequate to express what they were each feeling.

The three of them began their breakfast. Each slave doing her part of seeing that Master's breakfast was ready for Him before she began eating her own. kathy put the apple butter on His biscuits while dee put the cream in His coffee. They each piled food on His plate, and added the appropriate amount of pepper, just the way He liked it.

They sat at the table eating breakfast having some idle chit-chat as they ate, but not a lot of serious conversation. The slaves were avoiding the topic of dinner, pretending and hoping that He didn't know that they already knew. For His part, He was content to allow the illusion to go on for a bit longer.

"Excuse me, slaves. I will be back in a moment." He said as He left the table to go into the kitchen. He returned with three plates. Each plate contained a single serving of figgy pudding. It was a rare treat that He ate only on Christmas Day.

"My lovely slave girls, it has been an eventful year, filled with highs and lows, but mostly highs. Having you both live here with me has brought me much joy and happiness. Watching you grow and mature had been equally rewarding. Now, I need to explain what is going to happen today.

"As you know, we have guests coming today."

"Master, what are you talking about?" dee said trying to feign ignorance.

"You know what I am talking about. kathy overheard me making the travel arrangements three weeks ago. I had little doubt that she had told you. But, even that doubt was erased earlier when you didn't question my statement that you had to prepare for guests. If I had wanted to keep it a secret, I wouldn't have been talking about it when I knew that kathy was around and would soon bring in my breakfast."

"Yes, Master. I was only just told last night. But, you are correct that I knew."

"Okay, here's the deal. All three of our families are due here promptly at 1:00. In addition, Master Tom and slave suzie-q will be here as well as Master Vin and His new slave. At that time we will have Christmas dinner. After dinner, all slaves will leave the room and the Masters will explain about consensual slavery and I will explain that you are both my slaves by your own request and consent. I will no longer exclude one of you from family outings to make other people comfortable. That ends today. The emotional well-being of my property demands this, and there will be no discussion or debate. All three families will either accept it, or they won't. But, make no mistake, it is an all-or-nothing thing."

dee looked at Him in amazement. "Master, I couldn't bear being totally cut off from my family, I will obey as my vow to you demands, but PLEASE don't do it this way."

"girl, it is done. Besides, I am not stating that it will be a total cut off thing. Simply that if we are to attend 'family events' then all three of us will attend, or none of us will. You can still talk to your parents, send e-mail, even get together for coffee. But, I will not allow kathy to be left out." Then, looking at kathy He continued: "This goes both ways. You have the same options as dee has, but she will not be omitted from family functions. Period."

Both slaves were crying and trembling with the power of the raw emotions that they were processing right now. They could see the steel of His determination in His eyes and the set of His jaw. In this, He not lover or romantic, He was fully their Master and Owner, who had identified a threat to His property. He was a juggernaught who could not be reasoned or negotiated with. Only negation of the threat to them would stop Him, and nothing would keep Him from that goal. Their love for Him deepening by the second knowing the depths He would go to in order to care for their well-being, was balanced by the fear that their families will not accept the unusual situation.

"Now here's the plan…" With that he began to detail all of the preparations that had been made. In fact, they wouldn't be eating at the house. He had rented a private hall and hired a caterer to handle the food preparations and serving. "… after dessert is served and the caterer leaves, we will have the hall all to ourselves. It is then that all of the slaves will leave the room. Do you both understand what is going to happen?"

They both nodded that they did.

"One last thing, you are to be in 'ubber-slave' mode. Being servant to me and to our guests is the rule of the afternoon, as usual. But, even more so than normal, you are to project a posture and attitude of humility and servitude."

"Yes, Master." The two naked slaves said in unison with their heads bowed in submission.

"Now get me another cup of coffee, get the breakfast left-overs cleaned up, and the dishes in the dishwasher, and meet me in the living room to exchange presents."

dee and kathy made short work of getting the dining room and kitchen put to rights and joining their Master as He had commanded. The magic of opening Christmas presents was something that neither of the slaves had out-grown, and they were both excited about what they had purchased for their Master.

They entered the living room and found a number of new packages under the tree that were not there before.

The tree had been quite a series of "discussions" in its own right… colored lights or white lights… real or artificial… all the same kind or ornaments of a variety… star or angel… blinking lights or always on… Much of the debate centered on: "My family always had _____." Master had listened patiently for each of the disagreements, and had pronounced: "It doesn't matter what was in the past, we are doing _____."

In general, Master's philosophy was that it was important to understand the effect that the past has on the present. He didn't accept the argument "We've always done it that way." As sufficient justification for doing it the same way today. But, He didn't feel that change just for the sake of change itself was acceptable either. The most frustrating part for His slaves of their lives together were when He looked them straight in the eye and said: "Why do you believe that?" They had both learned from experience that this meant that He had found some nugget hidden in their personality that they were not aware of, and was requiring them to dig until they understood. It was not always a pleasant experience. Only after all of the decorating was done did Master observe that for slaves who didn't want to make decisions, who had given all control to Him, that they sure had a lot of opinions on how things should be. It was another of those uncomfortable moments. For as much as each of them had grown since being owned by Him, some times it seemed like they were just starting out all over again.

They sat on the floor at His feet and waited patiently (at least they tried to give the appearance of being patient).

The first gift was from Master to dee… She tore through the festive paper like a four-year-old girl!… It was a plush pink bath robe with matching slippers.

Master thought back on His first Christmas with slave dee. He had almost had to threaten to punish her to get her to rip the wrapping paper from the gifts. (She had wanted to gently remove each piece of tape and then carefully fold the paper to be recycled next year.)

The next gift was for Him from kathy. It was a framed lithograph from the New Yorker magazine. One of the rare older ones that were very hard to find.

On and on they went through the gifts. Each had been bought with special care to pick something suitable for the one receiving it. Even down to the chocolates that He had bought each of them.

After the gifts were unwrapped and the discarded wrappings stuffed into garbage bags (and more coffee consumed, of course), Master smiled warmly at both of His slaves and said: "Okay, girls, into the shower."

Shortly after He had purchased the house they lived in, He had remodeled the basement. The remodeling had included the dungeon, of course, but it also included a large bathroom. The shower could only be described as a communal shower. They had, at one party, had eight people in the shower at once. It was their custom to share their shower as often as possible. That is where they headed now.

The two naked slaves headed down the carpeted stairs to the basement to get the shower ready while Master took the now empty coffee cups to the kitchen and the bags of Christmas garbage out to the garage.

When he got to the bathroom in the basement, the water was running at the correct temperature, clean towels were laid out to dry with when the shower was done, and dee and kathy were kneeling in the shower waiting for Him. Master smiled to Himself thinking His life was very good indeed, due in a large part to these two women in front of Him.

He stepped into the shower.

His slaves cleaned His body beginning at the waist and moving down. After rinsing the soap off of Him, they both proceeded to give Him His Christmas blow job. The feeling of two mouths, four breasts, and four hands rubbing against Him was ecstasy. It was a shower tradition that He encouraged strongly. After His blow job was completed to His great satisfaction, the women continued washing Him from the waist up.

After He was clean, he exchanged places with slave dee. There were not many cases where He didn't treat His slaves exactly equal, but this was one. As the first slave to enter the household, dee was always bathed before her sister slave. kathy knelt on the floor again before dee with a razor in her skilled hands. She quickly and efficiently shaved dee's pubic hair and legs. Only once had she cut her sister while shaving. Master's punishment for carelessness with His property had been enough to make sure that she never did that again. While dee's lower half was tended to by her sister slave, Master washed her hair twice and then put cream rinse on it. Then it was time for kathy to make sure that the shave was sufficiently smooth. dee leaned back against Master as He wrapped His strong arms against her and grasped her breasts firmly. kathy then buried her face in dee's sweet pussy. At first her tongue searched the whole area to make sure that it was smooth. Satisfied with the quality of her work, kathy then started eating dee's pussy in earnest. As she enjoyed the treatment she was receiving more and more, dee put her legs over kathy's shoulders trapping her head to that she couldn't leave until the job was completed.

"Master, please, I need to cum." dee began to plead.

"Not yet, slave. You don't sound desperate enough yet." Was His simple reply.

Hearing her sister's need, kathy increased he ministrations to dee's beleaguered pussy. dee leaned back and moaned.

"M-M-MAST-ST-ER!!! P-P-PLE-E-E-ASE!!!!! I can't stop, I NEED to cum!!!"

"Okay, slave, you may cum." (He could tell that she was so far gone that there was no stopping the release now.)

dee released what little restraint she had left and moaned and screamed her pleasure for all to hear. Wave after wave wracked her body. It was all the other two could do to keep her from crashing to the floor. She couldn't help them, she was over the edge into subspace, and was only barely aware of her surroundings.

Gradually she recovered and stood on her not-so-stable legs. Master and kathy held and caressed her, gently kissing her in exquisite expressions of their genuine love.

After slave dee had sufficiently recovered, and switched places with kathy, and the sequence was repeated with their roles reversed. kathy reached the begging stage more quickly than dee had because she was already aroused by dee's orgasm and her participation in giving it to her.

"Oh my goodness… Master Pl…" the rest was lost to incoherent moaning as kathy soared with the waves of her climax. It didn't occur to her that she hadn't received permission. For that matter, she hadn't even completed the question. After her orgasm, dee wasn't up to the task of supporting kathy's weight and the three naked bodies tumbled to the floor. All three of them dissolved into a fit of giggles.

After they had recovered somewhat, Master said: "Position 6-J."

The two slaves hurried into the traditional "sixty-nine" position with kathy on top. Master then knelt behind kathy and presented His cock for dee to lick. Once He was hard again, dee began eating her sister's pussy again and Master slid His hard cock into kathy's ass. He could feel dee's head brushing against His balls as He pumped into kathy's ass. He finally exploded, shooting a second load of cum into her. As He slid out of her, dee eagerly sucked His cock clean. After He was clean, she asked respectfully: "Master, may I suck your cum out of kathy's asshole?"

"Well, slave. I don't know if you have earned that right. kathy, what do you think?"

kathy paused briefly from eating dee's pussy to say: "Master, I do not know if either of us has earner the right to do this, but I would very much like to feel my sister's tongue in my ass. Please, Master, I am begging you."

"Hmmmm… Both of you agree? Oh my!!!… Well, since I very much enjoy watching that too, and considering that it is Christmas day, I suppose that you can proceed. Slave dee, you have permission. But, make it a good show!"

"Yes, Master." dee mumbled as her tongue plunged into kathy's ass. Both women moaned with pleasure.

Master reached forward and pulled dee's legs up toward her head to tilt her hips forward.

"kathy, you can return the favor and get your tongue into her asshole as well."

"Yes, Master." kathy replied with a note of glee in her voice.

After everyone was clean (and pleasantly satisfied) they turned the water off and used the fresh towels to dry each other off.

They went up stairs to the bedroom to get dressed for the day. Master was wearing a nice black pin-striped suit with a red shirt and a Christmas tie with Rudolph on it. He told the slaves to wear identical green dresses. Of course, they were not allowed any undergarments. This was not unusual, since that was a rule for being His slave.

After all were dressed, He went down to the kitchen and retrieved Poinsettia corsages for each slave. He returned to the bedroom and pinned one to each slave's dress.

With all of the preparations completed, they all piled into the car. Both slaves shivered a little as they pulled their dresses up so that their bare asses were against the cold leather seat. But the car would warm up quickly.

They drove the short distance to the local grange hall which was the hall that He had rented for the afternoon. He could tell from the truck in the parking lot that the caterer was already there. Master Vin and His new slave were just getting out of their car. (A fire engine red Ford Mustang. Master Vin always did like flashy cars.)

To the left of the main entrance to the building was a coat room and to the right, through a double-hinged door was the kitchen. They could hear sounds of the catering crew preparing food coming from there. In the main hall, four rectangular tables had been set up and held place settings of fine china and silverware for each of the expected guests. Garlands of seasonal flowers lined the tables and several large pine wreathes lent their perfume to the air in the hall, adding to the festive mood. The lighting was subdued, mostly provided by Christmas lights around the room and candles on the tables.

Master, with slaves in tow, went into the kitchen to confer with the caterer. He had decided on Cornish Game Hens and Venison as the meat for tonight with fancy red potatoes, seasoned green beans and zucchini as the vegetables. The meal would begin with a nice Caesar salad, and end with a fine English triffel. All-in-all, it would be an event to remember even without the drama that would unfold here tonight.

Once all of the details were checked, Master greeted Master Vin and His new slave.

"Allow me to introduce my new girl. Her name is 'sugar cunt'. But, in light of the vanillas here tonight I will just shorten it to 'sugar'."

"Nice to meet you, sugar cunt. Perhaps some day, if your Master is willing, we shall get to test the appropriateness of that name."

"Greetings Mas…" she felt a hand slap the back of her head.

"That is NOT how you greet a Master who is serving us a holiday dinner." The young slave immediately dropped to her knees and with her legs spread so far that her pussy touched the floor, she kissed the floor between Master's feet. If it were possible, she would have crawled under the floor.

Master Vin continued: "Please forgive this cunt of mine. She is still learning. But, I promise she will get it right the next time." To punctuate His sentence, Master Vin nudged His toe against His cunt's bottom where her slacks concealed the butt plug that she was forced to wear today as a reminder of her chosen status as slave. she jumped and moaned as the plug moved inside of her. She was definitely not accustomed to the invasion into her asshole by the plug. He had used the medium-sized one today, and, to be honest, she liked the sensation, but it was unusual. He had a larger one that he had her wear as punishment one time. Her asshole had burned for a week after that. "Now greet Master Ivoree properly."

she kissed the floor… kissed Master Ivoree's shoes… kissed the crotch of His pants… and, with tears running down her face, said: "Greetings Master Ivoree, Sir. Please forgive this cunt for embarrassing her Master." She wouldn't meet Master Ivoree's eyes, her Master had been most insistent about that. After her greeting she returned her lips to the floor.

"she seems to have potential, at least." Master Ivoree said to Master Vin.

slave dee spoke up from her place behnd Master. "Master, may we be allowed to greet our new sister slave?"

"Yes, with Master Vin's permission."

"Master Vin, Sir, may we greet your slave?"

"Yes, but please do it in that corner over there. Your Master and I need to talk."

Master Vin's slave spoke up. "Am I excused, Master?"

"Yes, but don't get out of my sight."

"Yes, Master."

The three women moved off a short distance to talk.

As the women moved off, Master Vin asked: "Are you sure about this? What you are gong to do is a dangerous thing and could have serious consequences."

"It's a hell of a time to ask me that! But, yes, I'm sure."

"I know that any slaves that I have known would be mortified if their family were to find out. But, in a lot of ways, I can see your point. I hate having to conceal the most important part of my life to avoid the ridicule of others."

"Yeah. That too. But, you know that dee and I were always pretty open with a lot of people as a general rule. Although, very few, even in the lifestyle, know the full extent of what we do. Now that we have kathy here, it has presented some problems. she was never very open about her kinkier side. (And I LOVE the kinkier side she has!) But, I have to deal with the problem one way or another. The primary problem is when I have to pick which slave goes to family functions and who stays home alone. It simply devastated dee the last time."

"Yeah, I can see that would be an issue. Since I only have the one slave, I don't have that problem. We just have some code words that have extra meanings so that I can indicate that there is a problem with her behavior. But, to the rest of the world, we seem like a vanilla couple where she enjoys taking care of me."

"Exactly. I had the same deal with dee before I collared kathy. To be sure, I won't be giving the full disclosure after dinner today either. There are some things that they just don't need to know. On the plus side, there have been some mainstream movies and TV shows that put a positive spin on poly arrangements. What was that series on HBO? It was called "Big Love" if I recall correctly."

"Yes, that was it. There were a lot of religious overtones to it though. I assume that you are not converting to LDS."

Master Ivoree chuckled. "No, not at all. But, in all seriousness, I have made a study of the claims that the Christian Bible stresses monogamy. It doesn't, except in very limited cases. The heart of the matter is that I will not allow one of my girls to be alone on a holiday if it can be helped. I'm not asking that they let us stay at the house, we can get a hotel. But, I refuse to exclude one third of my family."

"Well, it sounds as if you have thought it out. I still think there is danger there. Something could backfire."

"We'll see." Ha noticed Master Tom and suzie-q come in "For now, there is someone else I want you to meet."

"Master Tom please meet Master Vin. Tom, Master Vin was a friend of my girl for some time before I came along. In fact, He was informally a protector/mentor who watched over her."

"Pleased to meet you."

suzie-q went over to join the other slaves and the Masters spent time in some small talk and chit-chat until the vanilla families arrived.

dee's parents arrived first. dee ran over to greet them for the holiday.

"Mom! Dad! Merry Christmas!!!"

"Hello sweetheart. Did you have a nice holiday with your man?"

"Yes, it was quite nice." Before she thought about what she was saying, she added: "He got me this gorgeous ring!" and she held her hand out for them to see.

Her parents just stared at it in shock. They knew full well what the "Story of O" was about.

Finally, dee's mother broke the trance. She opened her purse and pulled out a small pouch that would normally be used to hold coins. dee had seen the pouch hundreds of times. Slowly, her mother opened the pouch and retrieved something that dee couldn't see. Softly her mother spoke. "This is my most treasured possession. You have never seen it until now because I didn't think you would understand." She opened her hand and there in her palm was her own "Story of O" ring that dee's dad had commissioned many many years ago.

"Mom???" dee said as the full realization of what this small event meant dawned and blossomed in her mind.

"Daughter, we HAVE to talk." She turned to her husband with an attitude dee had never noticed before said: "Master, may i be excused, please?"

Suddenly, things started to click into place… little thing that she had never noticed before… He always ordered her food for her… any time there was a decision to make, she always deferred to Him (even where dee knew full well that her mother knew what decision He would make.)

"Yes, girl. I think that you had better." Was all her dad said.

The two women moved off with tears of joy streaming unnoticed down their faces to talk. They now had more in common than dee had ever dreamed possible.

Master Ivoree had noticed dee's parents arrive and had seen dee and her mother move off to get a little privacy. He assumed that dee wanted to break what he had to say to her a little more gently. Of all three sets of parents, hers were the ones that he expected to accept things the easiest.

dee's father walked over to Him and said: "Merry Christmas, **Master**. It seems that you have been keeping a lot of secrets from us."

Noting dee's father's tone of voice and not totally sure what to make of it, Master Ivoree responded: "Sir, do I understand you to mean that I am not the only **One** who has been keeping secrets."

Ignoring the direct query, dee's father replied: "Nice ring that you gave my **daughter** for Christmas."

Master Ivoree still wasn't sure where this conversation was headed. "Thank you, sir. It was custom made and has special meaning to us."

Feeling that His daughter's Master had been on the edge long enough, her father smiled and said: "Yes, son. I am quite sure that it does. Just like the one her mother sometimes wears has for me. It is surprisingly similar. It is done in silver not gold; and doesn't have the diamonds. But, other than that, it is the same. I am sure that the symbolism is generally the same as well."

No more words were needed. Both men now knew more about each other than they had ten minutes earlier. All because of a ring that originated in a fictional movie from thirty years ago.

Elsewhere in the room…

"mom, there is someone else that you need to meet." dee said. Then in a slightly louder voice to her sister slave: "kathy, can you come over here. I have someone that you need to meet."

dee's mother, not sure of who kathy was concealed her ring.

kathy came over to meet her sister slave's mother.

"sis, this is my mother… slave lois. Please show her what Master got you for Christmas."

kathy displayed the back of her hand, and dee extended hers as well to show that the rings were identical.

"mom, I want you to meet my sister, slave kathy."

"Pleased to meet you." She said to kathy and then to her daughter: "sister?"

"Yeah. It was a little weird initially. But, I have come to love her almost as much as I love Master. She has become such an important part of my life that I can't imagine life without her in it."

"Well, I won't pretend to understand, but if you are happy, I can accept it. It isn't like I haven't known poly couples in the past. To be sure, it is much harder to make a poly relationship work." Then addressing kathy: "slave kathy, on your sister's word, I accept you as her sister slave, and therefore as my daughter as well. I would be honored if you would call me mom as well."

kathy smiled, knowing that her sister couldn't be happier. "mom, I am happy to do that. At least when my biological mother won't hear and be offended. She can't be replaced, of course. But, is somewhat sensitive to thinking that she can."

All three women giggled like schoolgirls.

As the clock struck one o'clock, Master Ivoree's parents and kathy's parents walked through the door. Master Ivoree smiled. He had no doubt that His dad had made His mother sit in the car until it was exactly one o'clock. His dad had been that way about being exactly on time all of His life. It seemed as if His mother just accepted that as one of her husband's quirks.

"Dad, mom, you're just in time. We have a nice dinner ready. Please have a seat."

kathy saw her parents enter and met them with a wide smile. "Merry Christmas!!!" she shouted across the room. Turning back to dee and her mom, she said: "mom, I am so happy to really begin to get to know you. But, my folks just got here. Please excuse me."

"Of course, dear one, besides, it looks like we are about ready to eat. It is a pleasure having you in the family."

––––––––––––––––––––––––––––––––––––––

"My dear guests," Master said addressing the entire room. "Please be seated, the meal is about to be server."

As Master Ivoree's dad led his wife to the table, he leaned over and said in a low voice: "Probably some of that weird hippie food that the girlfriend of his makes him eat all the time."

"Fred! You promised you would behave today. It is Christmas Day, after all."

"I know, and I will. For the sake of the Day, if not for that worthless son of mine and that woman who has him wrapped around her scheming little fingers. But I don't have to like it, and I refuse to."

After all were seated, Master Ivoree raised a glass of champagne and continued: "Thank you for coming to dine with us today. It is our hope that that none of you go away hungry." Then he sipped His wine, saluted all, and took his seat between His two slaves.

The caterer, having been alerted that dinner was about to begin, shepherded his staff out of the kitchen with trays of Caesar salad. These were efficiently delivered to the guests, and the staff returned to the kitchen.

Someone pressed "PLAY" on the stereo and Handel's Messiah began playing softly in the background.

The dinner conversation revolved around mostly inconsequential things.... How the trip to come to the party was.... Family Christmas memories... Gifts exchanged now and in years gone by... All-in-all, it was pretty typical for a group of people who didn't know each other.

Master, dee, and kathy each had their share of embarrassing moments shared with everyone. You know, things like: "... and there was kathy, sitting at my dressing table, completely naked, covered head to toe in my make-up..." Each of the hosts had the opportunity to wonder why their parents' fondest memories seemed to be the most embarrassing for them.

The wait staff picked up the salad dishes and brought out the soup course. Master had selected a hearty French onion soup with a thick layer of cheese coating the top. As they placed the soup in front of each person, they asked whether they wanted the Cornish game hen or venison for their meal.

When Master's dad heard that venison was being served, he smiled his approval to his son and raised a glass in a silent toast of approval. Master Ivoree knew that venison was one of His dad's favorites. It didn't hurt that it was one of His favorites as well.

kathy was very relieved when the waiter placed a hearty vegetable soup in front of her instead of the French onion soup. She would have at least eaten part of it to not embarrass Master, but she was not fond of French onion soup at all. She had to admit that Master tried very hard to accommodate he dietary abhorations. Many wouldn't feel that she was worth the effort, and she adored Him for it. That was one of His hallmark characteristics. They both knew that she was, by her own choice, His property. Nothing more than chattel that He could do as He pleased with her. What amazed her was that, because she was HIS property, He consistently elected to make changes in her to make her better than she was before. His constant focus was in improving her and her sister slave. To her mind this was the same conundrum as her sister slave (and other slaves she knew) saying: "I have never felt so free as I am when I chose to become a slave." She too, knew that feeling. Being Master's slave had liberated her to acknowledge and indulge her true natural dispositions. It was a feeling of not having to wear a mask any more; of not pretending to be something that she wasn't.

The soup course was also generally uneventful. There were various light-hearted conversations, frequently punctuated by laughter. Master Ivoree noted that the families were talking to each other, and not just keeping to themselves. That was good. He had intentionally seated dee on His left, kathy's parents to her left, Master Tom and His slave next, His parents directly across the table from Himself. Master Vin and His slave to His parents' left and dee's parents between Master Vin and kathy. The seating plan had intentionally been designed to separate children from their parents and to pair the parents with people in the lifestyle. It seemed to be working well so far. It hadn't occurred to Him that, including Himself and His slaves, there were thirteen guests at dinner. Well, He had never been superstitious, but He hoped that thirteen wasn't an unlucky number for Him today!

After everyone finished eating the soup, the main course was served. The diners were split about evenly between the venison and the Cornish game hen. That seemed to indicate that having a choice between the two was a good decision. He had, of course, opted for the venison. It was served in a black pepper sauce, and was excellent. The red potatoes were served with butter and chopped parsley. The green beans had just a hint of curry, and the zucchini a hint of cinnamon. Each spice was added to perfection. Just enough to accent the primary flavor, but not enough to over power it. He had to smile as He noted that His dad was half way through eating his venison even before everyone was served.

There were a number of comments and even lively discussion among the women as to whether the proper spices had been used.... Was thyme or rosemary better than curry?... Should the cinnamon have been replaced with nutmeg or even garlic?... In the end, there was no final agreement. That is, other than a universal agreement that adding the spice to the vegetable was a definite change of pace, and that they would each try that later. There were even promises to e-mail each other with the results of their experiments.

As the dinner dishes were cleared away and the dessert was served, Master Ivoree remembered the purpose of this dinner, and realized that the clock was ticking away. If He had to make a guess, He would have said that His parents were going to be the ones to make a fuss. His father had never been one to allow anyone to tell him how things were going to be. On the plus side, the coffee served with dessert was the best He had drank in quite some time. He made a mental note to ask the caterer about it. English Triffel was one of His favorites. He didn't make it often because it involved a fair amount of work.

Once the dishes for the final course were cleared away, and coffee cups were filled once again, He stood up and tapped His coffee cup with His spoon to get everyone's attention. That was the sign for action. The slaves at the table stood up and left the room. Chairs had been provided in the coat room for this part of the dinner. He smiled as dee's mom stood and exited with her daughter. Master Tom and Master Vin stood and assumed a guard position blocking the door.

"My dear guests, I have a confession to make. I have an ulterior motive for bringing you all here today." There was a little fidgeting in those still seated at that pronouncement.

"As I'm sure you all noticed that I had two women sitting with me at dinner. This was no accident. dee, kathy, and I are members of a single poly family, and I love them both very much. That is the heart of the problem that I need to discuss. For the last year I have only been able to bring one of the two of them to family gatherings. Each time it has gotten harder on the one left at home because she is by herself. I cannot allow that harmful situation to continue. From this day forward, the three of us are a 'family' and will attend family functions as such. You can agree or disagree with the concept of a poly family. I don't much care one way or the other. I have satisfied myself that there is no sound basis against it. I have done the research, and we can discuss that at some other time." He finished and sat down.

Master Ivoree's father stood up and asked: "Are you quite finished?"

"Yes."

"Then I assume that you wouldn't mind if I shared my thoughts." He didn't wait for permission. "Are you a crack head or a pimp? What do you want with two women? How can you possibly think that you can give each of them the attention that they need and deserve if you have to divide your time between the two of them?" He sat down.

"I assure you that is not a problem. But, even if it is, why is that your concern?"

"Listen, son, I may be an old fuddy-duddy, and I freely admit that I disagree with this, what did you call it, 'poly family'. But, I will give you full marks for standing by your 'wives' at all costs. If you can stand alone in front of all of us to make it work, then you might just have a chance that it will. I worry that those two left you alone to deal with us all. That isn't the kind of support a wife should give."

"You misunderstand. They are not sitting here because I told them that they were not allowed to. I wish to protect them from anything said here. They do not need to hear themselves being referred to as whores, for example. I speak for my family, and I will defend it against anyone. They accept that, so should you."

kathy's dad spoke up. "I mean no disrespect, but I would like to hear her say that."

Master turned and clapped His hands twice. Both of His slaves walked out of the coat room and knelt at their Master's feet.

"kathy, your father is concerned that you are being coerced into something that you don't want. You are at liberty to say anything that is on your mind."

kathy stood and looked at her parents. "Dad, Mom, I trust this man with my very life. In the time I have lived in His home and in the friendship prior to that, He has shown Himself to consistently place the wellbeing of myself and dee above His own. His actions are constantly motivated by what is best for the three of us as a family. That is where His heart is today in organizing all of this." She turned to her Master and knelt before Him. "Sir, I pledge everything that I am to you, now and forever. Please speak in my defense and on my behalf until I draw my last breath." With the last syllable of her request she bowed her head to touch His foot.

dee, in order to show that it was her wish as well, bowed her head to His foot and said simply: "As I do as well."

His world contained only the three of them at that moment. With tears running down all three of their faces, He lifted them to stand in His arms. "Are there any other concerns?"

There weren't.

Chapter 10: Fantasy or reality?

Most of the time, having an active fantasy life enhances the relationship. But, not for all people. I know of a Master who has no interest as all in fantasy. There are those who assert that any long-distance relationship is just a fantasy. Let's start with the real fantasy aspects. (Things that everyone agrees are fantasy.)

Role Playing

For many couples role playing is a way to spice things up a bit. Some examples might be:
- Prison guard and prisoner
- Teacher (or principal) and student
- Priest and nun or parishioner
- Parent and child
- Police officer and criminal

These are but a few examples, I am sure that you can think of many more. The key to role playing successfully is getting your headspace into the role. Thinking and acting like a school principal, for example. These kinds of scenes work best the more elaborate they are. Costumes can be a great aid to acting a role out.

One of the key things to remember it that this is just a role you are playing. Just because a scene is role playing a mother having sex with her son, or her son's best friend, does not mean for a minute that the person playing the role of the mother is a pedophile.

"Littles"

There is a group of individuals in the BDSM community who are involved in something called age play. These are grown adults ACTING like children. Typically the dominant in this relationship is called "Daddy" or "Mommy". Once again, this is not about pedophilia. This group of people who thrive on acting like children are called: "littles." In a scene where a little is in the mode of being a pre-verbal child, they might cry, perhaps even soil their diaper (and need to be changed there in front of a room full of people). It is all part of the role they are playing. Most littles do not go to the pre-verbal stage. Typically, they will be playing with blocks or coloring in coloring books, etc. It isn't unusual for them to use an adult-sized pacifier. In the middle of the floor with their toys is where a little is happiest. Because of the parent-child nature in their relationship, there are some who refuse to have any sexual aspects of the play because that is not how a parent would interact with the child. Others may incorporate sex, but with the full realization that these are adults who are role-playing.

The word "NO" means "NO" (sometimes)

One of the threads woven into this book it that of informed consent. That consent can be, as we have seen explicit or implicit. But, because the submissive gives consent, she can also withdraw that consent. There may be consequences to doing so, but it can be done. This whole notion of consent is what separates BDSM from abuse. In a light D/s relationship the consent is an incident by incident one. The submissive gives consent for each and every act. This consent might be a blanket statement such as: "As long as we are together, I will give you a blow job any time you tell me to." But, the notion that consent is on an act-by-act basis is a central one.

On the other end of the scale, in the Master/slave realm, consent is given once when the collar is put on. When a slave is collared, she is effectively saying: "I will do ANYTHING you tell me to immediately, without question, and you may do anything to me that you wish and I will accept it." It is a one-time blanket consent for as long as she is collared. The key is that phrase: "as long as she is collared." As we have discussed, there are frequently limits placed on this consent. But, the fact remains that the slave can withdraw her consent at any time. In Master/slave, a refusal to obey a command is generally seen as expressing a desire to be released. I'm not talking about forgetting what you were told, I am talking about willful, conscious disobedience.

Having said all of that, what do I mean when I say: "No means No… sometimes"??? There are some situations where having the sub/slave protest what is being done is part of the fun of the scene. An example I heard once was that a Dom and sub were playing and He said that He was going to shave her pubic hair off. She started protesting: "No, you can't do that. Please, no." He replied: "Unless you use your safe word, I can." She heard Him and understood. She did not use her safe word, but continued to protest the shaving. This told the Dom that it really was okay for Him to shave her if He wanted, and that the protest was part of her getting into the scene.

A safe word is essential when playing with a new submissive. Most couples us a simple "Green", "Yellow", and "Red" system. "Green" means: "I like that, do it some more" or maybe just simply: "I'm okay." "Yellow" means: "Don't stop entirely, but back off a little because it is getting too intense." Of course, "Red" means: "Stop." ("Red, damn it!" means: "I should have said "Red" two minutes ago.)

If you have agreed on a safe word, and things get too intense, and you DON'T use your safe word, then you are just an idiot. You have no business complaining that evening or the next day that it was too much. The sub/slave has as much responsibility as the dominant for how far the scene goes.

But, by all means make protesting part of your scene if it is something you enjoy.

He's the Dom, He should know...

Heard that before, and frankly, it's bullshit. Yes, the Dom does learn to read the signs in a submissive's reactions over time. It is unreasonable to expect that the first few times you play together. Each sub/slave reacts differently to a given stimulus. That is a pure and simple fact. Doms are people just like subs are. They are not all-knowing gods that some subs expect them to be.

Now, having said that, the Dom needs to warm up to the sub and learn through observation how she reacts. There must be communication, but it is hard for the sub to talk with a penis-gag in her mouth. You have to learn to read her body language. Watch for her to react when the flogger hits her in an unexpected place. In a previous section I discussed "subspace." It is a very real state of mind and frequently a sub in subspace will literally be unable to communicate. You have to notice this and deal with it because she can't.

Our Story

Our story for this chapter involves a fantasy and the reality of having it made real. Many submissives have kidnap / rape fantasies. In fact, at a weekend retreat that I know of, there are sign-up sheets for people who want to be kidnapped and a separate list for those who want to perform the kidnapping.

Story: "Vacation"

Lori tried to wait patiently in the customs line with her husband, Bob. The baby was asleep in his car seat on the floor between them. Lori had fed the baby just after the flight had left Miami, and her breasts were now engorged with milk again, almost painfully so. It was a sure sign that feeding time was near. She loved the feeling of the baby drinking the milk from her body. In fact, Bob liked to drink her milk as well, but that was a very different feeling. They had discussed having her continuing to produce milk for him as long as that remained possible, even after the baby no longer needed it. Just the thought of becoming Bob's milk-cow was stirring feelings between her legs that had nothing to do with caring for her child.

Lori had never been to Chili before. In fact, she had never been outside of the south-eastern United States before. Bob came to Chili on business every three months or so. He assured her that she was safe, and that the delay in customs was quite normal. But she could feel her milk beginning to leak out. If things didn't move along faster, the top of her dress was going to be soaked!

They made it through customs, and took their luggage to the taxi stand. The driver stowed their bags in the trunk, and they piled into his vehicle.

"¿Dónde usted desea ir?" [*"Where do you want to go?"*] He asked them.

"Del Río del hotel, por favor." [*"Hotel Del Rio, please."*] Her husband replied, and the taxi merged into the airport traffic and accelerated.

At that point, the baby woke up and wanted fed. Lori unbuttoned the front of her dress and took a small blanket out to cover herself to keep from offending anyone. She took the baby out of the car seat, and while her hands were otherwise engaged, her husband removed the blanket to expose her breast to anyone who could see into the window. Her cheeks reddened in the unexpected exposure, but clearly he wanted this. So be it. She moved the baby to her nipple and allowed him to begin feeding.

Her husband smiled, indicating his pleasure.

The taxi driver smiled too.

The baby finished with the left breast, and Lori exposed the other one. Because her husband clearly wanted it, she left her left breast exposed as the baby fed from the right one.

The baby finished feeding just as they got to the hotel. Lori secured him in his car seat before adjusting her nursing bra and buttoning her dress. The driver was treated to an extended display of both breasts. She had always been a bit of an exhibitionist. She loved it when others feasted on her naked body.

"Well done, Lori." Her husband whispered to her, and turning to the driver asked: "¿usted tiene gusto de ver el resto de ella?" [*"Would you like to see the rest of her?"*]

"¡Sí, mucho!" ["Yes, very much!"] the driver replied with a wide grin on his face.

Lori didn't know what had just happened. But, she knew that it was her husband's idea, and that it was an idea that the driver liked very much.

"Ayúdenos por favor a traer el equipaje fuera del sitio, y ella le demostrará." [*"Please help us bring the luggage to our room, and she will show you."*] her husband instructed the driver.

"Sí, Señor." [*"Yes, sir."*] the driver smartly responded, and quickly tended to their luggage.

While Bob arranged for their accommodations at the hotel, Lori fussed over her son and tried to quiet her feelings of apprehension caused by the driver who was patiently waiting nearby. She didn't know what he was waiting for; their luggage had been transferred to the hotel's bell captain as soon as they had entered the lobby. She hoped that there wasn't going to be trouble over her showing her tits off.

Lori also noticed a woman that her husband was talking to, an attractive young woman with long brown hair. She assumed that it was the nurse that he had hired to help with caring for the baby. Back home, such a luxury was out of reach. She and Bob had a comfortable lifestyle, but they were by no means wealthy. The woman was well manicured and dressed quite smartly. She assumed that her husband had paid a premium price to get a nurse who was a cut above the norm. She hoped that she spoke English.

Bob returned with the room keys and the woman, bell captain (complete with a cart full of luggage) and the taxi driver following close behind.

"Lori, this is Hannah. She is the nurse I hired to care for Joey so we can have some fun of our own. Since you don't speak Spanish, I was careful to hire a nurse who spoke English so that you could talk to her."

"Hannah, this is my wife Lori, and our son Joey."

Lori spoke first. "Pleased to meet you, Hannah."

Hannah gave Lori a small curtsey and said: "Mistress, it is my pleasure to be allowed to care for your son."

Lori was immediately uncomfortable. Not by the woman herself, but rather by being addressed as "Mistress." Nobody who knew her secret would have made that mistake. Unless Bob...

She looked at her husband. Her eyes asked: "Does she *know* about us?"

Her husband calmed her with a gesture of his hand. She didn't know for sure if he meant that Hannah didn't know, that she did know, or if he was simply saying: "not here, not now." But, what she did know was that Master was aware and in control, and that was enough for her.

As they walked to their suite, she thought back over the last three years. It had been a long three years since Bob and she had met. There was an immediate "click" between them. It was something that she had never experienced before. She didn't understand what was different at first. For that matter, she didn't *understand* it now! But, what He had taught her was to see that she was "submissive" and He was "Dominant". At its most fundamental level, being submissive, she had learned, meant that it was her desire to yield her will to the desires of another, and that being Dominant meant that it was His desire to impose His will upon another who has consented to that action.

In the three years that she had known Him, He had taught her much. But, it went much, much deeper than that. He had shown her things about herself that she couldn't have guessed. Depths of her mind and emotions that even she had refused to admit were there. How He could see things in her own mind she couldn't see herself still amazed her. He had taught her that there were many levels of submission and dominance. The more He taught her, and the more He showed her about herself, the more her desire to submit to Him blossomed. She couldn't remember exactly how it happened, but today she wanted nothing more than to be His slave; to have Him Master her in every way possible. She had written in her journal: "As odd as it may sound, I have never felt as free as I am once I chose to become Master's totally owned slave." They had discussed the phenomena on several occasions. He had tried to explain it to her. He tried to explain that the freedom she felt was because she was able to indulge her basic nature. To be who she really was in the inside. It still didn't make sense to her. She had also learned that there was a whole culture of people like her. It was not out of the question to think that Hannah might actually be submissive herself.

Lori was shaken from her reverie when Bob opened the door to their rooms. It was truly a luxurious suite. There was a sitting room, with a small kitchen area, two bedrooms, and a huge bathroom. The bathroom surprised her. Not only was it huge, it was outdoors!!! There was, of course, a wall for privacy. But it had no ceiling! All she wanted right then was to fill the over-sized tub and soak under the clear blue sky. She loved being naked outside, and didn't get the opportunity to do so often.

Hannah took Joey into the bedroom, changed his diaper and put him to bed. After he was sleeping soundly, she unpacked her own clothes. Lori didn't know if it was intentional or not, but was pleased to see, when Hannah bent over to put some of her clothes in the dresser drawer, that she didn't have any panties on, and that her pussy was shaved! After the taxi ride, that was all Lori needed. Damn! Lori whispered to herself, I hope Master gets rid of these people so that I can get someone between my legs. At that point, she didn't much care who it was!

The bell captain, who had also noticed Hannah as she bent over, finished putting the bags in their bedroom and left with a sizable tip in his pocket, and a sizable hard-on in his pants. No doubt some lucky senorita was going to be pleased tonight.

"Hannah," Bob called, "would you please draw mistress a bath?"

"Yes, Sir." Hannah replied from her bedroom, and rushed to do as she had been asked. But, not so quickly that Lori didn't notice a smile on her face.

Bob leaned over and discretely whispered to Lori: "Hannah prefers girls instead of men."

Turning to the taxi driver who stood waiting patiently, Bob asked: "¿Ahora, cuál es él que yo le prometió?" [*"Now, what is it that I promised you?"*]

The driver looked embarrassed to have to ask and was about to leave when Bob added: "¡Oh sí, le prometí que podría ver a todo el cuerpo de mi esposa!" [*"Oh yes, I promised you could see all of my wife's body!"*]

"Sí el señor, de que era lo que usted dijo. Pero si la mujer de los jóvenes se opone, entenderé." [*"Yes sir, that was what you said. But if the young woman objects, I will understand."*] the driver replied politely.

Bob turned to his wife. "slave girl, this gentleman enjoyed your tits so much, that I have promised that he can see all of you. He is concerned that you might have some objection to being put on display. You don't do you?" (The last was NOT a question, and both of them knew it.)

To answer in a way that needed no translation, Lori reached under her dress and pulled her panties down. A smile lit the driver's face as he understood that she had absolutely no objection.

With her panties still around her ankles, Lori unbuttoned her dress and tossed it on the sofa. With her right hand she unfastened her bra. She hated the damn thing. Hated it! But, since she was nursing her son, she needed to wear it. It for no reason other than to hold the nursing pads in place that kept her milk from soaking her cloths. The bra joined the dress.

She stepped out of her shoes, leaving her panties on the floor where they were. She posed with her legs spread so that the stranger could see everything. Her husband bent over and picked up her panties, noticing that they were soaked from the juices of her excitement.

"¿usted tiene gusto de tomar éstos para recordarla?" [*"Would you like to take these to remember her?"*] her husband asked the driver.

The driver was speechless, staring at her. All he was able to do was nod his head in agreement and hold his hand out.

Bob placed the panties in the driver's hand, and the driver immediately lifted them to his nose and inhaled deeply.

Bob turned to his slave and said sternly: "You are on display." (He smiled to take some of the sting out of the sternness of his words.) He knew that he really needed no encouragement to show off, and he loved that about her.

She slowly slid her hands up her body. When she reached her nipples, she found that they were firm and erect. (It was not surprising to find them that way.) She pinched and twisted them, teasing droplets of milk from them. She caught the milk on the tip of her finger and brushed it on the lips of the taxi driver. It was all the driver could do to restrain himself from drinking all that she had to give. She raked her fingers through her long hair and turned slowly as she did to allow him to see her ass as well.

When her back was turned totally toward him, she spread her legs wide and bent over as far as she could. She watched his face as she reached around to spread her ass wide for him. She inserted a finger into her puckered asshole and then licked it. Then she spread her pussy to show him her swollen clit. She rubbed her clit slowly, but her mind was on his face. Slowly she stood back up and turned to face him again.

Bob pointed to the floor in front of the driver and said: "He has your panties to remember you by, now you need something to remember him by."

Lori knelt in front of the unsuspecting driver and unzipped his pants. She pulled his cock from its hiding place (it hadn't been hiding very well by that time) and put her lips around it. She had only made a few strokes with her mouth, taking him deep into her throat when he put his hands on the back of her head and pushed deeper. She could feel spasm after spasm as he pumped his cum down her throat. She swallowed it all. She loved it, and knew that her husband was enjoying it as well.

Just as the driver's cock was leaving her mouth, Lori felt a tongue on her pussy. Hannah had finished drawing her bath and had returned to the main living area. Seeing Lori naked on her knees was about all she could take, and she simply lay down on the floor and slid her head between Lori's legs. Lori ground her shaved pussy into Hannah's face and took the driver's cock into her mouth again. She was surprised to feel her husband rub against her back, and reach around to caress her breasts. She could tell from his movements that Hannah's mouth wasn't the only body cavity opening that was getting used.

Lori's mind exploded in climax as she felt her husband shudder as he came in Hannah's sweet pussy. The taxi driver was hard again and was fucking her mouth for all he was worth. Lori's moan in the ecstasy of her climax was all Hannah needed and she came alone with Lori. With all of the sexual energy the other three were releasing, the driver once again pumped his cum deep into Lori's throat. Finally, they all collapsed in a heap of bodies on the floor.

Hannah was the first to recover and said: "Mistress, your bath is ready." It was a wonderful luxurious bath, and Lori took the time to enjoy it. Hannah came into the bathroom with her and gently washed her body. It was a new experience. Lori had never had anyone else bathe her before. She thought belatedly about how grateful she was that her husband was not the jealous type.

Lori could hear her husband and the driver talking as the driver returned to his taxi…

"Muchas gracias, mi amigo. Su esposa es una mujer fina. Si usted necesita un taxi otra vez mientras que usted está aquí, pida Ricardo." [*Many thanks, my friend. Your wife is a fine woman. If you need a taxi again while you are here, ask for Ricardo.*"] the driver said as he left the room and closed the door behind him.

Hannah had removed her clothes so that they didn't get wet while she helped Lori bathe. Once Hannah had finished washing her body, Lori pulled Hannah into the tub with her. Hannah sat on her Mistress with her legs spread. Their shaved mounds pushed tightly against each other. Hannah leaned forward and put her tongue into Lori's mouth. As Lori returned the passionate kiss, she thought about how quickly this fire erupted between them. Eventually, both women simply lay peacefully in each other's arms, basking in the warm afternoon sunlight until the water in the tub was too cold to stay there any longer.

Bob came into the bathroom as the two women were toweling each other off. It seemed as if a warm afterglow was on each of their faces.

"Well, slave, it seems as if you are enjoying your vacation. Draw water while I shave so that I can take a bath and then get dressed for dinner."

"Yes, Master." Lori quickly replied.

She began filling the tub again and then, almost as an afterthought she asked: "Master…?"

"Yes?"

"I do hope that you are enjoying our vacation as well."

He chuckled. "Yes, my beloved, I am enjoying it immensely."

Lori fed Joey again while Master was taking His bath since it would be a while until they got back from dinner. Since it hadn't been very long since he had eaten, he wasn't very hungry. Lori was pleasantly surprised when Hannah drank what Joey didn't want. Hannah played with Lori's pussy the whole time she suckled milk from Lori's breasts. Lori simply relaxed and enjoyed what Hannah was doing to her.

When Lori's breasts would yield no more nourishment, Hannah looked up and smiled. "Mistress, your milk was delicious. Thank you for feeding me with it."

"Hannah?"

"Yes, Mistress?"

"Please…" Lori said, hoping the younger woman wouldn't be offended "Please do not address me as 'Mistress.' I am simply Master's slave girl, and have not earned the right to be addressed as Mistress by you or anyone else. Please just call me 'Lori'."

The younger woman's eyes began to fill with tears. She fell to her knees in the floor before Lori. "I am s-s-sorry, Mis-ummm-Lori. I meant no offence. P-p-please f-for-g-give m-me."

Lori took the younger woman's hands and pulled her up into her lap like she would a child. "Hannah, my sweet, sweet child. You did NOT offend me. I am a slave, nothing more. Do you know what a slave is?"

"Yes, Mis-… Yes." Hannah replied.

Lori continued. "Hannah, I am Master's slave because that is exactly what I choose to be. It is what we call 'consensual slavery'. Master may do anything to me that He wishes, I really am His slave. But, I have only to remove my consent, and all of that would end. I promise you, with all my heart, that I want nothing more than to be His slave. But, should I ever reach a point where I do not want that, I have but to say so. That is who I choose to be."

"I-I understand." The younger woman replied.

"But that isn't all." Lori continued. "Because I am a 'slave', I do not deserve the respect from you of being called Mistress. Indeed, I should call you Mistress because you are a free woman, and I am not."

"I wouldn't like that, Lori. It would make me uncomfortable."

"Do you understand now why I asked you to stop addressing me that way?"

"Yes."

"I was not offended. But I thought I was being dishonest to who I choose to be."

"I understand, I will call you Lori from now on."

"Thank you."

"Now, please allow me to help you dress for dinner."

The two naked women checked on the baby, who was sleeping soundly, and then went into the other bedroom arm-in-arm. It was a unique bonding that sometimes happens with submissives. Kind of a sharing of equal kindred spirits.

Lori snatched up the shoes, dress, and bra that had been discarded on the sofa, and threw the soaked nursing pads into the trash can. In the bedroom, she put fresh pads in, and put her detested bra back on while Hannah selected a dress for the evening. As she turned to face Lori once again, a bolt of inspiration hit her and she dashed back to her bedroom and returned holding a pair of hand-made lace panties.

Hannah knelt in front of Lori holding her panties out for Lori to put on. "My new friend Lori, I ask you to wear these as a way to remember ME, and please take them home with you when your vacation is over." When she finished speaking, she kissed Lori's washed and freshly shaved pussy.

Lori briefly spread her legs to give the younger woman better access. But, then she reached down and took Lori's hands in hers and helped her stand. She kissed the lips that were just against her pussy, and whispered: "Sister, I will treasure these as a gift from you as long as I wear them. But, I would have remembered you for the rest of my life even without them." To complete the spell that was weaving itself around them, Lori said: "Now would you help me put them on?"

The younger woman immediately complied with the simple request. They fit perfectly, and Lori thought they looked simply awesome.

Hannah kissed Lori again, and said: "Sister, I like the sound of that. They do look very nice on you, but it is a shame to have to cover your gorgeous body."

As she pulled the dress over her head, Lori had to agree, it was a shame.

Bob returned from His shower. He hugged and kissed His wife / slave and then the naked young woman standing next to her. He quickly dressed for dinner. He wore a white cotton suit and a sky blue shirt (open at the collar).

"Hannah, tonight we are just eating down stairs at the hotel restaurant. It has been a long day, and we want to get into bed early. You don't need to put clothes on, if you don't want to, and you can order yourself dinner from the room service menu."

"Thank you, Sir." Hannah replied politely. "And thank you for earlier too." She added.

Bob said as he opened the door for Lori: "Believe me, it was my pleasure."

The hotel's restaurant was, effectively, two restaurants in one; a five-star modern continental restaurant, and a small intimate sidewalk café. Bob selected the café to give at least the illusion of privacy. Bob had stayed at the Hotel Del Rio before, and knew that there was but one kitchen, and one menu.

When the waitress seated them, Lori couldn't help but notice her huge breasts. They were "liberated". That is, the waitress wasn't wearing a bra. Which reminded Lori of that damned contraption she had on. Damn things must have been invented by a sadist!

"I'll have a Black-Jack-and-Coke, and my wife will have a Margarita, and we will start with nachos del casa." Bob instructed the waitress and settled in to examine the menu.

Lori didn't give the menu even the most casual glance. Master selected her food for her, and she ate what He ordered. But, it gave her time to drink in her surroundings. Bob called it "making memories." But, it seemed only fair. He had been to Chili many times. This was her first time being in a place where the natives didn't have a southern drawl!

It was a warm evening, but a breeze was blowing. There were a few clouds in the sky, but mostly it was an expanse of azure blue. The calls of birds floated to her ears, singing songs of peace and contentment. The highway wasn't far away, but the sounds were all muted by lush vegetation. Planters of tropical flowers and potted palm trees made an informal wall around the veranda where they sat.

"Master?"

"Yes, girl?"

"Thank you for bringing me on such a wonderful trip. I also wanted you to know that I like the nurse you hired very much."

He leaned over and kissed His lovely slave. "I am glad, girl. It seems that Hannah, and a certain taxi driver, like you very much as well."

"Oh my goodness, Master," she replied breathlessly, "I loved his cock deep in my throat. But, I was wondering just how long I was going to have to hold my breath!"

They both laughed. It was the shared laughter that one used when both saw the humor in a situation. There was no malice in His tone, or in His mind.

Just then the waitress brought their drinks and nachos. "I'm sorry sir, the bar only has Green label Jack Daniels tonight. So, there is no charge for your drink. If you wish, I can bring you something else."

He paused for a moment thinking that the green wasn't quite as smooth as the black. Still, free is free. "No thank you, this will be okay. We are ready to order out meal, please."

"Very good, sir."

"I will have the seafood medley, without the miniature squid, with the house special potatoes and mixed vegetables."

"And for the lady, sir?"

Bob smiled to Himself and thought: "Ah, a civilized corner of the world that knows a gentleman takes care of his date."

"She will have the salsa pork medallions in orange glaze with the stir fry vegetables. Do you have bottled water?"

"Yes, sir, we do."

"Great. We will each have two bottles of water."

"Very good, sir. Will there be anything else?"

"Not at the moment, but we will probably order some coffee and dessert to take to our room when we are finished."

The waitress hurried off to see to their order.

Now that the necessities had been taken care of, Bob wanted to talk about their day tomorrow. "Well, slave, tomorrow we tour the castle. It is patterned after a castle in Madrid, Spain. It was built **about** one hundred and sixty years ago, but the original has been standing for almost a thousand **years.**"

"That sounds wonderful. Does it have a dungeon?"

"The tour guide said that there was a dungeon with all of the original equipment. However, I doubt that they will allow us to play on it."

Lori pouted mockingly.

"I am thinking of touring the beaches the day after that. There are several nice nude beaches here. It isn't like back in the states where the conservatives have everyone convinced that you can't see a naked body without wanting to hop in bed." His fingers tapped the table to emphasize the passion of His words. It was a topic that was dear to His heart.

"Be careful Master, they might hear you! They have spies everywhere!"

"girl, you know that my beliefs are as strong as the next guy, I just don't like those who claim false teachings and proclaim them as truth." Then, seeing the smile on her face, He knew that she had just been teasing Him.

Just then the waitress brought their dinner. Neither of them wasted and time getting down to business. It had been a long time since lunch in Miami.

When they had eaten their fill, the waitress returned.

"Would you still like coffee and dessert to take with you, sir?"

"Yes, we want coffee and cheesecake for three, please."

"For three, sir?"

"Yes, for three. Please charge dinner and the dessert to our room."

"Right away, sir."

Hannah was surprised that He had dessert for her. She had just had a cheeseburger brought up to the room for her dinner, and had been watching the news on television. She was still naked, and Joey was still asleep.

"I hope your dinner was well."

Lori spoke up as she served the coffee and cake: "Yes, it was quite nice. We were both starved."

"Good. The hotel's food isn't really authentic Chilean cuisine, but it is quite good in its own way."

Before she sat down to enjoy her dessert, Lori stripped off her clothes so that she was as naked as Hannah. Bob smiled His approval. Making Him happy was all that mattered to her. But, getting out of that damn torture device was good too.

As she sat on the floor beside Hannah, her Master picked up the lace panties that Hannah had given her earlier.

"Excuse me, slave, where did these come from?" Bob asked.

"Sorry, Master, I forgot that you didn't know." Lori said as she looked at the floor. "Hannah gave them to me the same way you gave Ricardo mine. Well, except that hers were clean. She wanted me to remember her."

"Did she explain to you what they mean?"

Lori looked at Hannah, and back to Bob. Hannah was looking at the floor.

"Lori, these panties were hand made by Hannah and her mother. Hannah's mother knows that Hannah likes women as well as men. It took several hundred hours to make them for both mother and daughter."

Lori nodded that she understood.

"Hannah wore these panties one time, and one time only. After that, she removed them and put them in a box. They were never to be worn by Hannah again. Instead, they were to be given to the first woman that Hannah made love to."

Lori took the lace panties from her Master and held them to her chest. With tears streaming down her cheeks, Lori turned to Hannah and said: "I had no idea how special these were to you. I am honored to receive such a gift. As slave I am not worthy…"

"SLAVE! You will accept the gift!!!" Master interrupted.

Lori looked at Bob, trembling.

"Yes, Master."

Lori took Hannah into her arms. Dessert was forgotten. The two women cried tears of joy.

Lori whispered to her sister: "This gift is beyond price. I shall treasure is always, and think of you every time I wear them."

Turning back to her Master she added: "Master, thank you from the bottom of my heart for allowing me to keep this gift. Even though I am not worthy, it is still something very important to me."

"Now, let's have dessert. I need milk in my coffee, slave."

Lori took his coffee cup and expressed milk into it until it reached the color that He liked it. When she returned the cup to Him, she asked Hannah: "Sis, do you want milk in your coffee?"

With a gleam in her eye, Hannah said: "Yes, please."

Lori added milk to Hannah's coffee and to her own.

There wasn't much conversation while they ate, but there was a pleasant feeling that they "belonged" together.

After they were all finished eating, and the garbage was put into the trash can, Bob stood up and took off His clothes and pointing to His erect cock, He said: "Okay, girls, it's time for the dessert to your dessert."

Both women immediately began licking and sucking His cock until He exploded into both mouths as they kissed each other around the end of His stiff member.

After they had serviced Him, the two women started performing "69" on each other while he watched and enjoyed the show. Hannah was on top and Lori on the bottom.

After both women had climaxed twice, Master was erect again, and He moved in behind Hannah's ass. He moved in close and inserted His cock into Hannah's tight asshole to fuck her ass while His slave ate her pussy. He quickly reached the point of no return, and pumped His cum into Hannah's body without reservation. Lori could tell that he was ready to climax and shifted her head to put her tongue up His ass, just the way he liked it.

As they all came one final time, the baby started to wake, wanting to be fed one last time before sleeping through the night. Lori excused herself to take care of him, and Hannah busied herself with licking Bob's cock clean.

After the baby was fed, and the discarded clothing was gathered up, they all trundled themselves off to bed.

In the morning, everyone was up and about getting ready for the day. They were all still naked from the night before. Hannah fed the baby formula while Lori prepared breakfast. Joey was eating, but was clearly not happy about the substitute beverage!!! Lori had pumped her breasts earlier so that he would have her milk to drink during the morning, and there just wasn't any left for him to drink now. Currently, she was standing at the stove was cooking eggs, sausages, and potatoes. She also had biscuits in the small oven. The coffee was ready, and Master was having His first cup, with her milk in it, of course, while He read the newspaper.

"It looks like they have been having some problems with quasi-military groups. They have threatened to kidnap American tourists if the United States doesn't denounce the government here. This sort of thing happens all the time. It probably means nothing, but we should be careful while we are out and about today."

"Yes, Master. Are you sure that is all it is?" Lori asked, thinking of her child's safety. (They were planning on taking Hannah and Joey with them to the castle today.)

"As safe as it ever is down here." Came His distracted reply.

Lori didn't know that His comment was a complete fabrication, intended to enhance what he had planned for her that afternoon. This vacation was her idea, but He has planned it to fulfill one of her kinkier fantasies. Thinking back on the last twenty-four hours, He wasn't sure just how much kinkier she could get. But, by the time they got on the plane to return to Florida, she would have had more than her wildest dreams.

Hannah brought the baby out and kissed Lori good morning. She kissed Bob as well, She started to bend over to kiss His cock, and He firmly put His hand on her shoulder.

"Not with the baby in the room."

He pulled her close to Him and hugged her. He didn't want her to feel rejected, but He had a firm rule that NOTHING sexual was to be done with the baby in the room. Nothing!!!

Hannah smiled. She understood. "Perhaps later then." She said.

He gave her a mischievous grin and said: "Definitely later."

Lori handed Hannah and her Master each a plate of food, and returned to the stove to retrieve her own. They were all hungry, and for the first little while everybody was too busy eating to talk.

Bob finished His breakfast first and sat back pleasantly satisfied. "slave, you did a good job."

Lori glowed with His words of praise. It was what gave meaning of her life, pleasing Him.

Bob picked up the baby, who had been playing on a blanket on the floor and gave him papa bear hugs. Then He took him into the bedroom to change his diaper and get him dressed for the day's outing. He selected a navy blue sailor suit for His son. He grabbed the bottles that Lori had filled. He thought about sampling Joey's lunch, since it was Lori's milk; but He decided against it. Joey would need the nourishment today. Putting the bottles and a few spare diapers in a bag, He picked up the baby and returned to the living room. The women were sitting, holding each other in their arms, and feeding each other the last of the biscuits and honey. He was delighted that His slave and Hannah got along so very well. He had hired Hannah to care for the baby. The rest was just icing on the cake.

He put the baby back on the blanket and announced: "All right ladies, move your cute asses. Time to get dressed and get out the door. I will watch the baby while you two get dressed."

The two women walked to Bob and Lori's bedroom. "Sis, I'll help you get ready first."

Hannah said as they walked.

Hannah picked out a white, light-weight sweater and a flower-print skirt. She got Lori's nursing bra and put fresh pads in it. She winked at Lori and said: "No panties today, I want to be able to reach your bare ass if the opportunity presents itself."

Lori kissed Hannah passionately and grabbed a hand full of the woman's shaved pussy and said: "I like pussy better than ass, so you don't wear panties either today."

Hannah giggled and teasingly said: "Yes, mistress." Then she quickly helped Lori get dressed. In a mildly more serious note she added: "I don't usually wear a bra either."

Lori caressed Hannah's breasts and responded: "I hate the damn things too. I wish that other women weren't so critical and condescending of those of us who like to go without."

As Hannah tied Lori's tennis shoes, she continued the conversation. "I think you will find that it is more accepted here in Chili. It is true that most women still wear them, but going without is more accepted."

Before she stood back up, she pulled Lori's skirt up and licked her clit.

A soft moan escaped Lori's lips, and she reached down to press the younger woman's face into her pussy.

Lori nearly jumped out of her skin as a male voice from the doorway said: "We don't have time for that!"

Lori backed away from Hannah's tongue that had been very busy and helped her to get to her feet. Let's get you dressed. Turning to Bob she said: "Master, I will take the baby into the room with us and watch him so that you can get dressed. Do you want me to get your clothes out first?"

He chuckled. "I'll manage."

It didn't take long for Lori to pick out a loose sun dress and pull it over Hannah's luscious body. She added a pair of comfortable slip-on walking shoes, and Hannah was ready to go. One more check to make sure the baby was still dry, and Lori called out light-heartedly: "We are ready, Master."

He walked out of the bedroom in shorts and a t-shirt and announced: "Good, so am I. Let's go."

It was a beautiful day outside, and the castle wasn't too far away, so they decided to walk. As they strolled along, a familiar taxi drove by. The driver blew his horn, and waved. The trio waved back and smiled.

Lori leaned over and said to her husband: "Master, we have GOT to have company over more often."

He smiled at her and said: "Cum slut."

Undaunted, she retorted: "I am YOUR cum slut, Master."

When they got to the castle, they found that there was a long flight of stone stairs. Not at all good for a stroller. But, there was also a wheel-chair ramp. It was also, unfortunately, much longer. They made it to the top, only mildly out of breath, and Bob paid for the tour while the women recovered.

"The next tour leaves in fifteen minutes."

They waited in comfortable silence. Bob was happy that Hannah fit in so nicely. (He was quite happy with the way He fit into Hannah too, come to think of it.) When his vacation was over, they might have to talk about inviting Hannah to visit them in the states. It was a plus that she liked the baby, and that Joey seemed to like her. He wondered if they could encourage her to produce milk too.

The tour started promptly on schedule, and included all of the public rooms of the castle, including the dungeon.

The great hall was immense. It could have easily accommodated a banquet for three thousand people. The vaulted ceiling was thirty foot overhead at its peak. There were balconies lining both of the long walls. There were also ten large fire places on each wall that were still used today for heating such a large space.

The hall of audiences where the Count had heard petitions was dwarfed by the dining hall, but was quite large in its own right. In its day, the castle had been the center of government in the region, and countless life-and-death decisions had been made in that very room.

The dungeon was interesting. It had ten cells for holding prisoners. Each cell measured about ten feet on a side. There was a torture room that had been used to "encourage" liars to tell the "truth" (according to the tour guide). Against one wall was a medieval rack. It was, very authentic, and resembled the one that He had plans to build at home. In one corner was an Iron Maiden. Although it was a reproduction, it was authentically placed in the room. Most of the time, an Iron Maiden was placed over a trap door that allowed the gore-covered body to be disposed of directly into the river below. There was a fire place, of course, and an assortment of pokers that were heated and used to burn the victim. Hanging on the walls were a wide assortment of whips and floggers. Some of the floggers had glass or metal embedded in them, which made them particularly nasty. Overhead there were various hooks and pulleys that had been used to suspend men and women who had the misfortune to find themselves in this room.

Lori's face was a picture of awe and wonder; much like a child in a toy store. He could tell that she loved the rack, and wished that she could try it out. There was also a cage that would have been barely large enough for her to fit into that caught her eye.

The last stop on the tour was, of course, the gift shop. Clearly the owner of the castle agreed with P. T. Barnum who is reported to have said: "It is morally wrong to allow a sucker to keep their money." They bought some postcards picturing the dungeon that said: "Wish you were here." on them. Little did the owners of the castle know that some of their friends wouldn't think of it as a joke.

After visiting the gift shop, it was time for a bite of lunch, and then the afternoon siesta. (As if there was going to be any sleeping going on.) Hannah was out front pushing the stroller, and Lori had lagged behind a little. Suddenly, He looked around, and Lori wasn't there any more. He looked around for her. Then He saw them. There were four men putting her into the back of a cargo van. He looked at His watch. They were ten minutes early. He caught up with Hannah and said: "It has started." And they continued to the hotel.

Lori woke up. The last thing she remembered was someone covering her mouth and nose with a rag that smelled strange. She was restrained. Her feet were spread wide and she was bent over. Her arms were held straight out from her shoulders with chains and handcuffs. Her hair was pulled back into a pony tail, and her head was being held back at a ninety-degree angle to her body. She could taste cum in her mouth and could feel that it had dripped down her chin. And she was naked.

As she swallowed the cum in her mouth she could also feel that her asshole and pussy were wet. She assumed they had been ravaged as well. In fact judging from the strong smell around her, there was a considerable amount of cum in the area. Clearly a number of men had used her body while she was unconscious.

"Hello, is anybody there?" she called into the darkness. "If there is someone there, I need to go to the bathroom?"

"¡Así pues, nuestro poco perra de la cogida es despierto!" ["So, our little fuck bitch is awake!"] A bass male voice said somewhere to the left of her.

"Pl-l-lease!!! I need to take a piss!" Lori pleaded, now that she knew someone was there.

"Ése no es mi problema. Si usted tiene que ir, después vaya a donde usted está." ["That is not my problem. If you have to go, then go where you are."] The disembodied voice replied.

Lori didn't understand. She wasn't even sure that they understood. But, it had reached the point where she couldn't hold it any more. She released her bladder and allowed her fluids fall where they may. In a way, the sound of her piss hitting the floor was pleasing. It was the one thing that these men couldn't stop her from doing. As it that thought occurred to her, she wished she had to shit too!

Another voice spoke up from her right side, but sounded like it was behind her.

"La pequeña perra habla solamente inglés, usted idiota." ["The little bitch only speaks English, you idiot."]

"Ése no es mi problema. " ["That is not my problem."] The first voice replied.

"Es su problema si usted desea conseguir pagado para su parte del trabajo. ¿Recuerde lo que nos dijeron? Nos requieren hablar inglés de modo que ella consiga la experiencia completa de ser secuestrado." ["It is your problem if you want to get paid for your part of the job. Remember what we were told? We are required to speak English so that she will get the full experience of being kidnapped."] the second voice responded.

"Yes, Sir." The first voice said, switching to English as ordered.

The second voice called out: "Lights!"

Glaring lights flooded Lori's face. She instinctively snapped her eyes shut.

Immediately a cane struck the back of her legs. "You will keep your eyes open!"

She opened her eyes. The bright light hurt her eyes because they had been adjusted to the darkness. Tears began to run down her face. The stinging on the back of her legs helped encourage her tears.

"Now," the voice continued, "we will discuss your lack of control. As punishment for pissing on my floor," the cane struck her ass, "you will get" it struck again "ten" and again, faster and harder this time "lashes" again "with the cane." The leader punctuated each word with a lash of the cane across her reddening ass cheeks.

Lori was determined to not give him the satisfaction of crying out in pain, but she couldn't. It felt like her whole ass was on fire. Tears flowed down her face as the waves of pain continued even after the lashes stopped.

"In addition," the leader added, "you will be required to drink one half gallon of water to replace what you put on my floor. You will hold it until you are given permission to let go. And you will not get permission until you have begged to MY satisfaction. Do you understand?"

With trembling lips, Lori replied: "Y-y-yes."

Suddenly she felt the cane again. "Yes what?" the leader demanded.

"Y-y-yes, s-s-sir." Lori replied. But, in her mind she said: *Yes, you fucking asshole.*

"Give her something to eat, and pump her tits." The leader commanded.

A table was placed in front of her, which she found confusing. Then a muscular female officer walked into view.

"This better be the best damn orgasm I've had this month." She told Lori sternly. Then she stripped off her clothes and climbed onto the table. Two men moved the table in so that the woman's cunt was against Lori's face. "Eat it, you bitch." The woman commanded.

Lori ate. She licked the woman's clit and put her tongue in her hole; doing her best to make the woman cum while her companions watched. She could taste cum in the woman's hole, and loved the taste.

"Faster!" and leader shouted, and the cane hit her ass again.

She gave herself totally into pleasuring the other woman. Then she felt the suction on her nipples. They were pumping the milk from her swollen breasts.

"This is for your son. We are not without concern that you keep feeding him. In fact, the one who hired us told us that we could have your body any way we wanted it, provided we increased the amount of milk you produce. As a consequence, you will be milked on a regular schedule."

She could feel the milk being pulled from her body. But, knowing that somehow, her son would be nourished by it, was comforting.

The woman on the table was starting to ride against Lori's face, and Lori knew that she was getting close to climax. She licked harder and deeper. The woman grabbed Lori's hair in a vice like grip and ground Lori's face into her wanton pussy. The woman's back arched and Lori felt liquid shoot into her mouth as the woman squirted her cum.

Just as Lori thought that part of her captivity was over, she felt one of the men come up behind her and slide his cock into her asshole. It seemed to slid in forever, he must have been huge! While he was pumping her ass, the two who had moved the table close to her moved it away, and another cock was shoved into her mouth. The two men fucked her in rhythm so that they were both thrusting in at the same time. She didn't think that she had ever been penetrated so deeply. She could feel pain in her ass as the back-door guy slammed against her reddened cheeks. She could feel the machine sucking the last of her milk from her body. Finally, she could feel it as both men started to jerk in the spasms of orgasm at the same time. She honestly wished that the one in her mouth would back off some so that she could taste him. But he was only concerned with seeing how deep he could go into her throat.

The process repeated itself seemingly for hours. She had had ten men who came in her ass, and seven in her pussy. She had lost count of how many cocks had squirted their load in her mouth. She had stopped caring how many a long time before they were finished. As it turned out, there were three women in the group who had each had their turn with her mouth too.

"Well, slut," the leader finally said to her "It seems that you have pleased my men, so we will give you some food and allow you to rest for a little while."

She felt something slide into her asshole, but it was too small to be one of the men's cocks.

"But," the leader continued "we can't have you being too comfortable while you eat."

She felt her colon begin filling with liquid. The realization dawned on her that they were giving her an enema.

Finally, when she was so full that she didn't think she could hold any more, the hose was removed, and a butt plug was inserted.

"That is to keep everything inside until I am ready to let it out." The leader admonished her. Then he removed her wrists from the cuffs.

Someone behind her pulled the rope tied to her pony tail, and forced her to stand up straight. She had been in the bent-over position for so long that just the act of standing up was agony. She screamed out in pain, but it quickly subsided. She could feel the cum dripping down her legs from her saturated pussy.

The leader gave her an egg salad sandwich, and offered her water, which she declined. Her bladder was full from the water he had forced her to drink earlier. Her insides were aching to pass the water they had just put inside of her. She really wished she could savor the sandwich after all of the cum she had ingested in the last few hours, but she was worried that the sandwich might be taken away. Besides, somehow, she knew that the leader would keep the enema inside of her until she was done eating. She ate as fast as she could.

After the sandwich was gone, the leader signaled one of the others to bring a bucket for her.

"Squat down over the bucket, but do not touch it." He commanded her.

She obeyed.

"Now you may release what we have put inside of you."

The plug was removed and fluid was forced out of both her colon and bladder. It was an explosive force that she couldn't have held it back if she had tried to. It seemed like it would never end.

Finally, when she was empty once again, the leader told her to stand up. She wasn't given the chance to obey, the person who controlled the rope in her hair helped by tugging her to her feet.

A table was put in front of her, the same one that the troop's women had used to position themselves in front of her. And the leader told her that she was allowed to lay down and sleep for four hours.

They cuffed her wrists to the far end of the table. She didn't think that she would be able to sleep on a hard table, but she was so tired that she promised herself to try. She was asleep in moments. It was a deep dreamless sleep, a sure signal that she was exhausted.

Lori awoke to the man she now thought of as "super dick" entering her sore asshole again. Deeper, and deeper he went. Then he started to fuck her ass. In and out he moved. Faster and faster. Super-dick seemed even bigger and longer than he had the last time. Then it happened. She felt a tongue on her clit. She couldn't stand it. Her mind exploded in climax. She lost all track of the world around her; even this hideous world.

When she returned to her senses, super-dick was no longer inside of her (she assumed that he had cum as well) and the tongue was gone.

TH-W-ACK !!! (The cane struck her ass.)

In fact, she received twenty lashes from the cane this time. Then the leader's voice was in her ear. "You will not climax without permission. Do you understand me?"

"Yes, sir." Lori whispered through her tears. But in her mind she was reliving the most glorious orgasm she had ever had in her life, coupled with a fantastic trip to subspace.

"Your voice lacks sincerity. Cuff her and milk her tits again, and then form the fuck lines again. Her body must be filled with your cum again!" the leader called to the whole troop.

It seemed like it went on for hours. In spite of the leader's warning, Lori climaxed several times even though she tried to hold back. It just wasn't possible to stop them from happening. She lost all track of how many times she was penetrated. Of how many cocks she sucked. Of how many pussies she licked. And she didn't care any more. She was their fuck bitch, and she decided to enjoy it.

"Milk her again." the leader commanded, and his troops moved to obey. But, this time the use of her body continued without pause. Her face and legs were rivers of cum, and her bladder was full again. She decided to just let go with one of them inside of her, and that is just what she did. Just as he started jerking in orgasm she released her bladder and her piss gushed out all over the man using her pussy for his pleasure.

"Enough." the leader said and they all backed away from her. "Hose her down and clean her off."

Her cuffs were released and she was once again jerked upright. Someone turned on a high-pressure hose that delivered a stream of ice-cold water to her naked body. A couple of the men moved in with soap and brushed and scrubbed her down. One of them turned his brush over and swatted her ass with it. Then they rinsed her off.

The three women then brought over oil and rubbed her body down gently. She felt totally refreshed.

"Release her." The leader commanded.

Then speaking to Lori: "Our patron wishes to have dinner with you. Follow me."

He led her into a small room that had an elegant table set for three. Her first thought was to trash it. But she just couldn't bring herself to do so.

"Sit here." The leader commanded pointing to the chair in the middle.

Her tender bottom was thankful for the padding on the chair. But, unfortunately, the padding was not entirely adequate to the task.

She sat there waiting. Her curiosity was mounting to see just what kind on monster would abduct her like this. Eventually, she noticed that there was an envelope on the table under her dinner plate. She pulled the envelope out and turned it over. It had one word written on it…

"slave"

She opened the envelope and found two pieces of paper. The first she recognized immediately. It was a letter she had written in her own hand to her Master describing her fantasy and wish to be kidnapped and gang-raped. All she could say was: "Holy shit! He really did it."

The second piece of paper was a note from Master. It read: "slave, It was my pleasure to arrange this fantasy of yours. I hope it was all that you wanted it to be. – Master"

She had to reflect that once she had accepted her situation, it had actually been enjoyable.

She looked up after reading Master's note to see Master and her son in the arms of his nurse.

"Hello slave." Her husband said.

"Greetings, sis." Hannah said.

Lori ran to their arms. Tears of joy were running down her face, and she couldn't speak.

"Sit down" Master commanded, but in a mild tone of voice.

Once they were seated, Master spoke to his slave. "slave, you need to understand that you were guarded at all times. One of us was constantly watching you."

Lori looked at the floor in shame. "You saw everything that happened?"

"Yes."

"I'm sorry, Master. I…" Lori stuttered trying to explain.

"Relax, slave, all happened as I planned. Well, all except the part where you pissed all over me."

Lori dropped to her knees. "MASTER, I'm sorry. Please forgive me!!!"

"You didn't know it was me. But, I didn't see why you should have all of the fun. Now get back in your chair. You're holding up dinner."

Dinner was served, and all three ate until they were filled. Well, actually, all four. Joey wanted to be fed too. It was a wonderful vacation.

Glossary

aftercare	Refers to the time taken after a scene to stabilize and ground the submissive.
alpha slave	Refers to the head slave in a house with multiple slaves. The alpha slave has authority over the beta slaves. Not all houses with multiple slaves have an alpha slave.
anal play	Activities that involve stimulating a person's anus, usually by penetration (finger, penis, tongue, or some other object). For this play to be less painful, some form of lubricant may be needed.
anal plug	A device designed to be worn in the anus while the wearer goes about their every-day tasks. There are also vibrating anal plugs that can be quite stimulating.
analingus	Sometimes called a "rim job", the act of one person inserting their tongue into another person's anus.
APE	Acronym. Stands for: "Absolute Power Exchange". Refers to a relationship where the submissive, who usually calls him/her self a "slave", gives all rights and control to the dominant. A "no limits" form of relationship where the slave will literally do anything asked of them. (See also: "TPE" and "power exchange".)
bastionado	The practice of whipping the feet.

BDSM	A three-way acronym that is typically broken into "BD" (bondage and discipline) "DS" (domination and submission) and "SM" (sado-masochism). Often used to refer to a lifestyle where these activities are practiced.
beastiality	"Love is a nice warm puppy." Refers to persons that perform sex acts with animals.
ben wa balls	These hollow balls contain smaller solid balls inside of them. They are inserted into the vagina. The movement of the inner weighted balls causes the outer ball to vibrate. This non-electrical device is one of the earliest forms of artificial vaginal stimulation.
bi, bisexual	A term indicating that an individual enjoys sexual activities with members of both sexes.
bondage	Using some device, like rope, chains, cling film, etc. to restrain the movements of another person.
branding	The act of using some heated device to permanently mark a slave as property. (Just like the cattle branding seen in many westerns.)
breath play	Any kind of activity that restricts a person's breathing. Even performing "deep throat" on a male is a mild form of breath play. Binding a person so that they can breathe, but can only take shallow breaths.
cage	A cage is a box used to confine a sub or slave. Typically, the cage has sides made of wooden or metal bars. They vary somewhat in size and shape, but all are intended to restrict the freedom of movement of the one inside of the cage.

cane, caning	A cane is a straight thin piece of rattan, bamboo, or acrylic. (I have one that is made from carbon fiber too.) The material determines how much is stings or marks when used.
cat	A multi-stranded whip. The name derives from "cat-o-nine-tails" that was used in ages past.
CBT	"Cock and Ball Torture" Consists of inflicting pain on a male's genetalia.
chastity device	A device used to prevent sexual intercourse. For a male, this device takes the form of a metal or rigid plastic device that fits over the penis and scrotum. It makes it painful for the male to even begin to have an erection, and makes vaginal penetration impossible. For the female, this device is a belt that goes around the waist and between the legs. It blocks the opening to the vagina so that the female cannot be accessed. Most of the time, it covers the clitoris so that she cannot even be stimulated.
clamps, nipple clamps	Nipple clamps range from mild to severe. The mildest are small tweezers clamps. Clover clamps are slightly above the middle on the scale. They are fairly popular. (See also: "clover clamps")
clover clamps	Clover clamps are a popular form of nipple clamp. They have the virtue of being difficult to pull off when you tug on them. In fact, tugging on them makes them tighter!
collar	A symbol of a D/s relationship. It can be actual fetish wear (leather, chains, etc.) or something as simple as a special necklace. Typically, a submissive will actually own several collars because no one collar is suitable for all situations.

cow, milk cow	This term is used to describe a female submissive or slave who is lactating (usually induced rather than as a result of child birth) and is routinely milked to provide milk for others to drink.
crop, riding crop	A rigid rod with a folded over piece of leather that slaps when a person is hit with the crop.
cuffs	Cuffs are typically leather straps that buckle closed around the submissive's wrists and ankles. They may be locked on using pad locks. Their principle use is to provide a safe, convenient way to restrain a submissive.
cunnilingus	The act of performing oral sex on a woman's clitoris and vulva.
cupping	Cupping is a process where small glass cups are placed against the skin, and the air is removed from them. That allows the suction to pull the slave's skin into the cup. This can be very stimulating.
D/s	The general category of relationships between dominant and submissive individuals.
dildo	A device, often molded to look like a penis, made to be inserted into the vagina. They are manufactured in various sizes and from various materials.
discipline	The act of using some form of punishment as negative re-enforcement in response to improper behavior in an effort to modify that behavior.

"Do me" sub	A person who claims to be submissive, but who wants to be the center of attention. I also call these people "passive dominants". Their goal is that their own needs be met, but without their own active participation.
Dom	Male dominant. (See also "dominant".)
Dominant	A dominant is a person who desires to control others. The degree of control will vary from one couple to another and often from one situation to another. Dominants can be either male or female.
Domme	Female dominant. (See also "dominant".)
dungeon	A space set aside as a dedicated play area. May be a space in the Master's home. May also be a public space that is available for rent for play events.
Dungeon Monitor (DM)	An experienced person in the lifestyle who volunteers their time at an event to help monitor what is going on and to deal with unsafe situations if they come up.
dungeon wheel	A piece of dungeon furniture that allows the submissive to be bound (to the wheel) and then turned at any angle desired.
edge play	The category of activities that involve higher levels of risk.
electrical play	Play activities that include electricity. See also "TENS Unit" and "Violet Wand".

fellatio	The act of performing oral sex on a man's penis. (Slang: "blow job".)
fetish	Some non-traditional thing that sexually excites a person.
fisting	Inserting a hand and wrist into vagina or anus and making a fist for stimulation.
flogger	A multi-tailed whip used to whip a submissive. Most of the time made of leather, but can be made of other materials as well.
fuck machine	A mechanical device with a dildo attached to it. Used to mimic sexual penetration by a human partner. Usually used with the vagina, but also very rarely in the anus.
gag	A device that is placed into / across a person's mouth to stop them from talking.
golden shower	The act of urinating on another person.
Gor, Gorean	Pertaining to a lifestyle based on the series of Gor novels by John Norman.
hood	An article of clothing used to confine a person's head. Typically covers the ears and diminishes hearing. May also cover they eyes and mouth or nose.
IM, instant message	A computer software program that allows two (or more) people to communicate using their computers and the internet.

impact play	Any kind of play that involves striking the submissive with a hand or some other implement.
insertable	Anything that can be inserted into the vagina or anus. Generally used to refer to things that were not intended to be used that way. (See also: "pervertable".)
IRC	"Internet Relay Chat" A group servers on the internet that has "rooms" where people come to chat with each other.
kajira	Gorean word for "slave girl".
kink	Any kind of non-traditional play activity. Usually used in a sexual context, but not totally limited to sexual activities.
knife play	Any kind of play that involves sharp edges, or the perception of using sharp edges. (For example, using the back of a knife, but allowing the submissive to think it is the edge of the blade.)
kurt (Gorean)	A five-tailed whip used in the Gor novels and by practitioners of the Gorean lifestyle.
limit	Some activity that the sub will not do. Limits are generally divided into hard and soft categories. A hard limit is something that there is no compromise on, and a soft limit is something that the sub might consider in the future. (Doms may also have limits.)
liquid latex	A product for painting rubber (latex) "clothes" onto a submissive. In some states, recognized as clothing.

lube, lubricant	A slippery product used to make it easier to get into tight body cavity openings. Perhaps the two most popular brands are "KY Jelly" and "Astroglide". There are others as well.
Marquis de Sade	Born Donatien Alphonse Francois comte de Sade on June 2, 1740 in Paris, France. His parents were French nobles and spoiled him throughout his childhood. He finally died in his sleep on July 21, 1814 at the age of seventy-four. He is noted for his "unusual" sexual practices. The word sadist is derrived from his name.
masochist	A person who enjoys having pain inflicted on them. (See also: "sadist" and "pain slut".)
Master	A male dominant involved in an APE or TPE relationship (or desiring to be so). Sometimes used to address any male dominant.
Mistress	A female dominant involved in an APE or TPE relationship (or desiring to be so). Sometimes used to address any female dominant.
MOTSS	Acronym. Stands for "Members Of The Same Sex"
needle play	Play that involves putting needles through the submissive's skin.
paddle	A rigid device for spanking a submissive's bottom. They come in various shapes and sizes, and are made of assorted materials.

pain slut	A person who enjoys having pain inflicted on them. (See also: "masochist".) Typically, a person who has been involved in masochistic activities long enough that their tolerance has deepened to a much higher than the norm.
penis gag	A gag that has a projection shaped like a penis that gets inserted into the submissive's mouth. Sometimes, with a hollow passage through the middle that allows liquid to be put into the submissive's mouth.
pervertable	Regular everyday items that can be used for non-traditional purposes. For example, inserting a candle, or even a soda can, into a submissive's vagina.
pillory	In a sense, a variant of "stocks". Designed to restrain both wrists and head. See also: "stocks".
piss play	See "water sports"
poly	A person, or persons, who have on-going relationships with multiple people. There are closed and open forms of poly relationships. In a closed relationship, all persons are only involved with the persons in that single relationship. In an open arrangement, the people in the relationship may be involved with people not in the same relationship.
pony, pony play	Refers to the activity of a sub / slave serving as a horse to pull a cart, or to carry riders on their back.

power exchange	A relationship that is based on one person granting another person power over them. See also: "TPE" and "APE".)
RACK	"Risk-Aware Consensual Kink"
role play	An activity where the players assume a role. They try to act out the person or object they are trying to be as faithfully as possible.
sadist	A person who derives pleasure from inflicting pain on others.
safe call	Refers to the practice of establishing a contact with a trusted friend who can alert the authorities in the event that it is suspected that something has happened on a visit to someone else.
Saint Andrew's Cross	An article of dungeon furniture. Typically two heavy boards nailed to form the letter X. It is used to bind the submissive's wrists and ankles while leaving the rest of the submissive's body available for play.
SAM	Acronym. Stands for "Smart-Assed Masochist". Refers to a submissive who will tease of make "smart remarks" in order to receive a spanking or other discipline.
Scat	Play activities that include the use of (usually human) fecal matter.
Scene	A sequence of activities of interaction between a dominant and submissive. Sometimes it is a scripted sequence, and other times the submissive just goes with the flow of what the dominant is doing. See also "role play".

self bondage	Bondage that you can do to your self. For example, using rope to tie your knees and ankles together. Often used in long-distance relationships. See also: "bondage".
sensory depravation	A play activity that involves limiting or greatly reducing the submissive's use of one or more of their senses. You can buy (or build) sensory depravation chambers that limit as much sensory input as possible. Some find these very relaxing.
service slave	A slave who serves Master and His guests in non-sexual ways. Typically serving food or beverages, showing the guests to various places in the house.
sex slave	A slave who is used for whatever sexual activity the Master chooses. This usually (but not always) includes uses that Master extends to His guests.
shit play	See: "scat"
single-tail	A leather whip with a single leather strip extending out of the end.
slapper	A device for whipping a submissive that consists of several wide leather strips arranged in layers so that they slap into each other as they impact the submissive's body.
slave	A person who surrenders most or all of their rights and privileges to another. (See also "TPE" and "APE".)

spanking bench	A piece of dungeon furniture that is used to restrain a submissive on hands and knees so that his/her bottom is held in perfect position for spanking.
SSC	"Safe, Sane, and Consensual" A mantra in the BDSM community that is used to communicate that the people involved are being as safe as possible, only do things that most would consider reasonable (sane), and do what they do by mutual consent. (See also "RACK".)
stocks	A rigid device for restraining hands and/or feet.
sub, submissive	Generally, a person who does not enjoy control and wants others to make decisions for them.
swinger, swinging	An individual who has casual sexual encounters with people that they are not involved with on a long-term basis. Do not confuse this with a poly relationship.
switch	Refers to a person who is sometimes dominant and sometimes submissive. Most switches will be predominantly submissive or predominantly dominant.
TENS Unit	A medical device used for deep tissue (muscle) therapy. In play it is used to trigger muscle twitches to stimulate the submissive.
toilet service	Using the submissive / slave's mouth as a toilet. Typically, the slave swallows whatever is deposited in it's mouth.
tongue bath	Using your tongue to clean every part of another's body.

TPE	Acronym. Stands for: "Total Power Exchange". This form of relationship allows a few limits. But, in general, anything else goes. (See also "APE" and "power exchange".)
verbal humiliation	Use of words usually humiliating (for example "slut" or "whore") in talking to a submissive. When done in the right context, it can be a real turn on for the submissive.
Violet Wand	A device used in electrical play. It is based on a Tesla Coil that drastically steps up the voltage to the electrical charge which consequently reduces the current being carried. (Current is the primary danger in electrical play.) It uses various attachments that shape the discharge to achieve different intensities.
water sports	Any type of play involving urine.
wax play	Dripping hot (liquid) wax onto a person's body. Of course, care must be exercised to not create serious burns.
WIITWD	Acronym. Stands for "What It Is That We Do".
zipper	A string of pinch clothes pins that are tied together in a manner that allows the clothes pins to be removed rapidly by just pulling on the string.

About the Author

Ralph White is a computer professional by trade, and a part-time college professor. He resides in the eastern mid-Atlantic states. He is a survivor of two failed vanilla marriages, and decided that this time he would do it the way he wanted to.

At this time he owns one slave by her consent. When this book was written, Master and slave were coping with a long distance relationship, working toward being 24/7.

While this is his first fictional work, Mr. White has published over fifty magazine articles on computer programming, has written 300 pages of lecture notes for an on-line computer programming course, and is working on a book discussing Bible teaching on marriage (which may never be published…smile). At the moment, Mr. White is more inclined to begin writing a sequel to this work.

Mr. White has interest in finding a second slave, eventually. But hasn't really found anyone totally suitable thus far.

Made in the USA